C000279073

The History of Fordingbridge
from Earliest Times to the Twenty-First Century

The History of Fordingbridge

from Earliest Times to the Twenty-First Century

by Anthony Light and Gerald Ponting

Charlewood Press

Copyright © 2001 Anthony Light and Gerald Ponting

The moral rights of the authors have been asserted

All rights reserved

Published by Charlewood Press
Middle Burgate House
Fordingbridge
SP6 1LX
http://home.clara.net/gponting/index-page10.html

British Library
Cataloguing in Publication Data
A catalogue record for this book is
available from the British Library

ISBN 0 9533955 2 9

Typesetting, scanning, layout and design
by the authors using :
Microsoft Works 4,
Microsoft Word 97,
Corel PhotoPaint 8
and Serif PagePlus 7

Printed by Hobbs the Printers
Totton, Hants

Front cover: A map of the Fordingbridge area, dated around 1605.
Note that south is at the top! This is taken from John Norden's map of Cranborne Chase – hence few details are shown on the New Forest side of the River Avon.
Of the notation 'PARTE OF HAM SHYRE', only the large letters 'OF' and 'HAM' appear on this section of the map. See also page 61.
Reproduced by courtesy of the Marquess of Salisbury

Back cover: Two hand-tinted post-cards from the 20th century
Above: The Market Place in about 1920.   *Below:* The Great Bridge in about 1960.

AUTHORS' PREFACE

It is the aim of this volume to provide a structured account of the development of the town of Fordingbridge; to tell something of the lives of its inhabitants over the centuries; and to record the main sources of information which are still available to us.

Many original documents (not only in Hampshire but also in Cambridge, Cornwall, Derbyshire, London, Nottingham and Wiltshire) have been consulted during the long-term research underlying this book. There is fascinating medieval material, while from the Tudor period onwards the quantity of detailed evidence is considerable. The vast bulk of this original documentary research has been carried out by one of the authors, Anthony Light.

We have not, however, attempted to give an exhaustive treatment of every aspect of the town's history – that would be impossible without a much larger book. There remains enormous scope for further research. Our bibliography contains lists of documents and their whereabouts, in the hope that this will assist others who may wish to extend our investigations in the future.

In compiling this book, we have tried to allow old documents to 'speak for themselves' as much as possible. **Where the records leave matters open to doubt or misinterpretation, where we have expressed opinions or made assumptions, and where, in a few rare cases, we have indulged in speculation, we hope that we have made this clear.** We trust our readers will realise that the frequency of caveats, such as *'it is likely that'*, is inevitable if we are not to present probability as fact.

Fordingbridge and its Hinterland

No settlement exists in isolation. Every town and village has always had economic, social and political interactions with its neighbours and these relationships cannot be ignored when compiling a history.

In some settlements, the boundaries of the village, the manor and the parish largely coincide, but this is certainly not the case with Fordingbridge. The manorial system in the town became increasingly complicated during the medieval period, with several manorial Lords involved. Adjoining properties often belonged to different estates. Fordingbridge parish was always large, encompassing several outlying villages and hamlets such as Godshill and Stuckton. They and other nearby villages were closely involved with the town's shops, markets and fairs, but it is beyond our scope to cover these smaller settlements in any detail.

Taking a wider view, government in London, county administration in Winchester, the port at Southampton, and the markets in Salisbury and Ringwood all had their effects on the life of the town. In addition, evidence for the earlier historical periods would be sparse indeed if we confined ourselves to the limits of the town or parish.

So our intention has been to deal primarily with the <u>town</u> of Fordingbridge, while viewing it in the context of its wider geographical setting and its economic hinterland.

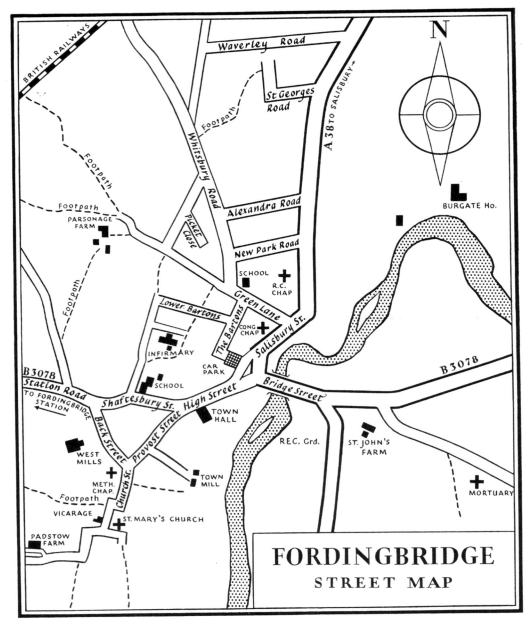

Street-plan of Fordingbridge, 1961-62

This map was originally published in a Guide issued by the former Ringwood and Fordingbridge Rural District Council. It shows the town before its expansion during the 1960s and the following decades and before construction of the by-pass. Even this plan shows several streets where Victorian inhabitants would have known only fields – Waverley Road, St George's Road, Alexandra Road, (New) Park Road, The Bartons and Lower Bartons.

The 'historic core' of the town, referred to from time to time in this book, consisted of Salisbury Street, Bridge Street, High Street, Shaftesbury Street, Provost Street, Back Street (West Street) and Church Street.

Reproduced with the permission of The British Publishing Company Ltd

INTRODUCTION

The River Avon flows through the Cathedral City of Salisbury and, in due course, enters the sea at Christchurch, 25 miles further south. The river valley is broad and fertile throughout this distance. East of the valley are the heaths and woodlands of the New Forest; to the west are the chalk downs and the heathlands of Dorset.

Ten miles south of Salisbury is one of the few natural crossing-places of the river. There has always been a ford, and the first bridge must have been constructed long before William the Conqueror became King of England. Thus the name, 'Fordingbridge', reflects the early existence of both a ford and a bridge.

A small Saxon village developed into the medieval settlement of Fordingbridge. While it never achieved borough status, by the 13th century it had all the characteristics of a market town. By that time, also, the street plan which we know today was established. While few people lived in some parts, population grew rapidly in Provost Street and near the Great Bridge, where homes were densely packed.

Regular markets and fairs attracted merchants from other towns. People from the nearby villages gathered in Fordingbridge for these events and also to attend the Hundred Courts. There, the customs which governed daily life were enforced and justice was dispensed. The Parish Church of St Mary's served a large and prosperous parish, and for centuries it was the centre of the local deanery.

Townsfolk in those days were still closely linked to agriculture. Everyone was dependent upon local farm produce for their day-to-day living; most people grew some food of their own, or kept a few animals. Town craftsmen used farming products such as leather, or produced items needed by farmers. This organic link between town and country was only broken relatively recently, following the industrial and technological advances of the 19th and 20th centuries.

The homes and lifestyles of Fordingbridge residents have varied greatly, both over the years and according to their rank in society. The limited excavations and fieldwork so far undertaken in the area, although restricted in scope, provide some information on past ways of life. Even more valuable are the many obscure documents that survive in various archives. Thanks to these records, we know the names, the businesses and the possessions of many former inhabitants, who are introduced in the succeeding chapters. They include the following:

- **Alfwy the Saxon** was an important landowner locally before the Norman Conquest, owing allegiance to no man other than King Edward.

- **Edward Scott**, an affluent vicar in the 16th century, owned not only horses, cattle and pigs, but also ten swans and six cygnets on the River Avon.

- **Elizabeth Silly** was sent to a House of Correction in Winchester in 1745, as she had given birth to a 'female bastard child'.

- **Thomas Knowles** was a 17th-century merchant. The success of his business enabled him to retire and to call himself a 'Gentleman'. His name survives in the town – Knowles Bridge in Provost Street was named after him.

- **Henry Eldridge** and **Joseph Arney** were transported to Australia for their part in an 1830 riot, when a mob broke up the machinery in East Mill.

CONTENTS

Picture Essays

Fordingbridge's Parish Church of St Mary the Virgin, although rebuilt on several occasions, has been a constant aspect of the town since Saxon times
James Coventry photograph 1897

CHAPTER 1 – LOCAL GEOLOGY AND LAND USAGE

The geology of any area is a vital component of its history. The bedrocks, soils, natural vegetation and river systems are the fundamentals that determine the suitability of a place for settlement.

A major part of the underlying local geology is a series of stepped **gravel terraces**. These were laid down at the end of the last ice age by a great river, formed from the melting snows to the north. Most of the historic core of Fordingbridge sits on the lowest and latest of the terraces, only a few metres above the flood plain of the Avon.

Due to the natural flooding of the valley, **river silts** have accumulated over the centuries, resulting in fertile soils. These low-lying areas have long been used as high quality meadowland. Known locally as *meads*, *marshes* or *moors*, they have traditionally been used for the pasturage of cattle and horses after the removal of the hay crop.

The gravel terraces above the flood plain of the Avon have been exploited as rich farming land at least since the Bronze Age. Roman sites, such as that at North Street, Breamore, were surrounded by large areas of arable land. The present-day valley villages on these terraces, which include Breamore and Bickton, originated in medieval times.

To the east, the gravel terraces climb from the valley to the **New Forest**. Geologically, this is an extensive area of gravels, clays and sands. It was once fertile, but since the Bronze Age the area has been used mainly for pasturage and hunting, and also exploited for its raw materials such as timber, clay, heather and bracken. Sites dating from the Roman period have been found at Armsley and at Crystal Hollow, Godshill. The scattered villages, hamlets, smallholdings and farms which abound along the valley edge to the east of Fordingbridge are mostly of relatively recent date; these include Woodgreen, Hyde Stuckton and Godshill Wood.

To the west lie the rolling **chalk downs**, utilised by prehistoric man for a variety of purposes. Occupation sites, cattle enclosures and ritual sites are all found there, dating from the Neolithic to the Iron Age. Many from the latter period continued in use into Roman times. The chalk soils were then, as now, ideally suited for the production of grain crops, and were able to support relatively substantial populations over many centuries. Visible earthworks and aerial photographs provide evidence for large areas of early field-systems on the chalk downland. After their decline, probably by the end of the Roman period, the downs reverted to the sheep pasture so familiar to generations of English people. Today, most of the downland consists of large arable fields, the pasture having been ploughed up, mostly during the 20th century.

Capping the chalk near its eastern boundary with the valley gravels, and running south-south-westwards through the area, are narrow and relatively thin **bands of clays** known as Reading Beds and London Clay. Although they are different in character, both have supported woodland through the centuries; Breamore Wood is a surviving example. The multicoloured clay of the Reading beds has often been exploited for pottery making, at least in historic times (for example, at Crendle). Areas of sand and water-worn pebbles occur within this clay. Above the pebble layer, the London Clay contains patches of brick earth; this has been used for brick-making since the late 16th century, as at Alderholt, and for tile-making from much earlier periods, as at Outwick.

The **heathlands of eastern Dorset** are composed of sands of later date than the valley gravels. There are small areas of other bedrocks, such as greensand and pipe clay, adding to the complex geology of the region. Geological maps of the area provide an insight into the overall nature of the various strata, but often fail to reveal the many localised surface outcrops which are so vital in determining both vegetation cover and land use.

CHAPTER 2 – PREHISTORY

By definition, the prehistoric period dates from before written records began. Thus the information in this chapter is inevitably based on inference from archaeological evidence, which itself is often sparse and patchy.

Palaeolithic period

     The Old Stone Age or Palaeolithic period included the last ice age, some 12,000 years ago, when the great southward-flowing river created the gravels already mentioned. So it is not surprising that evidence of Palaeolithic man comes from these gravel deposits. Stone axes and other tools have been found in a number of places, notably in the gravel workings at Blashford, at Woodgreen and at Godshill.

> In the summer of 2001, archaeologists working in the Avon Valley north of Ringwood discovered a remarkably well-preserved site, believed to be around 12,500 years old. It contained not only the tools of nomadic hunter-gatherers, but also hearths, engraved artwork, ancient footprints and even the outlines of tents. A news report described it as a 'Stone Age Marie Celeste'.

A Palaeolithic hand axe, 7.5 inches (189mm) long, found at West Park, Rockbourne.

Mesolithic period

     Most of the local evidence relating to the Middle Stone Age, or Mesolithic period, is dated around 5000-3000 BC. During this time, groups of hunters visited our area, settling in seasonal camps. Several thousand worked flints associated with a large pit, discovered at Godshill, represents one such short-term habitation area. Other camps and hunting areas are suggested by scattered groups of Mesolithic flints, which have commonly been found both within the valley and beyond.

A selection of Mesolithic flint tools from Crystal Hollow, Godshill, between 7.7 and 12 mm long.

Neolithic scrapers collected by one of the authors (AL) from field surfaces at Middle Burgate (scale in cms)

Neolithic period

     The New Stone Age or Neolithic period lasted from about 3000 BC to about 1800 BC. Semi-nomadic tribes lived in the area throughout this period, mainly in the valleys, with the nearest certainly-known settlement at Downton. Flint-working was carried out throughout the Avon valley and along its tributaries, as shown by the many flint tools and waste flakes which are readily found today.

     Little Neolithic worked flint remains on the higher ground of the chalk downs, areas which were reserved for grazing, hunting and funerary monuments. Visible remains of the period are few, the most spectacular being the long-barrows on the downs, including Giant's Grave at Breamore and Duck's Nest at Rockbourne.

A superb highly-polished jadeite Neolithic axe-head, on display in Devizes Museum, is labelled as having been found at Breamore. However, there is some doubt whether it even originated in Western Europe, let alone our corner of Hampshire. The museum bought it in 1916 from Joshua Brooke, whose family had previously had links with Breamore House, which probably gave rise to the idea of it being found in the village.

The Bronze Age

During the early Bronze Age (roughly 1800 BC-800 BC), settlement seems to have continued in much the same vein, but long before the end of the period there had been significant changes. Settled communities had gradually developed and the first steps had been taken in the formation of a landscape filled with fields, pastures, woods and farms. In the main these new homesteads were sited on the uplands, on both sides of the valley, with the lower ground apparently used from time to time by pastoral communities.

Surviving monuments from this time are relatively common. Numerous round barrows - burial mounds - exist on the chalk downs and on the Forest edge, while many more have been destroyed over the centuries. On the downs beyond Whitsbury is the massive Grim's Ditch enclosure, probably constructed to enclose cattle.

Both the Forest and the valley bottom, particularly at Harbridge, have produced another class of monument, known today as 'burnt mounds', some of which still stand up to a metre high. Most, if not all, date from the middle of the Bronze Age. Similar sites occur in many parts of the country, but many have been obliterated by later farming activity, and exist now only as scatters of burnt stones.

Each burnt mound consists of a kidney-shaped heap of fire-crazed flints alongside a small oblong trough, clay-lined to retain water. The usual interpretation is that they were a 'by-product' of a means of cooking meat, perhaps by hunting parties. Water from a nearby stream was used to fill the trough, while the stones were heated on an adjacent fire. Meat was placed in the water, which was then boiled by the immersion of hot stones. The stones inevitably cracked in the water and were discarded before the trough was used again, thus gradually forming the characteristic mounds.

The Iron Age

Through the Iron Age (from about 800 BC till the arrival of the Roman legions in 43 AD) there is increasing evidence for an intricate farming system. Settlements were well-established, often being in use for several centuries, and sometimes well into the Roman occupation. Both the uplands and the valley bottom were being farmed concurrently by the Celtic peoples of the time; previous societies had preferred to use one or the other. Pottery from the first two centuries of the period (about 800-600 BC) has been found at Breamore, Godshill, Bickton and Harbridge.

Between 750 and 500 BC the countryside was transformed by the construction of the great earthwork enclosures known as Iron Age hillforts. Locally, our biggest fort was at Whitsbury, with three banks and two ditches encompassing 6.5 hectares (16 acres), the central location of a large estate controlling thousands of acres of land to the west of the Avon.

An aerial view of Castle Ditches hill-fort, Whitsbury, taken in the summer of 1932. The banks and ditches are covered by trees.
Reproduced with the permission of the Ordnance Survey

Hillforts were probably permanently occupied, and were trading and religious centres. Some were military bases and, undoubtedly, places of retreat for the occupants of the surrounding countryside in times of trouble. In fact, they were the nearest equivalent to towns existing before the Roman conquest.

Two more hillforts existed near Godshill Wood and, unusually, they were quite close together. Frankenbury is a simple univallate promontory fort encompassing under 4.5 hectares (11 acres), while that at Armsley, about a kilometre to the north, is much smaller. They were probably in use at the same time, but the relationship between them can only be a subject for speculation, especially as neither has been investigated archaeologically. As both overlooked the eastern side of the valley, they could have exercised some control over the nearby river crossings.

> Long-term excavations at Danebury hillfort near Stockbridge – and about 18 miles from Fordingbridge – have given us our greatest knowledge of the hillfort settlements. The Museum of the Iron Age at Andover displays the results in a very effective manner.

The mature landscape of the later Iron Age was one of scattered farms, and probably villages, composed of round-houses. They were connected by lanes and tracks running through permanent arable and pasture fields, meadows and woodlands. In effect the countryside was beginning to take on an appearance that would not seem at all strange to us today, even though the actual buildings were so different.

Reconstructions of Iron Age roundhouses at the Cranborne Ancient Technology Centre, photographed after a snowfall. The hut in the foreground is a 'ring-ditch roundhouse' which has no vertical walls under the conical roof. It is based on evidence from an excavation at Godshill. The other houses in the background are constructed with three different types of walls - wattle and daub, chalk cob and a double wattle wall, stuffed with heather for insulation.

A considerable number of Iron Age settlements are now known in the area, mainly from pottery scatters on field surfaces. A site at Crystal Hollow, Godshill, however, has been excavated. The pottery recovered included a small, but significant, quantity of imported amphorae. This indicates that wine from Gaul or Spain was available to wealthier families before the Roman Conquest, probably via the port at Hengistbury.

Coinage had also been introduced, although it is doubtful whether it was, at first, used for day-to-day trade. Rather it was hoarded as accumulated wealth and used as gift exchange between chiefs. By the latter decades of the 1st century BC many of the tribes were issuing their own coinage in relatively large quantities, and it is possible that this process marks the first steps in what we would regard as a market economy.

Almost all the coins found locally have been Durotrigian in origin. It is usually postulated that the Avon was the boundary between the Durotrigian tribe to the west and the Atrebatic tribes to the east, but Durotrigian coins have been found in some quantity within the New Forest. However, pottery recovered from local sites contains only small quantities of the Durotrigian type vessels that predominate deeper into Dorset. Tribal associations are difficult to determine in peripheral areas such as ours, and the tidy fixed boundaries that we like to imagine may never have existed.

CHAPTER 3 – THE ROMAN PERIOD

The Invasion and Conquest

In 43 AD the relative peace and prosperity of the Iron Age countryside was disturbed by the Roman invasion – news of the impending disaster must have travelled rapidly and soon reached our area. It has long been thought that the original landings were at Richborough in Kent, but more recently Fishbourne (near Chichester) has been suggested.

As so often in war, the landings were followed by a lull while the invaders consolidated their bridge-head and accumulated equipment and food supplies. However, it was not long before the Second Legion Augusta, led by Vespasian, later to become emperor, made the inevitable push westward. Probably, this took place in 44 AD, with the camp at Fishbourne being used as the base. It has been suggested that Vespasian's route through the Fordingbridge area involved marching up the Avon valley from Christchurch.

The '*Second Legion of Augustus*', a re-enactment group at Rockbourne Roman Villa

There is, however, another possibility. The legion could have used a military road from Southampton Water, across the present-day New Forest, towards the ford at Fordingbridge. The troops would have subjugated the fort at Godshill, crossed the ford and then continued to the Whitsbury hillfort, along a route similar to the existing Fordingbridge-Whitsbury road. By this time, the majority of the local population would have retreated to the hillforts, with as many of their livestock and possessions as they could gather.

The might of the legions was impossible to overcome; they were experienced, well-trained professional soldiers. Even if resistance took place locally (and we have no way of knowing if resistance was attempted), the local forces would have been no better than an inexperienced part-time militia. No doubt terms for peace were soon dictated and a detachment was left to control and administer the area. Meanwhile the bulk of the Second Legion pressed on westwards into the heart of Durotrigian territory, culminating in the capture of the huge hillfort of Maiden Castle near Dorchester.

Gradual Romanisation

The Roman army required enormous quantities of grain. The simplest way of obtaining it was for the indigenous population to grow and harvest their crops as usual, but with a proportion being taken by the invaders as taxation in kind. Thus the local people would have been encouraged to return to their farms as soon as possible. However severe the trauma of the invasion and however deep the resentment of the taxation, for many families life soon returned to something approaching normality. Within a generation or two, prosperity returned, with a gradual 'Romanisation' of the population.

In due course, the Celtic tribal leaders or chiefs were given roles in local government. As a result, it was not long before they were enjoying the benefits of co-operation with the civil and military authorities. Many soon adopted a Roman lifestyle. Locally, the earlier native round-houses had been replaced by the first Roman-style stone buildings at Rockbourne Villa by about 80AD. The nearest civitas capitals, occupied by the Roman administrators, were Venta Belgarum (Winchester) and Durnovaria (Dorchester), but it is not clear on which side of the boundary our area lay.

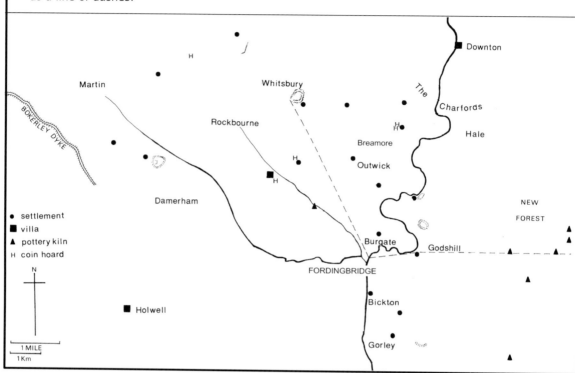

MAP OF KNOWN ROMAN SITES IN THE FORDINGBRIDGE AREA
Rockbourne Roman Villa must have had an extensive estate, including many of the lands to the west of the River Avon. The proposed military road past Godshill and on to Whitsbury is shown as a line of dashes.

- settlement
- villa
- pottery kiln
- coin hoard

1 MILE
1 Km

How soon did the lower grades of society, the local farming population, benefit from this process of 'Romanisation'? Many of their occupation sites are now known, simply from scatters of pottery and other artefacts, at Breamore, Rockbourne, Outwick, Burgate, Godshill, Bickton, Harbridge and elsewhere.

At Godshill there is more detailed evidence, from the excavation of actual house-plots. A hamlet or small village existed here, on the edge of the Forest at Crystal Hollow, its economy being pasture based, in contrast to the arable or mixed farms of the valley and downs. Here, the change from round-houses to Roman-style rectangular buildings seems to have occurred, along with planned streets, in the middle of the 2nd century AD. This was perhaps two or three generations later than the change had occurred at the wealthier Rockbourne Villa. However, the buildings were of timber; stone buildings were never an option for any but the wealthiest in this part of the country.

Imported pottery of the period, particularly Samian ware from Gaul, does occur, but in very small amounts. Surface collections of pottery sherds from many of the other sites tend to confirm this scarcity as the norm. In general, it seems that fine table wares did not reach the local population in quantity until the 3rd century AD, although at Rockbourne Villa they were available from the start.

Roman Fordingbridge

Where then does Fordingbridge itself fit into the overall picture of a rural landscape of hedged and fenced fields, with areas of woodland, populated with farms, hamlets and villages?

Over the years Roman finds have been made at a number of places in and near the town, but as yet no occupation site is known with certainty. Pottery is reputed to have been found near the Old Manor Court House in Salisbury Street and near the Hospital, while several stray coin finds have also been reported. The ford, just downstream from the medieval bridge, had long been an important crossing point of the Avon. Being at a focus of routes, it could well have been a major meeting place and the site of a market, as it was to become in later times. When sewerage pipes were laid in the 1950s, Roman pottery is said to have been found on the river-bed; the assumption was that it had fallen from a wagon which had capsized while crossing the ford.

The site now occupied by the town of Fordingbridge was very likely part of (or at least on the edge of) the large estate administered from the Rockbourne Villa. The estate is believed to have stretched from Martin and Damerham in the west, at least as far as the Avon in the east. It would have controlled and exacted rents in money or kind from virtually all the farms and villages in our area. The closest neighbouring villas were at Moot Lane, Downton (Wiltshire) and at Holwell near Cranborne (Dorset).

Rockbourne Roman Villa, excavated by A. T. Morley Hewitt in the 1950s and 1960s, had developed gradually over the years. By the later part of the 2nd century it was a large and imposing complex of buildings, the equivalent of the country house of more recent times. By the 4th century it had evolved into a courtyard villa, and was still growing in size (as shown in the artist's reconstruction above.) Extensive pottery scatters in the field behind it may indicate the existence of a further range of farm buildings. While it is generally assumed that the occupiers of the villa were the descendants of a wealthy local family, at least in the early days, this may not always have been the case. Large inputs of capital into new buildings on the site in the 2nd century, and also late in the 3rd century, are just as likely to have followed the arrival of new owners with wealth accumulated elsewhere. ('Owner' could be a misleading term, as the occupiers could have been tenants, perhaps even of an imperial estate.)

Reconstruction reproduced by permission of Hampshire Museums Service

Assuming that each of the villas at Rockbourne, Downton and Holwell was the centre of an estate, their boundaries must have been approximately where the present day county boundaries run.

A number of other excavations of Roman period sites have been carried out in the area. At Armsley near Folds Farm, an 'industrial' settlement was revealed, with working floors related to iron smelting and smithing. Sites within and near the Whitsbury hillfort provide evidence for occupation from the 2nd to 4th centuries, and possibly later. On Gorley Hill, pottery was being made during the 1st century AD, and there are doubtless other contemporary kilns to be found elsewhere in the area.

Soon after the middle of the 3rd century, a major local pottery industry developed, mostly within the area of the New Forest. The kilns produced an enormous range of fine table wares and coarser grey vessels for the kitchen. Several centres of production are known, the nearest to Fordingbridge being at Pitts Wood near Godshill. Others have been found at Sloden, Amberwood and Linwood. A contemporary site, outside the Forest, but producing identical wares, has been discovered at Allen's Farm, Rockbourne. The range of vessels declined during the later 4th century and production seems to have ceased before the end of the Roman occupation.

CHAPTER 4 – THE DARK AGES

The Sub-Roman Period

The century after the end of Roman rule in 410AD has long been known, with good reason, as the beginning of the Dark Ages. After the departure of the Legions, the monetary economy collapsed, and it became increasingly difficult for people to maintain their Roman lifestyle. In the countryside, although the amount of arable land may have decreased, farmers and villagers would have continued to cultivate their long established holdings. Perhaps, in some cases, they retreated to the hillforts for protection. For urban dwellers, things were more difficult. The towns established by the Romans gradually deteriorated and eventually were abandoned.

However, the term 'the Dark Ages' refers less to the lifestyles of the time than to our lack of knowledge of the period, resulting from the paucity both of contemporary documents and of archaeological information.

Early Saxon Settlements

Saxon mercenary soldiers had been present in the country since the 3rd century AD, and many had settled with their families. By the early years of the 6th century, larger westward movements of Germanic tribes resulted in attempts to settle our area. According to Bede's 8th century *Ecclesiastical History*, the Isle of Wight and areas of the nearby mainland were occupied by Jutes from Jutland (rather than by Saxons from Saxony). It is not known if Jutish influence extended as far north as our part of the Avon Valley. Our knowledge of the period depends largely on *The Anglo-Saxon Chronicles*. However, they were written in later centuries, based on oral traditions. Their validity is doubtful in view of their propaganda value to the Wessex kings.

The Battle of Cerdic's Ford

The *Chronicles* record a battle in 519 at Cerdic's Ford, which has long been identified with Charford, just to the north of Breamore (though some historians dispute this identification).

> *Cerdic and Cynric received the West Saxon kingdom, and the same year they fought with the Britons in the place now called Cerdicesford; the royal line of Wessex ruled from that day.*

If we accept the *Chronicle's* version of events, Cerdic was a Saxon leader who defeated the local British forces, which surely included many men from the Rockbourne Estate. It must be assumed that the survivors retreated into Dorset, constructing the major defensive earthwork, Bokerley Dyke, in an attempt to protect their remaining territory against the Saxon settlers.

The 'royal line of Wessex' (whether or not Cerdic was its ancestor) lasted for many generations. A little over four centuries after the supposed battle, Athelstan, a grandson of Alfred the Great, became the first King of a united England.

Archaeological Evidence for Saxon Settlements

Although archaeological evidence for the period is still sparse, much new information has come to light in recent years. Sherds of grass- or chaff-tempered ware, which dates from the early Saxon period, has been found at Breamore, Charford, Burgate, Bickton and Whitsbury. In the making of this type of pottery, the clay was tempered with grass or chaff, which burnt out during firing, leaving small voids. Thus, sherds are very friable; they soon disintegrate when exposed on the surface of fields, so they generally survive only in fragments.

In most cases this pottery has been found in the same fields as Roman material. This indicates either continuity of occupation through the sub-Roman period, or reoccupation of the sites in the early Saxon period. At Breamore, brooches (see below left) and other metallic finds have helped to define a probable occupation site.

Steve Bolger, using a metal detector in 1999, recovered an extremely rare Byzantine tin-plated brass 'bucket' from a field in Breamore. As a result, in August 2001 a 3-day live television excavation was carried out for *Time Team*, Channel 4's popular and well-respected archaeology programme. This revealed an early Saxon pagan cemetery with grave goods of very high status.

Ten adult burials were investigated, of which at least one was a female. Unusually, most were laid to rest in pairs. They were accompanied by a variety of iron weapons and shields. Other grave goods recovered, all of 6th century date, included a garnet-inlaid buckle and seven further 'buckets' or drinking vessels. These were of a more usual type, made of wooden slats with metal bindings.

These wonderful finds, recovered a little over two miles from Fordingbridge, are of major significance. Conservation and examination of each item will, in due course, greatly increase our knowledge of this still obscure period in our local and national history.

1 cm

ABOVE : An early 6th-century Saxon 'face' button brooch found at Breamore by Chris Gifford

RIGHT: the Byzantine 'bucket' or situla found at Breamore by Steve Bolger. It is covered with intricate designs of hunting scenes and carries an inscription in Greek. It was probably made in Antioch during the 6th century. It is fascinating to speculate on how it found its way from present-day Syria to our corner of Hampshire - and on the status of its Saxon (or perhaps Jutish) owner.

Photograph reproduced by permission of Hampshire Museums Service

The Norman Conquest and the Domesday Survey

Following the Battle of Hastings in 1066, the forces of William the Conqueror swept throughout England. Just as the Roman invasion in 43 AD had led to a complete restructuring of local society, so the Normans imposed their rule on the existing English kingdom. Land was re-distributed among William's Norman followers, adding a new upper tier to society.

Ironically, much of what is known about late Saxon times comes from William's amazing 'national census' of 1086, known as the Domesday Book. As well as recording contemporary land holdings, it also looked retrospectively at ownership and value before 1066, *'in King Edward's time'.*

Late Saxon Times

While we are now beginning to understand something of settlement patterns in early Saxon times, the same cannot be said of the 8th-10th centuries, the period in which the majority of our villages were being founded. The earliest Saxon place-names are thought to be those, such as Forde, which were derived from geographical features. There can be little doubt that the area was continuously cultivated from early in Saxon times, though there is no archaeological evidence, as yet, for what were probably scattered farmsteads. As the population increased, village communities began to be formed, as houses and farms became grouped together.

With no surviving contemporary Saxon documents, we can only guess that the settlement called Forde originated in the 8th or 9th century. It is clear from the evidence of Domesday Book, however, that the Manor of Forde was well established by 1086. Geographically it must have been formed out of the Burgate estate; we can infer that it was granted at some point to a courtier or thegn, probably during the 10th or early 11th centuries.

HD.
IN FORDINGEBRIGE

T.R.E. Iſd Robt̃ ten̄ FORDE.7 Robt̃ de eo.Aluui tenuit in alod de rege.E.

ualb Lx fol. 7 poſt xx. Tc̄ geld p.ii.hiđ 7 iii.virḡ.Modo p.ii.hiđ.Tra.ē.ii.car̄.In dn̄io.ē una.

m̃.Lx.fol. 7 xiii.borđ hn̄t.i.car̄.Ibi æccła 7 ii.molini de.xiiii.fol.7 ii.denar.

7 xxx.ac p̃ti.De iſto m̃ ſunt.iii.v in foreſta regis.7 totū nem̃.qđ ual.xx.fol.

The Manor of Forde in Domesday Book
ABOVE: the entry in its original abbreviated medieval Latin. The handwriting of King William's surveyors has been transcribed into printed text only once, in 1783, using type specially designed for the purpose.
From the Phillimore facsimile edition of the Domesday Book, Hampshire volume, 1982

BELOW: the entry transcribed into modern English

OPPOSITE: an explanation of each of the sections of the entry

---

Robert son of Gerold holds Forde and Robert holds it of him. Alfwy held it of King Edward as an alod. It was then assessed at 2 hides and 3 virgates and now at 2 hides. There is land for 2 ploughs. In demesne is 1 plough, and 13 bordars have 1 plough. There are a church, and 2 mills worth 14s 2d, and 30 acres of meadow. Of this manor, 3 virgates are in the King's Forest; also the whole woodland worth 20s. In King Edward's time it was worth 60s and afterwards 30s. It is now worth 60s.

Alfwy held it of King Edward as an alod

In 1066, before the Conquest, the estate was in the possession of a Saxon by the name of Alfwy, who held it in allodium, that is as a complete owner, having no powerful magnate as an overlord. He was a landowner of considerable importance, holding manors in several counties. Although many of his lands were taken from him after the Conquest, he continued to hold Lockerley in Hampshire. He may well have been the same Alfwy, son of Thurber, who held Midgham and parts of Charford and Rockbourne.

Robert son of Gerold holds Forde and Robert holds it of him

After the Conquest the manor passed into Norman hands. Robert son of Gerold, the son of Giroldus Dapifer of Roumare in Normandy, was a powerful landholder owning eight other manors in Hampshire, as well as 22 hides in Dorset and 55 hides in Wiltshire. Forde, like most of his holdings, was sublet, the tenant being another Robert, who is much more difficult to trace as the name is so common.

It was then assessed at 2 hides and 3 virgates and now at 2 hides

This assessment relates to money collected for Danegeld, a tax due each year, up until 1051. The Saxon kings paid it to the Danish kings as 'protection money', to prevent invasion. The payment was related to the area of arable land, the unit of measurement being the hide.

A hide was supposedly the amount of land needed to support a family for a year, and which could be ploughed by a team of eight oxen. In practice, this was a rather arbitrary measurement, with a large degree of variation. Some computations put the area at well under 100 acres, others say about 120 acres, but at Damerham it is put at 160. Clearly, the quality and nature of the land was vital. A virgate was a quarter of a hide.

It is difficult to see how more than a hundred acres at the very most could ever have been considered to be arable within the manor of Forde, and yet in the 1086 Survey it was assessed as having been 2¾ hides in Saxon times. Here, the hide seems unlikely to have been more than 40-50 acres of relatively good quality land – unless the arable land then extended down into the floodplain, into areas now considered to be meadow or pasture.

30 acres of meadow

This assessment of meadow, much smaller than would seem likely today, supports the idea, mentioned above, that some present-day meadow-land was arable at that time.

There is land for 2 ploughs. In demesne is 1 plough, and 13 bordars have 1 plough

Of the two ploughlands recorded, one was farmed directly by Alfwy himself, with the other split between the 13 families of bordars or cottagers. There is no evidence as to how these lands were distributed.

Of this manor, 3 virgates are in the King's Forest; also the whole woodland worth 20s

Several valley villages held lands in the New Forest, but these were taken away and subjected to Forest Law when it was refounded by King William in 1079. Forde had held three virgates (perhaps in the region of 90 acres) of land there and woodland worth 20 shillings a year.

2 mills worth 14s 2d

This may not imply that Fordingbridge had two mill buildings. The word mill is probably used in the sense of 'millstone', two being under one roof on the site of the later Town Mills on Ashford Water. Damerham had its own mills, as did Charford, Bickton, Ibsley and Ellingham. Burgate had two, one of which was at East Mill. Each had an annual value but those at Charford, Burgate and Ibsley were also assessed as paying 1250, 1000 and 700 eels respectively.

In King Edward's time it was worth 60s, and afterwards 30s. It is now worth 60s

This valuation refers to the whole Manor of Forde. It raises the question – why was the value of the property halved after the Conquest ? This is not uncommon, the same reduction being seen in the Domesday entry for some other local manors. There is no certain answer, but it may relate to some form of disruption which took place at the time of the Conquest. (In other parts of England, which were violently subjugated by the Normans, property damage resulted in drastic declines in value. There is, however, no evidence to suggest that the local population suffered greatly at the hands of the Norman conquerors.)

Royal Manors and Minster Churches

The county of Hampshire was first recorded as Hantescire as early as 757, and Forde was always within this county. The chief administrative officer was the county Sheriff, based in Winchester. He was responsible for administering the ancient demesnes of the crown. (Sheriffs also collected the Danegeld, dispensed the King's justice and oversaw the maintenance of local custom.)

It is clear from the Domesday Book that the lands of the former Rockbourne Villa Estate, as far as we can be certain of its extent, were in Crown hands, and had been so for many years. By 1086 the area was being administered as three distinct royal manors, based on Damerham, Rockbourne and Burgate respectively.

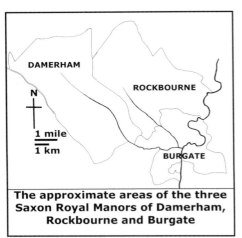

The approximate areas of the three Saxon Royal Manors of Damerham, Rockbourne and Burgate

Breamore was part of the manor of Rockbourne. As an ancient demesne of the crown, it was liable for a rent of 51s. 8d in lieu of *'firma noctis'*. This was an annual rent in kind – sufficient food to maintain the Royal Court for a night, a system dating from the 8th century or earlier. By the time of the Survey the system was certainly long defunct, but its former existence in the area implies that the whole group of local royal manors would have once paid this rent.

Forde is the only manor in our area to be credited with a church in the Domesday survey. Despite this, Breamore and Damerham are known to have had minster churches at the time, both being royal foundations. Minster churches ministered to much larger areas than did parish churches, areas which almost certainly corresponded closely with the estates in which they stood. Although Rockbourne was the head village, the minster was at Breamore, perhaps because it was nearer the centre of the area, and more easily accessible from the other villages.

Where Fordingbridge fitted into this system early on is unclear, but it must have been the ecclesiastical centre for the Burgate estate, at least by the 11th century. This would have given it equal status with the other two royal estates, so the church was presumably also regarded as a minster.

Each of these minsters would have been served by a community of priests based at the mother church, with responsibilities for its outlying villages. The important late Saxon structure at Breamore is well known and need not be discussed here, except to say that while it is still a large and impressive church of the period, it would have been all the more so when the chancel was its original height, when the western baptistry and the north porticus were still in place, and when the tower had its upper sections. At Damerham some of the existing structure may well date from late Saxon times, but it is difficult to gain any overall impression of the size and form of the early building due to later modification.

Breamore Church.

The Saxon Church of St Mary's, Breamore; and the inscription in Anglo-Saxon on the arch of the south porticus.

Both from picture postcards of around 1905

The Parish of Forde

The large parish of Forde included the villages of Midgham, Bickton, Gorley and Burgate as well as various hamlets in the Forest, an area that was to remain little altered for many centuries. Of the Domesday church itself there are no known remains, and it is currently impossible to tell whether there was once an imposing stone building here or a simple wooden one. It is assumed that it stood within the area of the present churchyard but until archaeological evidence is forthcoming even this cannot be confirmed.

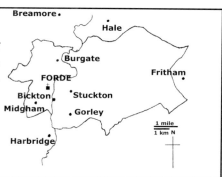

The Village of Forde

Although we have no direct information there is every reason to believe that the Manor of Forde occupied almost exactly those same areas that are later recorded as the Tything of Forde. There may well have been changes over the centuries but they are likely to have been relatively insignificant.

The earliest Saxon settlement is likely to have consisted of scattered farmsteads. We do not know when the first actual village, or nucleated settlement, was formed, or indeed where it was first situated. The most likely area is around the church where the land is well above the floodplain.

To the south-west of this is the large area of arable and pasture, known as Lulsey Field, one of the town's medieval open fields (see map on page 24). The name Lulsey is derived from the personal name Lulla, together with 'ey', the Old English word for an island, or land partly surrounded by water. Lulsey Field therefore took its name from its position as higher ground in the marshes of the valley, in the ownership of Lulla, who must have been one of the earliest inhabitants of the village of Forde.

The Hundred of Fordingbridge

By the 10th century the county was divided into Hundreds, the major unit of local administration. Forde became the centre of the local Hundred, probably for reasons of geographical convenience, as it lay at an important river crossing, allowing easy access from all directions. In the Domesday Survey, the Hundred, unlike the Manor, is recorded with the earliest instance of the name Fordingbridge, indicating that a bridge of some sort had already existed for a considerable time.

The Hundred consisted of the villages and manors shown. The householders of these places would have been expected to attend court regularly at Forde, probably every 4 weeks, at the ancient moot, or meeting place. This may perhaps have been on the west side of the river, near present-day Bridge Street, in the area which was later to become the town's market place. Interestingly, although the courts were apparently held within the Manor of Forde, the profits of dispensing justice there were always to be the property of the Lord of the Manor of Burgate. This anomaly must have dated from the time when Forde was part of the larger Crown estate.

Of the remaining villages of the old Royal estates, all of which were in Wiltshire until 1895, Damerham and Martin composed part of their own Hundred known as South Damerham, while Whitsbury was in the Wiltshire Hundred of Cawden and Cadworth, despite being in the Diocese of Winchester.

CHAPTER 5 – THE MEDIEVAL PERIOD

The duration of the 'Medieval Period' is open to debate. For the purposes of this history, we use the term to cover a period of just over four centuries, commencing after the Domesday Survey in 1086 and ending around 1500. By the latter date, King Henry VII had firmly established the House of Tudor on the throne of England. Inevitably, there were many changes both in and around Fordingbridge in this period.

> Our understanding of these changes is often limited by a paucity of surviving documents. We consequently depend upon interpreting those isolated records that do remain and on making assumptions concerning their factual correctness. (It is generally not possible, as can sometimes be done for later centuries when documents are more numerous, to double-check between different sources.)
>
> More concrete evidence is provided by the growing archaeological record. This is our best guide to the physical appearance of the town, bearing in mind that today we are left with little more than its street layout, the Parish Church and the Great Bridge.

The Church and the 'New Town'

Where were people living in medieval times? We have already seen that the location of the main settlement at the time of Domesday is uncertain. This is still true until around the middle of the 13th century, at which point information becomes more plentiful. We can reasonably infer that substantial changes were already taking place during the late 12th or early 13th centuries. The history of Forde as a 'town' rather than a village begins at this time.

Restoration work was carried out on St Mary's, the Parish Church of Fordingbridge, in 1903. The discovery at that time of fragments of stonework dating from the 12th century suggests that the church was rebuilt then, but as almost the entire 12th-century structure was itself later replaced, it is impossible to tell what came before it.

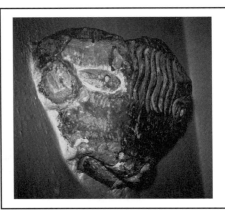

Now hidden away behind the organ in Fordingbridge Parish Church, this oxhead corbel is one of the oldest remaining pieces of stonework

In around 1230, in John Lovering's words:
'one feature of the obliterated 12th-century church was lovingly retained. The church had corbels, one of which was a little oxhead. Someone, the Lord, the Priest, perhaps the whole congregation, evidently had a deep affection for it, for it was brought into the extended church and mounted above the altar of the south chapel'

Other major changes in the town also took place in the 12th century. Their timing may have been partly coincidental, but it is tempting to think that they were part of an overall plan to reorganise and enlarge Forde. 'New towns' were becoming fashionable, for example the developments of New Alresford and of Downton. In each case, the intention would have been for the Lord of the Manor to maximise his income by establishing a planned market-town. However, if this was the case here, the plan was on a much smaller scale than at the other settlements mentioned – and also much less successful.

It is probable that most 12th-century houses were relatively near the church, stretching northwards as far as Provost Street, and perhaps to Shaftesbury Street and West Street. The widened area of Church Street, to the north of the churchyard, may well have originated at this time. Only archaeological investigations can determine whether this was in fact the case; so far the evidence is inconclusive. At the northern end of the 'square' occupation of about this period has been discovered, but on the western side the only plot yet excavated provided no evidence of medieval settlement.

Sites of the Market

The name 'Chopys Lane' was used until the 19th century for the track leading westwards from opposite the north-west corner of the churchyard. 'Chopys' is the Middle English form of 'shops', used during the Medieval period to refer, not to permanent shops, but to market-stalls. This is a strong indication that the 'church square' was the medieval market-place. But the market did not remain there. By the 16th century, and probably much earlier, it had moved to the area of today's Bridge Street, High Street and Roundhill.

The new site, just west of the Great Bridge, was clearly much more convenient for attracting new trade to the town; although there may have been other reasons for the move. Indeed, the bridge was an important catalyst for the development of the village into a town and for the success of its market. It provided easy access from the south and east for both traders and villagers. We have already noted that a bridge of some sort existed over the Avon at the time of the Domesday Survey of 1086. This structure, or a successor, must have continued in use throughout the 12th century.

The Houses of the Town

The development of Painter's Mews and Riverside Parade, completed in 2001, on the former Greyhound Inn and Albany Hotel sites to the west of the bridge, was preceded by excavation. Archaeology revealed that houses began to be built here in the last decade or two of the 13th century. This was to the north of present-day Bridge Street, adjacent to the space that was already, or was eventually to become, the market place. No evidence was found for settlement earlier than this date.

We can assume that most of the houses in the town would have been small half-timbered thatched cottages, closely resembling those in nearby villages. The few that have been excavated were built on flimsy stone foundations. There is, however, evidence that richer ones, such as that on the former Albany site, had tiled roofs with elaborate ridge tiles and decorated finials.

The land further south, in the region of the present High Street and perhaps as far as the top end of Provost Street, was largely undeveloped. It probably remained so until at least the

Excavations were carried out on the former sites of the Greyhound Inn (*left*) and of the Albany Hotel (*right*) in 1989 and in 1997, respectively.
The hearth in the first picture, made of clay roof tiles set vertically into the ground, was one of the earliest features revealed, probably dating from late in the 13th century. (Each division on the surveyors' rod is half a metre.) Extensive house foundations and evidence of a tanning industry were found on the Albany site.

16th century. Provost Street itself, however, was much more 'urbanised' and densely populated by the 13th century, with many of the houses probably having rear extensions and attached hovels.

The area on the eastern side of the bridge is still known as Horseport, a name which dates from the 14th century, if not earlier. This evocative name has never been fully explained. It may be that the earliest phases of the bridge were suitable only for foot passengers and horses, with wheeled traffic still using the ford downstream. The Old English word *'port'* was often used in the sense of 'town', and the meaning here would therefore be loosely, 'way to the town for horse traffic'.

Some other early place-names are recorded. A deed of 1342 refers to *La Bothelstrete* – its location is uncertain, but it probably led towards Sandleheath. Two other names were recorded in 1476. *Gomanyscrosse*, which cannot be located, was named after the family of William Gooman, a 15th-century tenant, while Frog Lane was then called *Grenelane*.

Population

The actual population of the town during any part of the medieval period is difficult to estimate. From the various documentary sources it seems unlikely that the housing stock would ever have exceeded seventy at the very most, and even this total would not have been reached until well into the 13th century. From then on, numbers probably remained fairly static, despite a sharp drop in population after the middle of the 14th century following the onset of plague. Some houses may have been lost during the economic decline of the first half of the following century, but by Tudor times expansion was again underway.

Clearly Fordingbridge was never a large town, and the population must have numbered hundreds rather than thousands, even at its peak during the 13th and early 14th centuries. Indeed there may not have been all that many more people here than in some of the larger villages such as Damerham and Rockbourne. Fordingbridge, however, had an importance which belied its size. This was due to its semi-urban nature, to its administrative and ecclesiastical status as the centre of the Hundred and of the Deanery (see page 23) and above all to its regular market.

Nor was it apparently a rich town. Historians can usually gain some degree of insight into the relative size and wealth of villages and towns from surviving tax rolls, some of which list individual taxpayers. Sadly, the poll-taxes of 1377-1381, potentially the most important and detailed rolls, do not survive for Hampshire. However, the Lay Subsidy Rolls for 1327 and 1333 survive to this day. Both list the taxpayers for Forde and for the other local villages, though, as their name suggests, clergy were exempted. The results are both fascinating and puzzling. For this district the 1333 list seems to be the fullest.

Taxpayers in 1333

The tax was levied at one fifteenth of the value of moveable goods owned by each householder, although some items such as craftsmen's tools and jewellery were exempted. No one with goods valued at a total below 15 shillings had to pay. This immediately excluded the vast majority of people, making the rolls impossible to use for assessing population totals.

Forde had only 16 taxpayers, rendering a total of 36s.7d. This number is surprisingly low, especially when compared with other local villages. Breamore's 22 taxpayers contributed 66s.2½d, Rockbourne had 40 paying 128s.4d, while even Bickton had 11 paying 33s.8d. These remarks must however be qualified by two points. Some of the taxpayers listed under Burgate could well have been living at Horseport which was really part of the town. Secondly, Maurice Brune, Lord of the Manor of Forde, was living at Midgham, as we shall see later, where he was paying 8s.8d.

Nevertheless, taking the assumption of 70 households in the town, and taking the Rolls at face value, it appears that more than three-quarters of the town's householders were too poor to pay the tax. Comparable figures for elsewhere are difficult to ascertain but at Breamore it is likely that between a third and a half were paying tax, while at Rockbourne it was almost certainly higher than that.

The Value of Money

Any attempt to convert cash values from earlier centuries into modern equivalents is fraught with difficulties. For a note on the £.s.d system (for those younger readers who have grown up with £.p) and for a rough yardstick of money values through the centuries, see page 164.

If the figures from this Lay Subsidy Roll were unique, we might suspect them as faulty, but they are confirmed time after time in later tax assessments. In 1379, Forde's total tax liability amounted to 40s.11d, while Breamore's was 73s.2½d, and Rockbourne's 144s.4d. Even the little village of Bickton was paying 38s.2d. Other similar comparisons can be made from rolls dating from the 15th century and the early part of the 16th century.

So there is little doubt that a high proportion of the town's householders, and probably an even higher proportion of the overall population, belonged to the poorer classes. Interesting confirmatory information comes from a Breamore Priory Deed of 1347 in which there is mention of bread being distributed annually to 144 poor people in Fordingbridge.

'Extent' documents of the 13th and 14th centuries also give a suggestion of the number of households. There were about 24 villeins (who rented their land by service – see page 26) plus up to 40 free-holders. But it would be unwise to assume that this gives a total of 64 households. Some of the free-holders may have held land in Forde but lived elsewhere. In addition, some of the freeholds may have belonged to villeins who had prospered sufficiently to purchase extra land, and thus they would be included in both categories.

Ownership of the Manor

We know that the Manor of Forde was held by Robert Fitz Gerold at the time of the Domesday Survey of 1086. During the reign of King John (that is, at some time between 1199 and 1216), William de Lingis is recorded as being in possession of the manor. From this time, the list is almost complete (see next page). The Lingis (or Linguire) family married into the Falaise family around 1240, and they held the manor for the next 37 years.

There are no records for the 12th century to tell us who held the Manor of Forde between Robert Fitz Gerold and William de Lingis. However, circumstantial evidence suggests that a family named de Roumare owned the manor, for at least part of the time. This depends upon a link between the Manor of Forde and the Manor of Corfe Mullen in Dorset.

At the time of Domesday, Robert Fitz Gerold held both manors; as did, more than a century later, the Lingis and Falaise families. William de Roumare was Fitz Gerold's nephew and heir and it is certain that he held the Lordship of Corfe Mullen in the 12th century. In all probability, the two properties were inherited together and the de Roumares held Fordingbridge as well.

When William de la Falaise was outlawed in 1277, for no reason that seems to be on record, the manor passed to William le Brune, the king's chamberlain, and Isolde his wife. Their descendants were to retain the Lordship until the middle of the 20th century. The Brunes, in common with most medieval landowners, had manors scattered across the countryside. Distant holdings included South Ockenden in Essex and Beckenham in Kent, while nearer Fordingbridge they held Rowner in Hampshire and Ranston in Dorset.

Inevitably, when manors were sufficiently close there was exchange of goods and produce between them and they tended to be administered by the same officials. There was certainly a degree of co-operation between Fordingbridge and Ranston, and before 1277 also between Fordingbridge and Corfe Mullen. (The latter manor did not go to the Brunes but followed an altogether different descent after 1277.)

Lords of the Manor of Forde

The following dates appear in various records, often at the death of the holder:

1086	Robert son of Gerold
12th C	possibly William de Roumare - held Corfe Mullen in the time of Henry I
Time of King John	William de Lingis
1231	Hugh de Linguire died
pre-1242	his niece Alice married William de la Falaise
1248	William de la Falaise died
1254	Elias de la Falaise died
1277	William de la Falaise outlawed for felony. Property taken by the Crown
1277	William le Brune and Isolde his wife granted manor
1301	William le Brune died
1307	Isolde le Brune died
1355	Maurice their son died
1358	William his son conveyed manor to Joan his daughter and Thomas de Overton her husband
1362	William le Brune died
1371	Joan released her rights to her husband and her brothers Ingram and Richard le Brune
1390	Ingram Brune took possession
1400	Elizabeth, wife of Ingram, held manor during minority of her son Maurice
1403	Elizabeth died
1407	Maurice Brune came of age
1461	Henry Brune died
1468	Maurice Brune died
1497	Thomas Brune his son died; William Brune his son takes possession

The Manor of Forde

It is probable that the original Manor of Forde consisted of the entire area shown in the map on page 24, stretching from what is now the top end of Salisbury Street down the west bank of the Avon as far as the Harbridge boundary, and westwards to Ashford, Bowerwood Hill and Midgham. By the end of the 12th century, however, grants of land to the new Rectory Manor, known as Woodfidley (see page 32-33), had reduced the area under the control of the Lord of the Manor of Forde. Over the years property sales and further grants produced a complex pattern of ownership, with many instances of neighbouring houses belonging to different manors.

The Lords of the Manor seem never to have lived in the town. (However, there are no records that either confirm or deny the existence of a Manor House before 1250.) By the middle of the 13th century the Falaise family were in possession of nearby North Midgham. It was there that they and their successors, the Brunes, established their Manor House, with gardens, and in due course, a park.

Quite why they never built within Fordingbridge is not clear, as we know that they owned a suitable site. In 1274 it is referred to as 'a certain place' within the 'villa de Forde', while in 1360 it is recorded as 'a certain site not built on'. From the Account Roll of 1277 it is also clear that a 'garden' existed here although the term is apparently used to refer to the Manor

Farm. The plot seems to have stretched along the north side of the road to Midgham, from the foot of Bowerwood Hill almost to Church Street.

While the undeveloped 'site' cannot be identified with certainty it must have been to the west of the churchyard adjoining the Vicarage, or just possibly a little to the north. This may explain why the western side of the 'church square' has not as yet produced evidence of medieval buildings. The post-medieval farm of the Brune's was in the field behind the Vicarage. It adjoined closes (enclosed fields) called Middlecroft, which are also referred to as being parcel of (i.e. part of) the demesne in an Account Roll of 1277.

The Church Building

We have already mentioned that the Saxon church was rebuilt during the 12th century, probably between 1160 and 1170 AD. It seems likely that the new structure consisted solely of a nave, similar in size to the present one but without the aisles, and a chancel of the same width as today, although not extending as far to the east. Parts of the west wall of the nave and of the south wall of the chancel remain from this building, the only fragments to have survived the second major rebuilding which took place between 1220 and 1240.

At this time aisles were added to the nave, the chancel was extended eastwards and a vestry was built to the south. A small chapel was added on the north, in the angle formed by the chancel and the north aisle. Eventually, in about 1270, this north chapel was extended to the same length as the chancel. At this stage, there was still no tower, although it must be assumed that a bell-cote of some form had long existed.

By around the middle of the 15th century, the tower was under construction, the south aisle had been rebuilt and the clerestory and north and south porches had been added. The church was beginning to take on the appearance which is familiar to us today, although the external walls were then covered in plaster.

We have few details of the internal arrangements of the church during the late medieval period, although much can be inferred from the fortunate survival of a volume of pre-Reformation Churchwarden's Accounts, beginning in 1490 (see page 52).

By the 14th century the church was the centre of a Deanery which embraced much of the western part of Hampshire, an arrangement which was still in place well into the 17th century. The parishes under its control stretched from Christchurch, Milford and Boldre in the south, through Sopley, Minstead, East Parley, Ringwood and Ellingham, to Whitsbury and the chapelry of North Charford.

Farming – Lords, Labourers and Tenants

In the medieval countryside almost everyone was, to some extent, involved in food production - the growing of crops, the keeping of animals or both. Few people had the available cash to purchase basic foodstuffs, so self-sufficiency was essential. Large scale farming was generally restricted to the bigger landowners, mostly manorial lords or monastic houses, but there were many small and medium tenants with anything from a few acres to forty or more. For those families without fields, their best hope was to grow a few vegetables in a cottage garden, but this would not always have been sufficient to supply a reasonable year-round diet.

In towns the situation tended to be very different. Here the landless population far outnumbered the farmers and smallholders. Those artisans and traders with a regular income could afford to purchase food. Those without a trade were in a more difficult position. There were basically three options: beg, borrow or rent a small patch of ground, and grow most of their

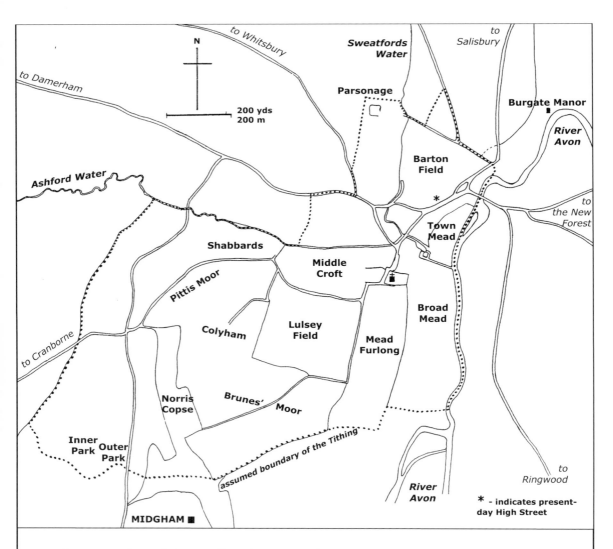

No map exists of the **medieval Manor of Forde**. However, the boundaries shown here, derived from 19th-century records of the **Tithing of Fordingbridge**, are probably similar to those of the original Manor. Some areas, however, were transferred to the new Rectory Manor of Woodfidley in the 12th and 13th centuries,

In medieval times the Brune family owned a manor house at Midgham. The names 'Inner Park' and 'Outer Park' are a survival from the park which adjoined this house.

The map also clearly shows the medieval Open Fields of the town, Lulsey Field, Mead Furlong and Barton Field (whose name is preserved today in 'The Bartons'). Middle Croft may originally have been part of Lulsey Field.

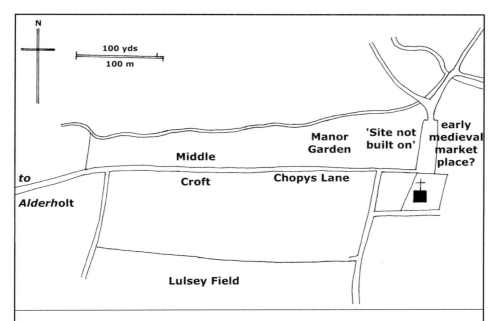

The suggested layout of fields and roads near the church in medieval times *(above)*, compared with the changes made in or before the 15th century *(below)*. The 'new' road layout largely survives today.
The wide section of Church Street was probably the first of three sites, over the centuries, for Fordingbridge Market (see also p 69).

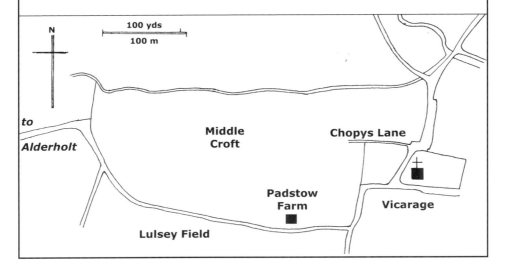

food; earn the money to pay for food; or rely on charity. The most readily available employment was as agricultural labourers, but the seasonal nature of agricultural work made this an unreliable source of income.

The biggest potential employers were the various Lords of the Manors, whose own farms were known as the *demesne*. However, before the drastic reduction in population caused by the Black Death of the mid-14th century, this work was not available to casual labourers, as it was carried out by the villeins (or customary tenants) and their families. They were the tenants of the ancient smallholdings of the manors; their 'customary services' on the demesne were effectively a form of rent for their holdings.

In Forde, the villeins' customary services seem to have been less onerous than on many manors, probably due to the relatively small area of demesne arable land (see next section). 'Week-work', with the villeins working on the demesne for two or more days every week, was

common on many manors. In the earliest records, dated 1277, there is no mention of week-work. When the Brune family took over the Manor of Forde in that year, they had twenty-four of these customary tenants. They had a commitment to work on two days of each week in August, in order to help with the harvest on the demesne, and there are also mentions of carting and mowing services. If some of the work was not needed, a small rent payment could be made in lieu.

In the records of the Manor of Burgate, tenants' services for carting, mowing, ploughing, haymaking and harvesting are mentioned. In Breamore, harvest work was apparently still being exacted from tenants of the old Priory lands as late as 1583.

After the middle of the 14th century, the reduction in population led to a disruption of demesne farming and of agriculture generally. As a result, customary services were frequently replaced by wage labour; in some places, this commuting of customary services occurred earlier. It is difficult to be precise about when the services were commuted at Forde in particular, but the Extents of 1354, 1360 and 1362 give some indications. Customary work is mentioned in 1354, but not in the other two. The demesne farm may even have been closed down around 1360, as the only arable recorded at that date was in the hands of bond tenants – and the manor had a much higher income from rents. By 1362 a degree of normality seems to have been restored, although freehold rents were then around 20% below those of eight years previously.

In many parts of the country demesne farming ceased early in the 15th century. Lords of Manors found it more profitable to let out their land to tenants, while the tenants took advantage of the increasing availability of wage labour. This change certainly happened in the Manor of Forde, but there is no information concerning its timing.

Harvesting, medieval style :
cutting the corn, tossing
sheaves, threshing with a flail

The Open Fields of Forde

Most of the manor's arable land was in the form of Open Fields; they were unfenced but divided into strips, each of about half an acre or one acre. In early times each tenant would have held a more or less equal quantity of strips in each field. Scattered among these were strips farmed directly by the Lord of the Manor using work services provided by these same tenants.

The overwhelming majority of the town's arable was to the south-west of the church in the open field known as Lulsey. The 42½ acres here were supplemented by 24½ acres in Mead Furlong, adjoining it on the east, and more than 23 acres in demesne to the north of the

A typical scene in a medieval open field as harvest nears its end

Bowerwood Road. These 90 acres had all at one time been part of Lulsey. Nearly half-a-mile to the north, in the area still known today as The Bartons, was Barton Field containing a further 23½ acres. (See map on page 24)

Across much of England it was usual for a two or three-field system to be in operation. One field was left fallow each year so that it could recover its fertility before being resown the following year. No record exists of how cultivation was organised in Fordingbridge but it seems likely that a two-field system operated, with Lulsey cultivated in one year and Mead Furlong and Barton (which together totalled a similar area) in the next.

The Demesne Lands of Forde

How big was the demesne held by the Lords of the Manor of Forde and where was it situated? Forty acres of arable land were recorded in 1274, increasing to 60 acres by 1300 and remaining at that level until at least 1362. Just over 20 acres of demesne land adjoined the Manor Farm between the town and Bowerwood Hill. The Brune family's remaining land, just under 40 acres, would have been in the form of strips in Lulsey and Barton fields. (The Lulsey holdings are recorded in a property deed of the mid-14th century.)

Further to the south, beyond Lulsey Field, was Brunesmoor, consisting of about 30 acres of good quality pasture. It is little mentioned in early documents. Its name suggests that the Brune family used it as part of their demesne farm, though parts at least were later let out to tenants.

The only woodland was on the slopes below Midgham, where about 10 acres were part of the demesne. Pigs were pastured there, a custom still continuing in the New Forest (although the present-day Bramshaw pigs in the picture are not a breed common in medieval times). Wood was, of course, a very important resource in medieval times, both for construction and for use as fuel. The name *Bowerwood*, still in use today, is interesting in that it implies that a 'bower' or cottage once existed there.

From at least the 14th century a large area of the New Forest lying beyond Godshill, and known as Brune's Purlieu, was part of the manor.

How Big Was an Acre?

It is uncertain whether the 'acres' of these medieval records were standard acres as used in more modern times based on length measurements of one perch equal to 16½ feet. On some medieval manors, which may or may not include Forde, arable was measured using a perch of 18 feet, while in meadow and pastureland a 15 foot length was used. Consequently an acre of arable would have been about 20% larger than we are used to, while an acre of pasture would have been about 20% smaller. If a standard acre was in use, the available arable in Forde was shared almost equally between the Lord of the Manor's demesne, on the one hand, and the holdings of the customary and freehold tenants on the other.

MEADOW ACRE, perch =15 feet

STANDARD ACRE, perch =16½ feet

ARABLE ACRE, perch =18 feet

Tenant Farming

In Burgate, Breamore, Rockbourne and other more fully rural parishes, tenant farming was on a much larger scale than in the Manor of Forde. Only about 60 or 70 acres of arable were available within the manor and few tenants had more than ten acres at any one time. But this should not be taken to mean that they had continuous blocks of land. The few property deeds that survive for the town show that householders commonly had only an acre or two attached to their holdings. The rest of their land was just as likely to be in Open Fields belonging to the Manor of Burgate or elsewhere. Trade in land was commonplace, particularly amongst the freeholders of the town, and because of this landholdings were constantly changing.

A few of the wealthier tenants were able to produce a hay crop for their animals from a share of the meadows near the Avon. Town Mead, north of the mill and extending towards the market-place (present-day Bridge Street), contained only about 8 acres. Broad Mead was a much larger meadow, of about 45 acres, situated south of the mill. Six or more of these acres were farmed directly by the Lord of the Manor throughout the medieval period. A figure of 17 acres is quoted as belonging to him in 1274.

Few tenants had access to any pasture for their animals within the manor, but they did have rights within the New Forest. (Forest rights have always been attached to land-holdings, not to individuals.) We have no details of these rights for the medieval period, but if later records are a guide they consisted of pasturage for pigs, cattle and horses as well as the right of turbary (see picture).

Over many centuries, Fordingbridge tenants exercised common rights in the New Forest. This inn-sign at East Boldre is a reminder of **the right of turbary** – cutting 'turf' for fuel.

Three customary tenements of the Brunes' estate, situated on the west side of the Great Bridge, seem to have had wider common rights than other holdings within the manor. They had *'common of turbary on the open wastes and furzy ground of the manor'*, while the others had turbary rights only in a close called Closepitts near Godshill (which was in the Forest but part of Fordingbridge Manor). We can be sure that one of these tenements was on the site of the present day George Inn, and another was probably opposite, while the site of the third is uncertain. All, however, were ancient messuages of the manor.

Now that there is archaeological information showing that settlement began around the Bridge towards the end of the 13th century, it seems likely that these messuages would have originated at this time. Eventually they were to become an integral part of that growing community around the market place, but whether they pre-dated it or were built adjacent to it is at present open to question.

The Market

The origins of the market and its move from Church Street are lost in the mists of time. The focus of routes at the river crossing produced a natural trading place. As a result, regular markets became established and were eventually enshrined in customary law. Unlike Salisbury and Ringwood they never were confirmed by a royal charter.

Our knowledge of the nature and size of the market is extremely limited, due to the small number of surviving documentary references. Some of these follow.

1274	*Rents of stallholders and profits of Court 20s.0d*
1277	*Rents of stallholders 27s. 3d*
1280	The Crown confirmed the rights to the market to William Brune as the new Lord of the Manor.
1405-7	Several entries in Court Rolls demanding that stall-holders repair their stalls.
Aug 15th 1406	*Profits of the Pie Powder Court of the market 9d.*
Sept 6th 1406	*To this Court comes Lawrence Peverell and gives the Lord for a fine 2 capons to have entry into one parcel of land in the market place from the Lord's waste, on the south part of a stall of Richard Muriet, containing in length 20 feet and in breadth 16 feet. To have and to hold the said parcel of waste land for term of his life and that of his wife, according to the custom of the manor. Paying yearly to the Lord 12d at the four principal terms of the year. And he did fealty.*
Sept 6th 1406	*To this court came Paynot Horne and gave the Lord for a fine 12d to have entry into one stall which John Ludelow Jnr formerly held within the Market of Forde, to hold for the term of his life according to the custom of the manor. Paying for rent 2d at the Feast of Michaelmas for all services.*

Repairing the Great Bridge

As we have already seen, a bridge must have existed before 1086, as the name *Fordingbridge* was in use for the Hundred at that time. We have no way of knowing whether the earliest structures were of stone or timber.

Certainly, in 1252, the bridge was in need of repair. In that year, the Bailiff and men of Fordingbridge received a grant of pontage from the Crown for 1 year:

> *'towards its repairs in consideration of the traffic, and because the bridge would shortly suffer ruin unless a helping hand provide a remedy'.*

Over the next 200 years six further grants of pontage were made.

The 14th-century stonework of the Great Bridge, when looked at from below, is clearly distinguishable from the wider arches which were added on top in 1841

The grant made in 1385 may well have been that which led to the building of the existing arches of the bridge, which are certainly of 14th-century origin.

The Town Mill

A mill has existed on the site of the Town Mills since at least the 11th century. There is no further reference until 1254, but from that date on it is mentioned in various Extents of the Manor. At that time it was valued at 13s.4d per annum, rising to 26s.8d by 1300 and to 40s.0d by the middle of the century. After 1360 there is a dramatic drop back to 13s.4d, the same value as it is given a century later, reflecting the fall in population and subsequent economic decline following the ravages of the plague.

As this mill belonged to the Manor of Fordingbridge, any tenant growing corn on land belonging to the manor was expected to have it ground here rather than at other local mills. Medieval millers had a reputation, often deserved, for dishonesty. Their fees were usually paid as a proportion of the grain submitted, but tenants had no real way of knowing whether they received the full quantity of flour in return. The few Fordingbridge court rolls that survive do not mention any particular problems of this sort, but it would be surprising if they had not occurred from time to time.

The Town Mills, photographed in the early part of the 20th century. There had been a mill here since Saxon times

Southampton Port Books

Although most goods were produced locally throughout the medieval period, some foodstuffs, craft materials and luxury items were brought from other parts of the country or from abroad. Much of this came through the port of Southampton. While there are no surviving details from the early part of the period, some Southampton brokage books survive from the 15th century. They include interesting details of goods destined for Fordingbridge.

While some were clearly bound for the houses of the well-to-do, others were probably brought for sale in the market. The following extracts are typical of other entries. The first name given in each entry is that of the carter.

25th June 1440	*William Angor to Fordingbridge with 12 cwt of iron of Richard Smyth.*
5th July 1440	*Thomas Swalf to Fordingbridge with 4 balets of woad and 1 bale of alum of Thomas Ede, merchant of Bruton.*
	John Dorent to Fordingbridge with 2 puncheons of white soap and 2 balets of woad of Thomas Ede.
3rd March 1443	*William Elynge to Fordingbridge with 1 barrel of salmon.*
9th June 1443	*Richard Smyth of Fordingbridge with 6 cwt of iron in his own cart.*
6th Feb 1444	*William Elynge to Fordingbridge with 1 barrel and 7 casks of herrings.*
5th Sept 1478	*The servants of John Worthton going to Fordingbridge with 4 quarters of salt for the said John in his own cart.*
24th Sept 1478	*William Spigot going to Fordingbridge with 1 millstone of John Werthton.*

Courts and Court Rolls

The Manor of Forde held Manorial Courts every three weeks. They were presided over by the Steward. We do not know where the courts were held; but generally such courts were convened at the Lord of the Manor's house. However, as this was at Midgham, somewhere more convenient may have been found.

Only three Court Rolls survive for the 15th century; they provide details of the proceedings of courts held in 1405-7, 1428-9 and 1444. Most entries refer to disputes between tenants, with pleas of debt and trespass being the most common. Bakers were frequently fined for selling loaves underweight, as were brewers for selling ale in unauthorised vessels.

The Manorial Court appointed various officials from amongst the tenants. The Ale Tasters tested the ale brewed at the various establishments and ensured that it was sold in correct measures. The Tythingman acted as a sort of policeman, presenting the misdemeanours of his fellow townspeople to the court for punishment. The hayward ensured that hedges and fences were kept under repair so that animals could not stray. Any that did were put into the pound and released only on payment of a fee.

The Hundred Court

In early times it is probable that the courts of the Hundred were held at the market place in the open air. Where they were convened later is not known but, as the lordship of the Hundred was held with that of Burgate manor, the manor-house there is a possibility. A large number of 15th-century court rolls exist within the archives of the Coventry family of Burgate, now held in the Hampshire Record Office.

The tythingmen of Forde, Burgate, North Charford, South Charford, Hale, Ibsley and Ellingham were expected to attend the Hundred Court at three week intervals. There, they made their presentments of breaches of custom, and of more serious crimes in these villages. Many of the offences were relatively trivial, relating to encroachment into fields and roads, the blocking of ditches, repairs to bridges, and non-compliance with a variety of other customs.

Here too, much of the court's time was taken up by disputes over non-payment of debts, both with local people and with traders from surrounding towns and villages. Hardly anyone could escape from this form of justice. In 1453 William Stroode, vicar of Fordingbridge, entered a plea of debt against Peter, rector of Ashmore. Just occasionally, more serious crimes were encountered. In the same year, Henry Pelley and Katermain his wife were arrested and sent to the jail at Winchester for stealing 9 shillings in money and a silver-gilt ring from Henry Smyth.

Assault was a relatively common crime. Fist fights were occasionally recorded, but perhaps more frequent were attacks with sticks, stones and daggers. Few years passed without at least one incident and often there were several. Amazingly that same vicar, William Stroode, had been brought before the Hundred in 1450 for assaulting Thomas Chaplayn with a rake.

Although both Breamore and Rockbourne had been within the Hundred in earlier times, they had long been given the right to dispense their own justice, and are consequently not mentioned in the surviving rolls.

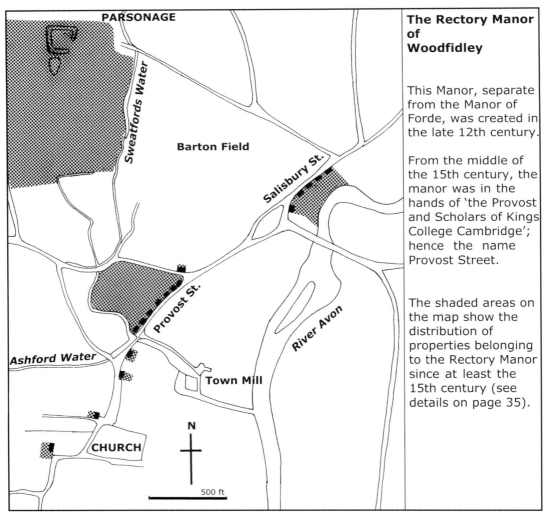

PARSONAGE

Sweatfords Water

Barton Field

Salisbury St.

Provost St.

Ashford Water

River Avon

Town Mill

N

CHURCH

500 ft

The Rectory Manor of Woodfidley

This Manor, separate from the Manor of Forde, was created in the late 12th century.

From the middle of the 15th century, the manor was in the hands of 'the Provost and Scholars of Kings College Cambridge'; hence the name Provost Street.

The shaded areas on the map show the distribution of properties belonging to the Rectory Manor since at least the 15th century (see details on page 35).

The Rectory Manor of Woodfidley

The history of Fordingbridge is complicated, over many centuries, by the distribution of properties in the town between three manors – the Manor of Forde itself, the Manor of Burgate, and Woodfidley.

The Rectory Manor of Woodfidley was apparently founded during the reign of Richard I (that is, at some time in the years 1189-1199), and a 'manor-house' was later built on the site of the present-day Parsonage Farm. In accordance with the widespread practice of the time, it was surrounded by a defensive moat, which still largely survives to the rear of the existing house.

The usual version of the name – Woodfidley – is a corruption of the earlier 'Wollfidley' which was in use by the mid-15th century, and probably much earlier. (The name Woodfidley also exists in the New Forest, about two miles south of Beaulieu Road Station, but there is no connection between the two sites.) The word is formed from the Old English '*leah*', meaning a wood, together with the female personal name '*Wulfhild*'. There is, however, no surviving independent record of a woman of that name in Fordingbridge. The original manor-house at Parsonage Farm was presumably built in or near a wood already known as *Wulfhildsleah.*

There are few contemporary records, but it seems likely that Parsonage Farm was the main home of most of the 13th-15th-century lay rectors of Fordingbridge. From here they administered the affairs of the church and the day to day lives of their tenants in Woodfidley.

The courts of Woodfidley Manor were similar in nature to those of Forde and were held at the Parsonage. A number of 15th-century rolls survive in the archives of King's College, Cambridge.

Lay Rectors, Vicars and Tithes

Lords of Manors in medieval times (and much later in some places), often also held the 'advowson' of a parish which, more or less, corresponded to the area of their manor. As the advowson could be sold, inherited or leased in the same way as a piece of land, it did not always belong to a local lord, but could be owned by any individual or institution.

Until 1256, the advowson of Fordingbridge parish was held by the Lords of the Manor of Forde. They appointed Lay Rectors who held Woodfidley Manor for a fixed rent. Lay Rectors took on the administration of the manor and received the rents of Woodfidley tenants. They were responsible for repairing the rectory site and the chancel of the parish church, which in some years could be a considerable drain on resources. They also had the responsibility of appointing a Vicar, who was the actual parish priest, in charge of church services and of the spiritual welfare of their parishioners.

Everyone in the parish contributed to ecclesiastical finances by paying tithes, originally in kind as a tenth of all the produce of the land. Fordingbridge, as a large and relatively wealthy parish, provided the lay rector with a considerable income; however, he had to arrange an income for the vicar from the same source. It was usual for the rector to keep the so-called 'great tithes' – corn and hay – and for the vicar to be given the 'small tithes' – livestock, wool and non-cereal crops – but it is not clear whether this was the case in Fordingbridge at this time.

From 1256 till 1446, the same system continued in operation, but with the addition of a separate 'tier'. Initially the Lords of Forde leased the advowson to Richard de Clare, and so he and his successors appointed the Lay Rectors throughout this period. The rent for the advowson was purely nominal – an annual payment of one rose!

Elias de la Falaise was the Lord of Forde who started this arrangement. Richard de Clare was Earl of Gloucester and Hertford, and the advowson continued to be held by the Earls of Gloucester until it came by marriage to Ralph Lord Stafford. He was created Earl of Stafford in 1350, and the property descended eventually to Henry, Duke of Buckingham.

Henry transferred both the Manor of Woodfidley and the advowson of the church of Fordingbridge to King Henry VI. Only a few days later, on 1st March 1447, the King gave it to a Cambridge college as part of its foundation grant. The College of St Mary and St Nicholas only later acquired its more familiar title of King's College.

The College did not, however, actually gain possession of the advowson until 1463, following the death of Henry Brune, Lord of the Manor of Fordingbridge, in 1461. The College as an institution then became the Lay Rector. It has had the responsibility of appointing the vicars of Fordingbridge from that time, right up to the present day.

At the time that the college took over, the vicar was John Irysshe. The college drew up an agreement with the vicar which defined the future distribution of tithes. The vicar was allowed the small and personal tithes from Fryern Court, but excluding those of wool, lambs or wood; the small and great tithes from Godshill, Folds Farm and Midgham; the small and great tithes from those areas of Fordingbridge known as Meadfurlong, Lulsey Field, Bowerwood, Middlecrofte and Barton Field. The remaining tithes from the entire parish belonged to the College.

An Account of 1464-5, the second year of the College's ownership, records that the rental income of the manor was 113s.2d, but that the profits of the Manor Court were nil. The bulk of the income came from the tithes of hay (11s.10d) and the tithes of sheaves of corn (£28.6s.8d). A total of 6s.7d was spent on repairs to buildings and 13s.4d on alms for the poor. The clear annual profit was £35.1s.9d.

The College did not administer the manor directly. Instead it rented the property out to a succession of local farmers. (At this time, the meaning of the word 'farmer' was someone who rented some kind of concession, taking on responsibilities and making a profit from it if he could – it did not necessarily have anything to do with agriculture.) The earliest was a yeoman by the name of Ralph Panter, who was in possession until 1481. He was succeeded by the Prior of Breamore who held jointly with a Thomas North. These individuals not only had the benefit of collecting the rents from Woodfidley Manor tenants and the appropriate tithes from all residents of the parish of Fordingbridge, but also took on responsibility for repairs to the chancel of the church and to the Rectory where they lived. (See 'Tenants of the Rectory', page 56)

Lay Rectors of Fordingbridge

There are many gaps in the list and exact dates are often unknown. Some are dates of first entry into the Rectory; others are mentions in documents.

Time of King John	Thomas de Lingis
Time of Henry III	William de Kywenny
1268	John le Fauconer
1279	Thomas de Gunneys (Rector or Vicar?)
1280	Bogo de Clare
1294	William de Weterhill
1300	John de Mouthermer
1335	Baldwin de Mohaurr
1348	Edmund de Morteyn
1365	Thomas Stafford
1386	John Welle
1387	Richard de Clyfforde
1394	Thomas de Feriby
1440s	Gilbert Kymer
1447	Granted to College of St Mary and St Nicholas

The Rectory Lands

The map on page 32 shows some of the lands of the Manor of Woodfidley. These included the moated manor-house site at Parsonage Farm and its adjacent lands; and the lands and houses adjoining the west side of Provost Street and the south side of Shaftesbury Street. In addition, the Manor held a large block of arable and pasture on the western side of Lulsey Field (not shown on the map); the land between Salisbury Street and the River Avon; and a number of other scattered properties and fields, as well as two outlying tenements in Rockbourne and Ibsley.

It is interesting to note that the name 'Provost Street' originated from the ownership of the manor and specifically of land adjoining the street by, to use the full designation, the 'Provost and Scholars of King's College, Cambridge'.

During the 15th century there would appear to have been sixteen houses belonging to the manor within the town, although only ten survived a century later. A fire is recorded in the College records for 1517 and it would appear that six or seven houses were destroyed along Salisbury Street. Most do not seem to have been rebuilt until near the end of the 16th century. At the southern end of the row, however, on the old Greyhound site, excavation has shown that occupation was more or less continuous from the later 13th century.

The Hospital of St John

The Hospital of St John was a wayfarer's hospital, located at Horseport. Apparently, it was founded by a Lord of the Manor of Burgate during the 13th century. However, the right to appoint its Wardens belonged to the Bishops of Winchester, a fact that was hotly disputed by Lords of the Manor of Burgate on at least two occasions during the 13th and 14th centuries, but without success.

Very little is known of the actual hospital or of how it was financed. Even its site is uncertain. In the Register of Bishop Pontissara dated 1283, it was described as being at the foot of the bridge of Fordingbridge. However, piecing together evidence from land ownership records and from continuity of place-names, it is clear that it must have been near the junction of the Ringwood and Godshill roads. As no sign of it was found during construction of the Fordingbridge by-pass, its remains probably lie under, or near, the present St John's Cottages.

Although the post of Warden was still being filled during the early 15th century, the hospital and its lands were granted to the Hospital of St Cross at Winchester in 1446. There is no indication whether or not it continued to function as a working hospital after this date, although by the 16th century it was being leased as a farm.

The probable site of St John's Hospital was near this road junction, just off to the right in this postcard from the early 20th century.

The road ahead leads to Godshill and the Forest. The right fork, leading to Stuckton, now also serves as the access road to the A338 southbound. The cottages pictured here survive, but the sheds and barns have long gone.

Southampton Rd. Fordingbridge

Medieval hospitals were semi-religious in function, and most had chapels attached to them. This was undoubtedly the case here, with the dedication to St John. The situation was complicated in that the hospital also appears to have possessed, or at least had rights in, the North Chapel of Fordingbridge Parish Church. The Hospital of St Cross succeeded to these rights in due course.

Since the late 16th century there has been a misconception that the premises had once been owned by the Knights Hospitaller of St John of Jerusalem. This probably came about because of a mis-interpretation of the St John dedication. The Victoria County History of Hampshire went even further and stated that the hospital had been owned in turn by the Knights Templar and the Knights Hospitaller. In reality there is no evidence that either organisation ever possessed it.

A New Barn for Parsonage Farm

In 1434 the Provost of King's College signed a contract with a carpenter, John Wyseman of Harbridge, to construct a new barn at Parsonage Farm. The details of the contract, transcribed on the opposite page, make fascinating reading, as it specifies the exact responsibilities on each side.

As elsewhere, the meanings of obscure words may be checked in the Glossary. Three in particular here are worth noting, as they are relevant to the style of construction of the barn. *'Coupell'* or couple, refers to the pair of cruck beams used on each end wall (see photograph on page 46); the *grounsellis* or ground-sills were the lowest timbers in the construction; while the *'enterteise'* or inter-ties were short horizontal timbers.

Parsonage Farm, from the south-west. The barn built following the agreement of 1434 had no doubt disappeared long before this photograph was taken for a picture postcard in about 1905.

The houses of Whitsbury Road, quite newly-built at that date, are clearly visible in the background.

Contract for a new barn at Parsonage Farm, 17th July 1434

This indenture made the 17th day of Juyll the 12th yere of the regne of Kyng Herry the 7th betwixt Walter Steele, Provost of the Kyngs College of Cambrigge of that on parte and John Wyseman of Harbrigge in the Countie of Southampton, Carpenter of that other parte. Witnesseth that it is concennted and aggreed betwixt the saide parties that the same John shall make newe or cause sufficiently to be made newe, a barne for the saide Walter and the same barne sett upp at the parsonage of Fordyngbrigge in the saide Countie of Southampton with all thyngs thereunto belonging of carpentre Werke and dors to the same. Which barne shal be in length from the coupell of the est syde of the dore of the olde barne of the saide parsonage unto Weste side of the same barne and the seide new barne to be in brede within the grounsellis 24 feet and in heigth from the underpynnyng to the upper syde of the wall plate 10 fote and the seide John shall make a renge of enterteise throughout the same house in the myddes of the wall. And the same John shall take down the seide olde barne of the seide Parsonage at his owne charge and take all soch tymber as is in the same as can be thought convenyent for hym and sufficient for the same, and the seide provost shall fynde the residue of all other tymber to the saide barne belongyng and carry it or cause it to be carried to the saide parsonage at his owne proper coste and charge and all Iren Werke for the Dors of the same barne and the seid Walter Steele granteth by these presents that he shall paye or cause to be payed to the seid John Wyseman for the making and settyng upp of the seide new barne for his werke 100 shillings of good and lawfull money of England to be payde at 2 tymes, that is to sey at the begynnyng of his werk 50 shillings and when he hath fynesshyd the werke of the seide barne 50 shillings so that it be fynesshed at the Fest of Pentecost next comyng after the date hereof, Which consented wele and truly to be kepte the seide parties byndeth theym their heires and executours eyther to other in £10 of lawful money of England. In Witness whereof the seide parties to theis indentures interchangeably have putte their seales the day and yere aboveseide.

CHAPTER 6 – THE SIXTEENTH CENTURY

The Tudor period began with the accession to the throne of King Henry VII in 1485 and ended with the accession of James I in 1603. So the whole of the 16th century fell within the reign of this dynasty, including the long reigns of Henry VIII and of his daughter Queen Elizabeth I. The religious upheavals of the period, notably the Dissolution of the Monasteries and the establishment of the Church of England, are well-known. These events inevitably had their influence on Fordingbridge, though the changes were less drastic than in settlements, like Romsey, which were closely linked to monastic establishments.

Even so, the replacement here of Catholicism by Protestantism must have been as horrifying to some, as it was welcome to others. In the 1540s the interior of the parish church was transformed from its colourful medieval state into a much plainer house of worship, with the statues and side-chapels removed, and with the wall-paintings covered in whitewash.

In the town, the market declined in importance as permanent shops began to open. Medieval-type houses were replaced or modernised by the insertion of upper floors, staircases and chimney stacks. A new society, which flourished on individual enterprise, was emerging.

Tudor bureaucracy, both governmental and ecclesiastical, recorded the lives and activities of ordinary people to an extent unprecedented in previous centuries. The result, for the modern historian, is a dramatic increase in the quantity of documentary information that has survived. Details of houses and their contents, taxation records, court cases and wills are readily available. Registration of births, marriages and deaths became obligatory nationally in 1538, but sadly Fordingbridge's records survive only from 1640 onwards.

Despite this unfortunate loss, we can for the first time begin to reconstruct the lives of individual people. Occasionally we can work out exactly where they lived, discover their occupations, and look at their family relationships. We can see how wealthy they were and understand the role they played in the life of the community. The poorer classes are less well recorded than the well-to-do; and the lack of detail, in those documents that do mention them, makes it difficult to appreciate their hardships and everyday problems.

Market Stalls and Shops

Throughout the 16th century, Fordingbridge's markets were held in the area around the present-day junction of Bridge Street, Salisbury Street and High Street. This part of the town was less developed then, and at first few houses existed on the block of land between Roundhill and Bridge Street. But in 1568 John Whelbrook occupied a house, described as standing *'right before the Market Cross'*. Later documents reveal that this house was at the northern end of Roundhill, at 5 & 7 Salisbury Street.

We have no information concerning the frequency of markets but can assume that they were held regularly on at least one day each week. Today, the idea of a market suggests a collection of stalls, erected on a temporary basis. While such stalls undoubtedly made up much of our Tudor market, it probably included a wider range of trading

The surviving Borough Cross at Downton may give us a good idea of the appearance of **the Market Cross which once stood at Fordingbridge**, while it has been suggested that the large stone, part of the steps into St Mary's churchyard, may be the re-used base of the old cross

methods. On the one hand, many smallholders and cottagers would have sold their spare produce from baskets spread on the ground around the market-cross. On the other, there was a tendency for stalls to become semi-permanent and eventually to develop into permanent shops, some even with dwelling-houses attached.

Traders, particularly the mercers with their large and often expensive stocks, needed premises that were bigger and better than mere stalls – and they needed to do business six days a week. Although six-day trading benefited the Lord of the Manor, as it helped to guarantee his rents, it contributed to the continuing decline of the manorial system.

> The conversion of stalls to shops is well-known from many market towns. There is even a term for it – **'market infill'**. Most, if not all, of Fordingbridge's first shops would have been in or near the market-place. The fact that none of the modern shops and houses in the 'Roundhill block' have substantial gardens or yards is a sure indication of their market-stall origins. Notable local parallels are Fish Row and Butcher Row in Salisbury and the block between the Market Place, Bell Street and the Cornmarket in Romsey.

There are documentary references to various shops from around the middle of the 16th century. The widow Gleva Green owned a property which was described as a *'tenement'* in 1533, but by 1546 it had become a *'tenement and shop'* (and continued to be recorded as such in subsequent references). Another shop, occupied by Richard Goddinge, was recorded in 1568; it probably stood at the southern end of the Roundhill block, on or near the site of the present-day baker's and confectioner's shop at the junction of High Street and Roundhill. Only two shops are mentioned in the 1593 Survey of the Manor of Fordingbridge, and these stood together *'in the west part of the market'*. They were occupied by William Fowle in 1571 and measured *'in length 24 feet and in breadth 20 feet'*. Their small size clearly indicates that they had replaced market stalls. Others must have existed, probably as freeholds, which are less well recorded.

The weakness in the market system, at least from the point of view of the Lords of the Manor of Forde, was that they had no authority over those parts of the town which belonged to the Rectory Manor. Much of Salisbury Street and Provost Street, as well as a few properties around Church Street, were beyond their jurisdiction, and trade had long been carried on from a number of these premises. The Court Rolls of Woodfidley show that Provost Street contained at least one alehouse, a butcher's shop and a baker's shop throughout much of the 16th century. By the last years of Elizabeth's reign, Thomas Knowles was establishing his mercer's business near the bridge which has since taken his name – see pages 78-9. Almost certainly there were other traders whom we cannot now trace.

Butchers and the Shambles

There are few documentary references to the market stalls, but some are very informative, notably these two extracts from the Court Books of 1548/49:

> *'all butchers are to sell their meat in the shambles in the common market place under pain of the statute'* ... *'the tenement of Richard Barnes and his Shamelles are in default of roofing with straw'*

Use of the term *Shamelles* or *shambles* clearly shows that there was a specific area of the Fordingbridge market where most of the local butchers operated. They slaughtered their livestock there, sold their meat from stalls, and, in at least some cases, they may have been living there as well.

The processes of butchery were messy and required good drainage. There is some evidence to suggest that the shambles may have stretched from the corner of Bridge Street along the eastern side of High Street as far as no.19 (at present a fishmonger's). This would seem to have been the most suitable area, as the slope would have allowed drainage away from the rest of the market towards the river.

The order for all butchers to sell their meat in the shambles is significant in that it implies that some had not been doing so, and that the market system was beginning to break down. As already mentioned, the Lord of the Manor wished to restrict trade to its customary position in the market place in order to maintain his income from tolls and rents. It was a battle that in the longer term could not be won, as the increasingly wealthy and influential merchants were prepared to defy the ancient customs and to go their own way.

At any one time, there seem to have been between three and five butchers in the town. Sometimes they are identified in Court Rolls; but wills and inventories can be revealing, even when the occupation is not mentioned. Nicholas Norris and Richard Veale, who died in 1551 and 1552 respectively, were clearly butchers from the lists of their belongings. Nicholas's shop contained:

> *'2 axes, 2 rondding knyffes, the beames, skales and wayghts with all other necessarys appertaining to the shop'*. His *'kyllyng ropes'* were in the barn.

He also had over forty cattle of his own and presumably bought in from other local farmers as well. Richard Veale's shop had almost identical equipment listed, but unlike Nicholas he does not seem to have been farming and certainly had no cattle. Nicholas was comparatively wealthy with assets of £81.14s.4d, but Richard died with debts of £12.11s.10d, which exceeded his assets of £8.8s.9d. Perhaps he had been forced to retire from work due to ill health.

Tradesmen and Merchants

While we know that there were butchers' stalls in Fordingbridge, surviving documents do not mention other trades. It is, however, easy to speculate that bakers, chapmen and mercers must have predominated, and that root vegetables, fruit and freshwater fish must have been brought in by local people on a regular basis. More exotic foods and products, as well as such essentials as salt and iron, continued to reach the town through the port of Southampton, as did herrings and other sea fish.

There were many other craftsmen in the district, notably those involved in the various aspects of the leather trade, as well as tailors, shoemakers and coopers. Some may have dealt directly with the public from their own workshops, others would have sold their goods to chapmen, who acted as middlemen, re-selling the items at the market. Others such as blacksmiths, carpenters and wheelwrights must have worked largely from their own premises.

There is circumstantial evidence for dyers operating in the town, including the delivery of woad and alum (a dyers' mordant) mentioned in the Southampton brokage books, quoted on page 31.

Christopher Phetyplace of Wimborne Minster was one of the first merchants to own property in Fordingbridge, though as far as we know he never lived here. During the middle decades of the century, he accumulated a number of properties in the town, several of which were in or near the market place. In 1568, he sold them to another merchant, John Lyne of Ringwood. There can be little doubt that these two wealthy landowners were instrumental in developing houses and shops around the periphery of the market and encroaching upon the space used for stalls.

One of the earliest merchants actually living in Fordingbridge was Francis Odwaye. When he died in 1599, he owned various properties in the town and was lease-holder of the nearby Manor of Alderholt. William Hatcher, a linen-draper who had died two years earlier, owned less land but the inventory of his shop taken after his death suggests that he was, for all practical purposes, a mercer. We do not know where either man lived and can only assume that it was near the market.

William's shop inventory (opposite) makes fascinating reading. Despite the unfamiliar spellings, such as 'peece' for piece and 'corse' for coarse, much of it is understandable, especially if read aloud. An ell was a measure of about 45 inches; other unfamiliar words are explained in the Glossary at the back of the book.

The Stock of a Linen-Draper's Shop
(Inventory on the death of William Hatcher, 1597)

Item a peece of Fyne Holland of 14½ Elles at 3s.4d the Ell 44s. 4d
a peece of corse hollande of 10 Elles at 2s the Ell..........................20s. 0d
a peece of corse hollande of 11 Elles at 2s the Ell 22s. 0d
a peece of corse hollande of 10 Elles at 20d the Ell 16s. 8d
a peece of corse hollande of 6 Elles and a half at 22d the Ell 11s.11d
a peece of Locoram of 15½ Elles at 13d the Ell 16s. 3d
a Remnante of 4 Elles at 10d the Ell...3s. 4d
3 smale Remnants of corse clouthe being 5 Elles.............................4s. 0d
14 Elles of corse canvas in remnante at 10d the Ell.....................11s. 10d
a remnante of corse canvas of 6 Elles at 10d the Ell.......................5s. 0d
20 Elles of corse clouth to lyne horse collers at 4d the Ell 6s. 8d
Browne Hollands 8 Elles and a half at 20d the Ell 14s. 2d
a peece of Russett Sackcloathe of 9 yeardes at 8d the yearde........6s. 0d
2 other peeces of Sackcloathe of 15 yeardes at 8d the yearde 10s. 0d
a remnant of black durans of 5 yearde and a half at 20d
          the yearde 9s. 2d
a remnant of durans of 2 yeardes at 3s..6s. 0d
a remnant of purple baffine of 9 yeardes at 12d the yearde 9s. 0d
a remnant of crane cullered holmnes fustian of 5 yeardes
          and a half at 12d the yearde...1s. 6d
a remnant of crane cullered fustian of 12 yeardes at
          12d the yeard 12s. 0d
a remnant of russett fustian of 7 yeardes at 12d the yeard............7s. 0d
a remnant of Strawe cullered fustian of 5 yeardes at
          12d the yearde...5s. 0d
a dosen and a half of pinnes at 6s. 6d
2 pownde of - - - thread at...6s. 8d
a parcel of velvite [?] threade at..20d
Remnants of brayde [?] Incle..2s.
of gartering remnants..2s.
Half a gross of thred points..8d
Caventre thred...15d
a pownde of - - - ruse Incle..16d
a pownde of currants...4d
a pownde of figges...3d
6 quires of writtinge paper...14d
a quateren of pepper and ozce of cloves, 2 ozces of ginger...................15d
2 dozen of wodden combes..16d
half a pownd of Mayles...5d
6 dozen of thred buttones...4d
Eyle hooks and knitting needles..4d
a pownde of gunpowder and half a ponde of Matche..........................10d
8 quires of narrow browne paper..6d
of Treacle half a pownde 6d
Bales of packthredd..3d
a flaggen bottle of glass..12d
3 payre of smale scales with smale weight of brasse............................2s.
a cheste, a case of small boxis with bordes and shilves in the shoppe.10s.
of Shewger, a pownde and half..18d

Bakers and Innkeepers

Butchers, bakers and brewers were important members of the community, as in any similar settlement. Court Books record the names of a considerable number of bakers, and sometimes they can be identified from lists of their possessions in inventories, even though the same individuals are rarely described as 'bakers' in wills or other documents. Furthermore, it is often very difficult to tell if their production of bread, etc., was on a commercial scale. Many bakers also seem to have been involved in brewing ale, and some at least must have sold this through their own alehouses.

It comes as no surprise that the inns and alehouses that we know of were near the Market Place. The George Inn was already long established on its present site and in 1593 was owned by Edward Odware. However, he may not have been the actual occupier as it seems that Brian Greene was the innkeeper by the early part of the 17th century.

The site of the later Greyhound Hotel, a Rectory Manor property, was occupied by an inn, of which we do not know the name. It was run by Nicholas Norris (perhaps related to the butcher of the same name). In his will of 1587 he described himself as a yeoman, but the contents of his Inventory clearly show that he was first and foremost an innkeeper. The extracts below, from the Inventory taken on 8th March 1587, are those which relate to the contents of the inn:

Furnishings and Equipment of an Inn

IN THE HAWLE AND PARLOUR
2 long joyned Tables, 1 shorte joyned table, 4 joyned formes, 6 stooles, one plane forme, one joyned bedsteade, one Trucle bedd, certen sealing glasse and two curtens for windowes...........................£3. 4s. 8d

IN THE CHAMBERS
2 joyned Bedsteades, 4 truckle bedds, 6 plaine bedsteades, 2 little joyned Tables, 3 chests, 3 coffers, one strawing chair ....49s.
4 fether beddes, 7 flock beddes, 7 fether bolsters, 5 flock bolsters, 11 fether pillies, 16 coverlates, 8 pare of blancketts, thre carpets, thre stayned clothes, 12 cushens, 20 pare of shetes, 4 pare of pillities, 1 lynnen Teaster, 8 Table clothes, 4 dozen of napkines £18.17s.

IN THE KITCHEN ETC
5 kettells, 4 brasse pannes, 5 crockes, 3 skillets, 1 frying pan, 4 broches, 2 pare of Andiers, 1 Rack, 2 hangings, 2 pothooks, 1 furnes, 1 gridiron...................£5. 4s. 8d
6 putor potts, 8 candelsticks, one mortar, one chaffing dishe, 6 saltesellers, 6 windowe potts, 18 platters, 12 pottingers, 12 sawcers, 10 spice plats, 2 washing Basons, 1 bason and ewer, 2 silver spoones, 9 Tynning dishes, 18 putor spoones....................58s.8d
2 Brewing vats, 2 keaves, 6 Trendales, 6 hoggesheades, 6 Barrells and firkins, 6 Ale vessells, 3 pales, 2 yoting vates, 1 bushell, 1 peck, certane old tubbes, 4 stands, certen shelves and planks, 2 Tubbes of strawe, 2 powdring Tubbes, 6 chese vates, 1 cherne, 3 lether Bottells..£3. 9s. 4d
Butter, chese, Bacon and Lardd....................................£3.

CHAFING DISH

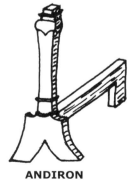

ANDIRON

SKILLET

Farming

Prominent as the market traders were in the life of the town, we must not forget that this was essentially a rural community and that almost everyone was involved to a greater or lesser extent in farming. A few of the wealthiest merchants and professional men had little time for such work and could afford to buy their own food, but most others kept a few cattle and pigs and grew an acre or two of corn and peas. The back garden was used to keep a few chickens and to grow apples, root crops and some other vegetables.

For those whose income came entirely from farming, the size of holdings varied from a few acres of arable land and meadow, belonging to the smallholders, up to twenty or more acres owned by the more prosperous husbandmen and yeoman farmers.

Townspeople often kept pigs, so they may sometimes have been seen in the streets

Arable Land and Equipment

The arable land of the Manor of Forde was still held mainly in the two ancient open fields of Lulsey, Mead Furlong and Barton. These were divided into acre and half-acre strips as they had been for centuries, and it seems that they remained unenclosed throughout the Tudor period. There were, however, a number of closes on the edges of the open fields, more particularly towards Bowerwood and Ashford. After harvest and until the winter ploughing, the stubble in all of these fields was available for grazing by the tenants' cattle.

The Manor of Nether Burgate, to the north and east of the town, included more extensive areas of arable land, so average holdings there were much larger than they could be within the Manor of Forde. The tenants of Woodfidley Manor were the least fortunate of all, as few had more than an acre or two of arable, although in general they had access to more pasture than was available on the Town Manor. Any tenant who wished to expand his farming activities often rented land in more than one manor.

It is generally supposed that ploughing was still done by oxen rather than horses in the 16th century. 'Oxen' are listed only infrequently in inventories, but they may have been more numerous than this suggests, as they could have been included in the general totals of *rother beasts* and *kyne*. Anyone with arable land must have owned a plough and many are recorded as *sulles*, together with their *chains*, *coulters*, *shares*, *mold wheels*, *eythes* [harrows], and *other plough gear*.

The large range of basic tools and equipment included many items still familiar to us today. Most, if not all, were made by local blacksmiths. Those listed in inventories include spades, shovels, prongs, dungpicks, saws, sieves, wedges, pickaxes, axes, rakes, riphooks, knives, grapples, scythes, shears and hedging bills, as well as grind stones, troughs, yokes, sacks, ropes, ladders and winnowing sheets. Threshing flails do not seem to have been considered worth mentioning, although they must have been used on every holding.

Thus the local blacksmith, who made many of these tools, was an important member of every rural community. John Clement was a Fordingbridge blacksmith who died in 1580.

A Blacksmith's Tools and Stock

When John Clement's inventory was taken on 25th October 1580, its value totalled £20.14s.1d. The excerpts from the list, on the next page, include all his equipment and stock in trade, which made up £8. 19s. 3d of the total.

John Clement's Inventory (excerpts)

Item six quarters of Smythes Coole ....30s.
Item in newe Iron 2 hundred and 43 pounds ....24s.
Item 3 whyppe Sawes ....12s.
Item fyve horse shoes 5d
Item an yron beame and a wooden Beame with scales 12d
Item 14 horse Collers 18d
Item Tenn leadon weights conteyninge 22 pounds 22d
Item a Browne Bill 6d
Item 14 shovells ....2s.
Item a lytle chayre and a lytle Tryvet ....4d.
Item a payer of Smythes Byllowes 13s. 4d
Item fyve smythes sledges 6s. 8d
Item one Anvell, 2 Bychornes and 2 vyces ....50s.
Item a nayling stake and a Doule stake 3s. 4d
Item the old yron in the shoppe 2s. 8d
Item seven hamers and fyve nayle Tacles ....4s.
Item eight payer of tonges, a spyncer and a butteres ....4s.
Item 16 prytchells and Clyftes 12d
Item 2 newe gredyrons and a tryvet 8d
Item a Dogg and a newe pothengles 12d
Item a Donge pyke and 3 payer of mollen Bytts 8d
Item a payer of Twysts and 2 handesawes 2d
Item 32 fyles ....2s.
Item eight hookes, 4 smytbylls and one Borryer ....2s.
Item 4 Boulsters and 4 fyles 12d
Item a payer of plate sheares and 2 Ladders 12d
Item six kytts and one Boate ....6s.
Item one slyce, a payer of compasse, a hearth staffe,
a sornyer and a marking yron 8d
Item 2 hedginge Bylls 6d
Item One Gryne stone with a Troughe ....4s.
Item the Woode 12d

'fyle'   'hamer'   'tonges'   'spyncer' (pincers)

Livestock

The larger farms kept a full range of livestock, including cattle, sheep, pigs, poultry and working horses. Not surprisingly, there were few flocks of sheep in the immediate area of the town; but large numbers were raised on the chalk downlands of the villages to the west.

The smaller holdings had a few cattle, variously described in documents as *kyne, bullocks, steers, 'heffers'* and, occasionally, *oxen*.

Most people who kept pigs and piglets [*shutes*] reared only a small number in a sty in the back yard. An exception was Edward Scott, who was the vicar of Fordingbridge from 1560 until his death in 1579. At that time, he owned a boar, a sow and no less than eighteen shutes.

The majority of households had a few chickens running around the farmyard to supply eggs – and eventually a tasty meal. Mr Scott was the exception here also, as he owned 13 ducks as well as a few hens.

Horses were used for riding, or more commonly for pulling a variety of carts for general work on the farms, as well as transport of goods over long distances to other towns and markets. *Horse harnesses, bridles, halters, road saddles, side saddles* and *pack saddles* are all mentioned in inventories.

William Hugman, a blacksmith who died in 1571, had little time for farming but did have five sheep and four hives of bees. His bee-keeping activities seem to have been unusual, if not unique, within the town, although hives must have been common in the surrounding villages and heathlands.

Every farm had a barn for the storage of grain and/or equipment. There are no recorded mentions of buildings specifically intended for housing animals, apart from the stables owned by the better-off farmers. Occasionally, there is a suggestion that cattle were being kept in barns.

Pasture and Woodland

All tenants with livestock needed the use of pasture for grazing. Only the luckiest (or most well-off) tenants had their own closes of pasture, although a few did exist in the Ashford area. Most grazing was on the common pasture, much of which was available only for part of the year. As well as the post-harvest grazing on the arable fields, the common meadows of Broad Mead and Town Meadow were grazed, once haymaking had been completed. The majority of tenants on the Forde Manor also had the right to pasture two cows in Brunesmore, a high quality meadow to the south of Lulsey Field, and most could exercise pasturage rights in the New Forest on payment of a fee.

The meadows, where hay was cut to provide winter feed for the animals, were held in common in the same manner as the arable fields. Depending on the size of their holdings, most tenants had between half-an-acre and two acres. The meadows were not yet 'water-meadows'. (This system of deliberate irrigation, using an elaborate system of ditches, originated in the 17th century.) However, the value of floodwater was already appreciated, especially the subsequent deposits of chalky soil washed down from upstream. John Norden, the map-maker whose work features on the front cover of this book, reported in his *Surveyor's Dialogue* (1607) that river mud was spread on fields to improve their fertility: *'mawme or malm, a light loamy soil obtained from the slub or slushy mud of the River Avon between Fordingbridge and Ringwood, was used by many'*.

There was little large-scale woodland near the town, but at Midgham there were a number of coppices, and a few tenants were able to obtain coppice-wood there and to graze their pigs.

Homes and Furnishings

No Fordingbridge dwelling from the 16th century has survived, complete, into the 21st century. Serious fires in the late 17th and early 18th centuries destroyed any older houses that remained at that time. A picture of the homes of the period can be built up, however, by combining the evidence from documents and from the small amount of archaeological evidence available. Inevitably there is a bias in our knowledge towards the better-off families, as the poorer members of the community, with few possessions of value, are rarely recorded.

Until the middle of the 16th century, the vast majority of domestic buildings were of the medieval cruck type, and of either two or three bays. Some larger houses, such as the Rectory and the Vicarage would have been of box-frame construction, and increasingly the wealthier merchants would have seen this type as more suited to their status.

We know from the Court Books that some houses were still being built in cruck form as late as 1546, but within a few decades the 'great Tudor rebuild' had begun. Gradually the

Two popular local eating houses demonstrate the change-over in house styles which occurred after the middle of the 16th century. The Old Beams Inn at Ibsley *(left)* shows the earlier **cruck construction**, with two great curved beams in the end wall. The Hour Glass Restaurant at Burgate *(right)* is an example of the **box-frame style of construction** which became more general in Tudor times.

medieval stock was replaced or upgraded into timber-framed thatched cottages, of a type still familiar in neighbouring villages today. Most houses were thatched but there was an increasing use of clay roof-tiles as time went on. Excavation in the town has shown that tiles must have been widely available long before the Tudor period, as larger houses had been built with tiled roofs for several centuries before this.

Floors were still strewn with straw, after the medieval fashion, well into the 16th century. When this practice died out locally is not known. Windows were generally small, shuttered and unglazed, but in the last few decades of the century a new process of making window-glass brought the price within the range of the middle classes. Window-glass, being of some value, gradually began to appear in inventories (see that of Nicholas Norris 1587 on page 42, where it is called *sealing glasse*).

Traditionally, before the great rebuilding, most dwellings had only one main room, the 'hall', open right up to the rafters. If there was a sleeping loft at one end, a simple ladder was the usual means of access. In the newer homes, upstairs chambers were built over the hall. Occasionally one of the chambers seems to have been downstairs at the end of the hall. Larger houses had stairways up to the chambers from an early date, but it was not till almost the end of the 16th century that they became common in more humble cottages.

In the 'hall-houses', a central hearth was the norm, undoubtedly producing smoky conditions at times. The fire on this hearth was used for cooking as well as heating. From around the middle of the century, and in the wealthier homes, open fireplaces of brick began to replace the old-fashioned open hearths. This change was accompanied by the introduction of a separate kitchen. At first, kitchens were often detached from the actual house, in order to reduce the risk of fire in the main part of the dwelling. As today, kitchens varied in size and complexity. Some contained several ovens and furnaces, with large collections of implements and utensils, as well as ample quantities of foodstuffs. Others had no more than a furnace, a few tubs and chests and a small selection of pots and pans. Other specialist rooms, or out-houses, included butteries, milkhouses, brewhouses and boulting-houses – where flour was sifted.

Although Fordingbridge was essentially a rural market centre, it had inevitably acquired some of the characteristics of an urban settlement. One of these was the crowding of more than one family unit into what was originally a single dwelling. In some cases this had happened by division of the original building and in others by the addition of a jumble of extra rooms and annexes. Documents often reveal a situation in which a family seems to be inhabiting only part of a house, and possibly only a single room.

Rooms in all classes of houses were sparsely furnished by today's standards. Every household had at least one table in the hall, and some had several. The number of forms, chairs and stools depended upon the size of the family and the standard of living of the owner, which in turn led to enormous variations in the quality of furniture from house to house. A real chair, with arms and a back, would have been reserved for the head of the household – the origin of the word 'chairman' as the leading figure in a group.

The commonest form of furniture, found in most, but not all, houses, was an open cupboard for plates and other vessels. Some also had separate shelves. Often there was little else in the hall, apart from the fire-dogs, cooking utensils and a few personal belongings.

Some houses had carpets or hangings on the walls. Occasionally, there were settles, table cloths and napkins, and in one instance a cradle. In the houses of the better off inhabitants there were more sophisticated pieces of furniture and possessions, such as round tables, books, cushions and window curtains. The vicarage boasted a clock as early as 1555.

The number of beds per chamber generally varied from one to three – occasionally there were even more. Sometimes there was a truckle bed, a low bed on wheels, pushed under a higher one when not in use. These were either used by servants or for extra accommodation. Chambers often contained a jumble of other objects, apparently stored there for want of somewhere better.

Two Farmers, John Read and John Stevens

It is interesting to compare the farming activity of tenants with very different standards of living. John Read, described as a husbandman on his death in 1570, had been living in quite modest circumstances. His farming stock and equipment were valued at almost ten pounds, but after his debts had been paid, the total value of his possessions was only £9.2s.9d. He had lived at South Lane, just beyond the church. The agricultural items in his inventory were:

An ax, 2 Ierne Wedges, 2 Ryphokes and an olde sythe	2s. 4d.
A soole, a chayne, a pere of Croks, a yoke, 2 eithen and 2 boryers	5s. 8d.
Horse harness, halters and Ropes	4s.
A shovell, a dungpyke and a prang	6d.
A wymshete, syvys and sackes	2s. 6d.
For pullen	2s.
8 shepe	16s.
A heffer, 2 bullocks and a Calfe	34s. 2d.
an olde Cart	6s. 8d.
Wood	3s. 4d.
Heye	6s. 8d.
For Wheat, barley, peson and Fatchys	£ 5.
For one geldyng	15s.

In complete contrast, John Stevens Inventory of 1560 recorded goods valued at over £114, making him one of the wealthiest men in the town, on a par with the vicar, Edward Scott. Eight years before his death, he had inherited a considerable farm with lands in the Midgham area from his father, as well as a shop and interests in both brewing and baking. We list (on the next page) only his property connected with farming. This totalled over £83, around three-quarters of his total wealth.

John Stevens' Farm, 1560

IN THE BARNE
In the barne of wheat onthreysshid by estimation 5 quarters .£ 5.
Of Rye onthreysshid by estimation 5 quarters ....£ 3. 6s. 8d.

IN THE FELDES
Of wheat 19 acres ....£ 8.10s.
Of Barley 32 acres ....£10.13s. 4d.
Of Rye 5 acres ....33s. 4d.
Of peeses 6½ acres ....40s.
3 sowes, 11 shutts and 15 wenelyng pyggs ....50s.
2 cartes yern bownd, 1 plow, 3 chaynes with
*   appurtenances ....36s. 8d.*

IN THE LEESES
12 Kyne and heffers, 2 bulls, 1 oxe, 5 weneling calves
*   and 4 sucking calves ....£20.*
8 yerlyngs ....£ 4.
3 coultes of 2 yeres age...£ 3. 6s. 8d.
1 nag and 1 geldyng ....53s. 4d.
4 coultes whereof 3 be twelve months olde, the other of
*   2 yeres age, 1 more of 3 yeres age and 1 grey gelding ..£ 4.*
In the heath of all sortes of shepe ....25s.
More in the leese 21 shepe, viz. 3 Rammes, 1 ewe and
*   17 wethers...£ 5.*
2 winnowing shets and 12 sacks ....10s.
the poultry and geese ....8s.
3 basketts ....12d.
the gryndingstone ....3s.
1 yern Rake, 1 grappull and the woode ....8s.
24 cheses ....8s.
5 quarters malt ....40s.
2 spades, 1 pick ax and the w - - - t spades ....12d.
In the forest 12 bullocks and heffers, the youngest of
*   2 yeres of age and the eldest of 5 yers age ....£ 9.*

The Local Militia

During the 16th century and into the 17th, all able-bodied men between the ages of 16 and 60 were expected to serve in the local militia. All members were expected to supply their own weapons, and to serve their country in time of war if called upon to do so. It was the duty of the Lord Lieutenant of each county to organise his potential troops. From time to time, muster rolls were drawn up. Three rolls survive for this district, dated 1522 , 1569 and 1637. They record the names of the men who attended the musters, together with the arms and equipment they had.

The overall attendance levels were consistently low. (This is clear, even though different recording methods were used in the various documents, making direct comparisons between the musters difficult.) In theory, attendance was compulsory, but avoidance was clearly widespread, even more so in the town than in the surrounding villages.

In Tudor times the long-bow was still regarded as vital for the defence of the realm, and archery practice was made compulsory at butts set up in each parish. The 1522 muster for the combined villages of Fordingbridge and Burgate reflects this, listing 10 archers and 10 bilmen.

The latter wielded pikes or halberds, then known as 'bills'. Between them, the twenty men had only 15 leather jerkins of various types and a single coat of mail.

The 1569 muster lists the names of all those in the Hundred of Fordingbridge with their arms, but does not separate them into villages. There were said to be 98 *'able menne'* within the Hundred and 58 *'unable menne'*. Archers still dominated with 46 bows and 34 sheaves of arrows, but there were now 18 guns as well as nine pikes, 62 bills, 69 swords and 65 daggers. The weaponry may have been improving, but the protective clothing still left a lot to be desired. Only 9 corselets, 18 almain rivets, 16 morrions, five jacks and three coats of plate are recorded, so that more than a half of the men apparently had no protective clothing whatever.

The 1637 roll is considered in the next chapter, but it is worth noting here that, in the intervening 68 years, bows and arrows had been replaced by muskets.

The Reformation

The history of any church during the Tudor period is dominated by the religious upheavals of the Reformation, which culminated in the replacement of the Catholic faith by Protestantism. The break with Rome came during the reign of Henry VIII in 1532, but it was fifteen years later, following the accession of Edward VI, that a serious attempt was made to replace Catholic rituals in parish churches. This resulted in the destruction, throughout the kingdom and over a quite short period, of many of the treasures of medieval churches.

Rood lofts, chantry chapels and images of saints were removed. Brightly coloured wall-paintings were covered with whitewash. Large numbers of books were burned. The Crown took possession of much valuable church plate. Although we have no detail exactly what occurred at the Parish Church of Fordingbridge, the effects were certainly as severe here as elsewhere, and as sudden in their accomplishment.

St Mary the Virgin Parish Church, in an engraving by G N Shepherd.
This is dated 1838 and shows finials at the corners of the tower,
which were removed only a few years later.

The short lived and bloody attempt of Mary to restore Catholicism, between 1553 and 1558, was followed within a few years by the permanent establishment of the Church of England during the reign of Elizabeth I.

> The Parish of Fordingbridge is fortunate that a volume of pre-Reformation Churchwardens' Accounts has survived the centuries and is now preserved in the Hampshire Record Office. Using this valuable document together with numerous wills and a few other miscellaneous records it is possible to picture the church as it was in the 1490s, at the very end of the medieval period. Details of the ornaments, vestments and other possessions of the pre-Reformation church provide an insight into the ritual of worship before there was any hint of the changes to come over the following five or six decades.

Building the Church Tower

Externally the building looked much as it does today, although the flintwork was covered with plaster. The tower was still a relatively new addition and had probably not achieved its present appearance until early in the 16th century. The earliest known reference to it dates from 1463 when the rector spent 12d to '*embellish*' it, while a will of 1483 mentions '*the new work on the bell tower*'.

A record of 1536 (see pages 54-55) mentions an earlier, undated, document which has since been lost. Its evocative title – '*A Reconsiliacion for a Suspence of the Church*' – implies that worship was suspended for some considerable time during major building works. This was almost certainly caused by the construction of the tower (or at least the lower part of it) around the middle of the 15th century. On completion, a Service of Reconciliation would have been necessary to restore the previous status of the church.

Other records suggest that the tower still required more work at later dates. During the 1490s the roof of the tower was thatched, probably a temporary measure due to lack of funds for its completion. The church received money for '*building the new tower*' in 1504. In the same year William Cotterell left 6s.8d in his will towards '*the new building and edifying of the tower of the church of Fordingbridge*'. As late as 1515 there were similar bequests from Richard Asley and from '*the village of Gorley*'.

The accounts for 1515 detail gifts of considerable quantities of building materials from local landowners. Chalk, timber, oak trees and lead were given by Mr Bulkeley, Mr Brune, Mr Calwey (or Kelway) of Rockbourne, by the vicar and by several other parishioners. It seems reasonable to infer that the freestone upper section of the tower dates from this time; and that the roofing of the tower and also of the North Chapel was completed during these works.

The Interior of St Mary's

The internal appearance of the church in medieval and early Tudor times was very different from that familiar in our own time. Until the Reformation, many of the walls were decorated with brightly coloured paintings, of which scant remains now survive. The aisles contained a number of '*images of saints*'. Some of these may have been paintings, but most would have been carved wooden figures, themselves brightly painted. In front of each image and at the font and the sepulchre, a

The fine chestnut timbers of the North Chapel appear to form a hammer-beam roof. Actually, this is the much more common construction of a tie-beam roof, with the addition of religious figures as 'false hammers'.

The interior of St Mary's, illustrated in a picture postcard of about 1905

'light' was kept burning constantly. The cost of the unending supply of candles was borne by particular villages or by bequests (see next page).

We know that in the 15th century the floor of the church was strewn with straw, according to ancient custom, and there is every reason to believe that this practice was continued well into the Tudor period.

There was also a Guild of St Mary attached to the church and this would certainly have had its own chapel for the use of its members. There is some evidence to suggest this may have been the North Chapel. Membership of the guild would have been open to all parishioners, on payment of an annual fee. In return they would have expected spiritual support,

At the east end of the south aisle of the Parish Church, where the organ is situated in the present day, there was a small chapel before the Reformation, with its altar against the east wall. It is not clear to which saint this was dedicated, although a chapel of St John and St James is mentioned in one document. This **piscina** remains in place, and the corbel shown on page 18 is higher up on the same wall.

pensions, and in times of great hardship, financial aid. Such guilds were the forerunners of later Friendly Societies, but like so many features of the early church, they were abolished in 1548.

A prominent feature of the church would have been the rood loft, situated across the front of the chancel arch, facing the nave. It took its name from the 'rood', a large wooden sculpture of the crucifixion, which was probably fixed to the arch above the rood loft. In front of the rood hung the trendle wheel, with up to twelve candles, each 'sponsored' by various villages in the parish. The 'rood lights' of Bickton, Gorley, Burgate, and of the town itself are all mentioned in wills. The rood loft was entered from a door in the south wall; it was used for preaching on important feast days. St Mary's possessed an organ as early as 1492, but this was most likely positioned in the choir, rather than the rood loft, as is believed to be common in some other churches.

The focal point of the church was, of course, the High Altar and for this was reserved the church's only lamp, made of brass. In 1492, the churchwardens paid 1s.4d for a new lamp and 17½d for 2 barrels of oil, while in the following year they bought a new glass for the lamp.

The Church Lights

Each light was looked after by two wardens, who were appointed annually. Their task was to purchase the candles needed to keep the light burning. They also did any maintenance work necessary on the actual 'image' of the saint. They paid for this work out of gifts and bequests from parishioners, kept accounts of their income and spending – and handed over any surplus to the churchwardens.

From the accounts kept by the churchwardens and from the bequests made in various wills, we can draw up a list of the known 'lights'. This provides us with knowledge of which saints were represented by the colourful images, at least sixteen of them, which ornamented the church.

IMAGE OF THE SAINT	SPONSORED BY	EVIDENCE FROM (including bequests)
St Anthony		John Molens' Will, 1483
St Michael the Archangel		John Molens' Will, 1483
St Mary of the Bellhouse	Fordingbridge	Churchwardens' accounts, 1504
The Trinity	Fordingbridge	Churchwardens' accounts, 1504
St George	Fordingbridge	Churchwardens' accounts, 1504
All Souls	Fordingbridge	Churchwardens' accounts, 1504
St Mary	Fordingbridge	Churchwardens' accounts, 1504
Crucifix light	Burgate	Churchwardens' accounts, 1504
St Margaret's	Burgate	Churchwardens' accounts, 1504
St Cross	Gorley	Churchwardens' accounts, 1504
Saints John and James		John Bisshop's Will, 1506
{ St Mary *(north part of church)*		John Bisshop's Will, 1506
{ Our Lady of the North Aisle		Churchwardens' accounts, 1520
Our Lady of Piety		Churchwardens' accounts, 1520
St Christopher		Churchwardens' accounts, 1520
St Michael		Churchwardens' accounts, 1520
St Katherine		Churchwardens' accounts, 1520
St Nicholas		John Barlett's Will, 1530 – a bequest of 2d

In most cases, we do not know where the various images were positioned. However, the image of St Cross must have been in the North Chapel, as this was in the possession of the Hospital of St Cross at Winchester. (This had come about through its ownership of the old wayfarers' hospital at Horseport – see page 35.)

We can reasonably assume that *'Our Lady of the North Aisle'* was the same as the *'image of St Mary in the north part of the church'*, mentioned in the will of John Bisshop of Gorley. He also provided for the *'sustenance and maintenance of the candle perpetuated in front of the image of Saints John and James'* to be financed from his bequest of a *'cow and two beehives with bees'*. One hopes that the wardens of this light were experienced with cattle and bees.

John Molens was Lord of the Manor of Sandhill (Sandleheath). His will locates the image of St Michael the Archangel, as he expressed a wish to be buried under it, *'in the east part of the church called Our Lady Aisle'*.

Churchwardens' Accounts - Income

The accounts provide many examples of both income and expenditure, all of which help us to build up a picture of the day to day life of the early Tudor church. Their income came from four sources.

Bequests came in a variety of forms, but mainly from the wills of better-off parishioners. Corn, malt, utensils, silver rings and cattle were the most common gifts. In all cases, the churchwardens would have sold these items for cash. Occasionally, bequests came from further afield – *Feyre Wode* [Verwood], *Emsam* [Edmondsham?] and *Terrande Henten* [Tarrant Hinton] are all mentioned. Most wills of the 16th century contained bequests for the upkeep of the town's two bridges, which fell within the churchwardens' responsibility. As with the church lights, wardens were appointed to collect the money and to expend whatever was necessary on the repair and maintenance of the structures.

The hire of 'brewing-leads' to parishioners wishing to brew their own ale for events such as weddings. Some leaden troughs were kept specifically for this purpose, while others were used by the churchwardens themselves at the 'church ales' (see page 58).

Mortuary fees. The standard charge for a grave was 6s. 8d. Inevitably, the accounts include numerous examples of such payments.

Collections. As today, these were regularly taken at church services. At Easter 1493, as much as nine shillings was collected. In addition, special collections were taken for specific purposes each year. These included Lamp Money, Torch Money, the maintenance of the font light, and the Paschal (Easter) Candle. One oddly-named collection was *'Smoke-Pennies'* – a tax of 1d per hearth or household, levied on householders each Whitsun for the benefit of the diocese.

A similar tax of 1d per hearth was taken throughout the country each year at Lammas, the first day of August. This was known as *'Peter's Pence'* and its purpose was to support the English College in Rome. By the late 15th century, the tax was very unpopular and many churches had problems in collecting the full amount. The page of the parish accounts, reproduced on the right, shows that the churchwardens, no doubt reluctantly, had accepted the inevitability of being unable to 'gather up' seven pence underpayment . The tax was abolished in 1534.

Churchwardens' Accounts – Expenditure

Similarly, spending fell into several categories, which are listed here with examples of each.

Buildings. In addition to the sort of large scale building work already mentioned, there was, of course, a continuous programme of maintenance on the fabric, as well as the replacement of items damaged through wear and tear. New locks were bought for the vestry door; the church gate was mended; as was the gate at the church stile. In 1493

A sample page from the Churchwardens' Accounts for 1492. The highlighted section records a bad debt.

The ancient handwriting reads:
'Itm for ye lackeyth off ye pet' hys mony yt wekannat gedyrhyt ope viid'.

This translates as:
'Item for the lacketh of the Peter his money that we-cannot gather-it up 7d'.

some new leaded lights were cast. For this purpose solder was bought, as were two loads of sand – and a basket to carry it in.

Repair of major items. The organ was taken down and mended, with its bellows, in 1490, and glue was purchased for it three years later. The clock was taken down and repaired, apparently by William Hugman the blacksmith, while a new clapper was made for the second bell. New ropes were bought for the clock, for a bell and for the trendle. Among the numerous items acquired were nails, coal, paper for making a book, frankincense, wax for candles and straw for thatching.

Vestments. In each year's accounts there is an item for washing clothes, while new garments were made from time to time. There is a record of cloth which was bought for making surplices, while a gown, a veil and two new baudricks were made.

Travel and provisions. The costs of travelling to visitations at Breamore and Christchurch are on record. Bishops made visitations every three years, and archdeacons every year. Wherever these were held, all local churchwardens were summoned to account for the moral and spiritual welfare of their parishes and for the physical condition of their churches. Grain was taken to Breamore and trips were made to Winchester and to Chalke. In each year there were entries for drink for the clerks at Lent and for their dinners at Easter.

The bridges. As already mentioned, the churchwardens were responsible for expenditure on the upkeep both of the Great Bridge over the Avon and of the Lesser or Lytch Bridge over Sweatfords Water. The latter bridge, at the lower end of Provost Street, is known today as Knowles Bridge after a 17th-century mercer who lived nearby (see page 79). The old name Lytch is interesting as it is derived from the Old English word 'lich' meaning corpse. This bridge is on the route along which many coffins would have been carried. Perhaps there was a resting place here for the coffin to enable the bearers to pause before the final leg of the journey to the church. (The 'lych-gate' at Minstead has a platform for this purpose.)

Bells and a theft

There are several references in the accounts to the bells in the tower, but only in a 1549 Inventory of Church Goods are they mentioned in any detail. Perhaps surprisingly there were only three bells at that time. The great bell was 3ft 8ins broad and 2ft 6ins deep, while the middle bell was 3ft 3ins broad and 2ft 6ins deep. The little bell served the clock and was 3ft broad and 2ft 2ins deep.

In the accounts for 1515, there is a note of the theft of a silver chalice and paten from a chest in the chancel near the vicar's stall. After removing them the thief left through the south door of the chancel.

Church Inventories, 1490 and 1536

The same Account Books include inventories of church goods, which fortunately cover both the pre-Reformation and post-Reformation periods. The inventory taken by the Churchwardens in 1490, when Catholic ritual was still very much the norm, is both the earliest and fullest of these lists of church property.

A bag with reputed '*relics*' of saints is listed. This would undoubtedly have been a proud possession of the parish, but no doubt it would have been one of the first items to be destroyed at the Reformation.

The silver and gilt vessels included two *pyxis*, four *challices*, two *cruetts*, a standing cup, 14 rings, a little cross and a *pax*. Other valuable items were an ivory box mounted with silver, three crystal stones and a knife of St John of Bridlington. Vessels in less precious metals included two copper crosses, four cruets and three basins as well as six candlesticks and a lamp with a tin bottle for oil.

There were eight suits of vestments and two copes as well as a red chasuble for use on Good Friday. A long list of hangings contained 12 altar cloths, a font cloth, two palls and a cloth for the rood, with eight banners and two streamers.

Important legal documents were contained in a *'box with evidences'* in 1490. Forty-six years later, in a 1536 inventory listing property in the hands of the churchwardens, Nicholas Norris and John Sanger, it is referred to as a box with *'nine poles* [items] *of evidence and writtings'*. Most of the items related to church lands, and none are known to have survived. The *'Reconsiliacion for a Suspence of the Church'*, already mentioned was one of them. There was also *'a Charter for the Churchyard'*, the significance of which is now difficult to determine. It may have related to an eastward extension of the graveyard, perhaps in the 15th century.

Books owned by the Church in 1490	Books owned by the Church in 1536
two Massbooks	*A paraphrase of Erasmus upon the epistells*
- - - Grayls	*Mr Bridges answere against Stapleton and*
a Psalter	*Sanders*
an Ordinal	*two bokes of Injunctions and articles*
A Dirge Book	*two old bokes of homylies*
four Processionals	*Copers Expositions*
a Portesse called the monke	*four psalters*
a Logion	*two olde Comunyon Bokes*
an Epistle Book	*A Bible*
a Manual	
an old Massbook	
two Antiphoners	
a Pye	Note that, rather strangely, the earlier list
a Hymner	includes no mention of a Bible!
an old Antiphoner	

Church Inventories, 1549 and 1582

Following the accession of Edward VI, the Crown wished to establish the extent of church possessions. An inventory taken for this purpose in 1549 was compiled by the churchwardens. It is now in the Public Record Office, within the papers of the *Department of the Queen's Remembrancer*. Valuables over and above what was deemed 'necessary' were to be forfeited to the Crown.

Most of the silver and gilt listed previously was still present, although the two cruetts and the 14 rings were gone. The reduction in the number of chalices from four to three was clearly the result of the church robbery in 1515. Two new censers had been acquired, as had a silver ship.

Some garments and hangings had undoubtedly been disposed of, due to wear and tear, and not replaced, and this satisfactorily accounts for a slight loss of such items since 1490. There is no mention of the lamp or of some of the less valuable vessels. The brewing equipment is not listed, nor is the bag with relics. Perhaps we should not read too much significance into these missing items, as the *'box with evidences'* is omitted, despite the fact that it was listed again over thirty years later.

The inventories do not reveal which items were considered to be *'unnecessary'*, but this becomes clear from another source. When Queen Mary made an attempt to reintroduce Catholicism, items which had been confiscated were ordered to be returned to churches. A Warrant of 1556 lists these items to be returned to Fordingbridge – a cross, a pyx, two censers, a ship, a sacring-bell and a pax. However, there is no record to show whether they ever were actually returned, or what their eventual fate was.

The last of the churchwardens' inventories is dated 1582. The box with the same nine documents still survived at that time, as did most of the books from 1536. One of the old communion books had been replaced and three of the psalters were gone. There was an additional book of Articles, which must have been the Thirty Nine Articles, issued in 1563 as the basis of the new Protestant church. Three account books are listed; the two which survive today have provided much of the foregoing information. Sadly, the third account book, which covered the period of the greatest changes, is now missing. The Register Book of the church, listed in 1582 but also now lost, would have contained details of baptisms, marriages and burials from 1560, and possibly from 1538.

Tenants of the Rectory

The institution formally known as *'the Provost and Scholars of King's College, Cambridge'* was Lay Rector of Fordingbridge parish, as explained in the previous chapter. However, its responsibilities were generally 'farmed out' to local laymen. They took on the college's privileges and responsibilities, lived in the Rectory and farmed its lands, administered Woodfidley Manor – and thus, although actually tenants of the college, were the effective rectors of the parish. They had to provide accommodation for college Bursars on their inspection visits.

The tenancy did not always go to local men. In 1583, it was leased to Charles Smith of New Windsor, Berkshire. His annual rent to the college was £29 per annum, supplemented by payments in kind – 15 quarters of good quality wheat and *'20 quarters of good and merchandisable malt of barlye, well dryed and cleane'*. This produce from the Rectory Farm was to be delivered annually to the college baker, but if the delivery could not be made, the tenant had to pay the monetary value of the grain, as determined by prices at the market in Cambridge on the Saturday before rent-day.

> A measure of 35 quarters of grain is nearly 9 hundredweights or, in metric terms, nearly 450kg. It is not difficult to imagine the enormous problems involved in taking a heavy wagon-load of grain, 150 miles from Fordingbridge to Cambridge, on the poor roads of the day. But it is probable that this was not the intention. The monetary option would generally, if not always, have been taken. Including such a clause, specifying that part of the rent was to be paid in kind, was probably a hedge against inflation, with more cash due if the price of grain was high.

Charles was also expected to re-build the Rectory House, near the site of the former moated house. His construction probably forms the core of the present-day Parsonage House, with 17th-century alterations and additions.

> *... the said Charles Smith within the space of six years next ensueing the date hereof at his and their own proper costs and charges, build repayre and mende the Dwelling house or Mansion of the said Parsonage of Fordingbridge aforesaid, bestowing thereof the least, to the value of one Hundrede Markes of lawful money of England to make yt a convenient, habitable and sufficient howse to dwell in.*

The barn, stables and other outbuildings were also to be *'maynteyned'*.

Vicars of Fordingbridge

Successive vicars were chosen, not surprisingly, from the ranks of past scholars of King's College, Cambridge. A complete sequence of incumbents is known for the Tudor period (see box on next page).

Vicars of Fordingbridge	
1447 - 1495	William Lyvyng
1495 - 1512	Robert Ellesmere
1512 - ?	Thomas Stephens
	(still incumbent in 1517, date of transfer unknown)
? - 1521	Brian Rouse
1521 - 1530	John Elmham
1530 - 1555	William Dussing
1555 - 1560	William Winke *(removed for neglect of the Living)*
1560 - 1579	Edward Scott
1579 - 1626	William Henson

The Vicarage at the time of Edward Scott

The 16th-century vicarage stood opposite the west door of the church. Some idea of the size and layout of the vicarage, and of the lifestyles of the vicars, can be obtained from their surviving wills and inventories of goods, especially that of Edward Scott, who died in 1579.

The vicarage was a large house by the standards of the time and probably one of the most imposing in the town. The rooms consisted of a hall and parlour, with two chambers, a buttery and a maids' chamber. A farmyard at the rear contained buildings known as the Little House and the New House, as well as a stable; it is probable that the kitchen was also a detached building in this area.

The farm yard was occupied by twenty pigs, as well as geese, ducks and other poultry. Twelve horses and 24 head of cattle must been pastured in the fields belonging to the vicarage, but a few of the former were used for riding or for pulling carts. By ancient custom the vicar held a *'game of swan'* on the River Avon, at this time consisting of ten white swans and six cygnets.

The furniture in the vicarage was more sophisticated and varied than that found elsewhere in the town. Besides the expected tables, forms and a chair, the hall contained a pair of virginals, nine cushions and a desk. His wearing apparel, appraised at £6.13s.4d, was several times more valuable than that of most of the townsfolk.

The parlour contained *'a standing bed'* as well as a *'truckle bed'* amongst the tables and chairs, and there can be no doubt that this was the vicar's own bedroom. In sleeping, and probably dining and entertaining

guests there, he was almost certainly the last vicar to continue the social traditions of the medieval household. As would be expected, the chambers contained bedsteads and bedding, but the one over the loft was rather less conventional in that it also held weaponry in the form of a crossbow with bolts and a pair of pistols and a powder flask. Alongside these was distilling equipment, and a library of written and printed books in both Latin and English.

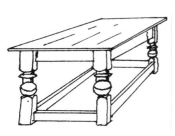

The buttery contained a diverse collection of utensils and vessels, while the well-appointed kitchen held all the cooking equipment that would be expected in a house of this standing. The Little House was used for preparing and spinning wool and linen while the New House seems to have been used for curing meat and as a store for corn and peas.

In total Edward Scott's estate amounted to £129.6s.4d. Few of his contemporaries in the town could match this.

Deacons, Curates and Clerks

As Fordingbridge was a large parish, most vicars found it necessary to employ a curate or chaplain to assist with their parish duties. We know the names of a few of them. Henry Traske was a curate living at Criddlestyle. His will, dated 1604, reveals that he also owned land at Winterslow; bequests to his son included *'my whole study of books and things relating to learning'*.

The Inventory of church goods taken in 1549 (see page 55) mentions vestments for a deacon and sub-deacon, while there are surplices for two priests and two clerks. The post of clerk was one of the few pre-Reformation posts to survive into the reformed church, eventually emerging as the Parish Clerk of later centuries. By Elizabethan times, he had taken on the roles of sexton and verger in some churches, while continuing to lead the singing and responses, as well as assisting the vicar in pastoral duties.

The Church House

St. Mary's Hall stands today on the site of the old Church House, opposite the north-west corner of the churchyard. The churchwardens held both the house and its lands as a freehold of the Manor of Fordingbridge at an annual rent of 1d. The earliest record of the property occurs in 1498 when it was occupied by Thomas Wyte, who was paying a yearly rent of 10 shillings to the wardens.

The churchwardens' box of documents, already mentioned, contained *'a deed for the church house and lands'*. Although that document has not survived, a 1581 lease of the property to Nicholas Bounde does exist. This states that the house is bounded by the Vicarage on the south, by Chopps lane on the north and by the King's Highway on the east.

One of the conditions of the lease was that Nicholas Bounde would:

> *at all times hereafter, as their occasion shall require, quietly permit and suffer them the said churchwardens of the said parish of Fordingbridge to have use and occupy all the convenient rooms in upon or about the said tenement or church house before demised at Whitsuntide yearly, when and so often as they shall hold and keep the Church Ale or Church Feast there, meet and convenient chambers and rooms for the said Nicholas and his assignes and all their family, always during the said time and term aforesaid to be reserved and allowed.*

Church Ales were, in effect, fund-raising events for which beer was specially brewed by the churchwardens. Parishioners were then expected to attend and to buy the beer and any food available, the resultant funds being used for the benefit of the church. This was one medieval festivity that did, for a time, survive the Reformation. Not surprisingly the drunkenness which such events were reputed to have encouraged, throughout the country, soon fell foul of the increasing Puritan influence on church life.

St Mary's Church Hall, on the right of the picture, occupies the site of the former Church House, used by the Churchwardens.
Beyond it are the vicarage of 1817 and its former stables, both now converted into flats.

The Bulkeley Family of Burgate House

The Bulkeley family had inherited the large Manor of (Nether) Burgate in 1446. The site of their relatively modest manor house is thought to have been just to the north of the early 19th-century house built by their successors, the Coventrys. The family also owned the profits from the Hundred of Forde, and from 1520 until 1573 leased the actual Manor of Fordingbridge from the Brunes who were absentee landlords. Throughout this period the Bulkeleys were thus the leading family of the town.

John Bulkeley was the head of the family at the end of the sixteenth century. He had become notorious, both locally and nationally, for his long running, almost obsessional, disputes with a neighbouring landowner, William Dodington of Breamore House.

This engraving of a fine Tudor brass in St Mary's Church shows William Bulkeley, his wife Jane, their three sons and their five daughters. Note the pious positions of all concerned and William's armour. His helmet is on the ground beside the stand for his bible. The date 1568 is something of a mystery. One would assume it to be the date of William's death, but there is a document that suggests he was still alive in 1573, while the Victoria County History states that he did not die until 1581.

The Bulkeley / Dodington Feud

The background to the bitter dispute between John Bulkeley and William Dodington is complex, and a number of issues were involved, but it centred around a disagreement over the ownership of East Mill, which had started as far back as 1593.

When, in January 1597, Commissioners met in Ringwood to examine witnesses in the case, a conflict occurred outside the meeting place. John Bulkeley confronted William Dodington and '*railed against him with diverse bitter and hard speeches, terming him a Jew and such like*'. Bulkeley drew his rapier and four of his servants also drew weapons. They taunted Dodington's followers with '*many other quarrelsome speeches*'. The Commissioners were disturbed by these events – they emerged from their meeting to ensure that Bulkeley's followers kept the peace.

The dispute seems to have led to bad feeling between the two men's workers. There was even an armed dispute in the meadows about the ownership of hay-fields! It is recorded that Henry Edmundes and Edward Burrough, who were workers on William Dodington's estate, were cutting hay in New Gore meadow. This is believed to have been somewhere alongside the River Avon, below the escarpment of Sandyballs Wood, near two meadows called Newlands and New Ground, which were part of the land dispute. John Bulkeley and some of his supporters rowed across the river in a boat, armed with guns, and assaulted them. They refused to let them leave New Gore with their carts for a time.

John Bulkeley and his men arriving to assault William Dodington's men while they were working in the hayfield

An interpretation of the incident by Phil Anderton, cartoonist, commissioned for this book

The feud and unrelated financial problems must have weighed heavily on Dodington's mind for a number of years. On April 11th 1600, the Star Chamber was due to hear another case between the two men. William, now in his 60s, climbed to the top of the tower of St Sepulchre's Church near his London home. Before he committed suicide by throwing himself from the tower, he left a note which read, in part:

> *...... John Bulkeley and his fellows by perjury and other bad means have brought me to this end ... ... after they had thus slandered me, every day that I lived was to me an hundred deaths; which caused me to choose to die with Infamy, than to live with Infamy and Torment ... ... The Unhappy William Dodington*

Needless to say, the suicide caused something of a sensation in Elizabethan London – and no doubt was a talking point in Fordingbridge for weeks.

CHAPTER 7 – THE SEVENTEENTH CENTURY

Just as the Tudor dynasty dominated the history of England during the previous century, so the Stuarts dominated the seventeenth. Following the death of Elizabeth I in 1603, King James VI of Scotland became also James I of England. His son, Charles I, attempted to rule without reference to Parliament, resulting in the Civil War and ultimately in his own execution. During the Commonwealth period which followed, under the rule of Oliver Cromwell, Puritan values held sway.

The Restoration of the Monarchy brought Charles II to the throne. His reign was marred by the Great Plague of 1665 and by the Great Fire of London in the following year. The reign of James II threatened a return to Catholicism. The abortive rebellion of 1685 had local consequences with the capture of the Duke of Monmouth in Ringwood and the execution of Dame Alice Lisle of Moyles Court. James was replaced by the staunchly Protestant William and Mary in the bloodless Glorious Revolution of 1689. William III was still on the throne at the end of the century.

The Fordingbridge section of Norden's map of around 1605, as seen on the front cover, here printed upside down so that north is, more familiarly, at the top. Note the open space at the junction of Bridge Street, Salisbury Street and High Street which was used as the market place before 'infill' divided off Roundhill as a separate street (see page 39).
Moxham's Mill is correctly shown on Sweatfords Water to the west of the town, but Shaftesbury Street, which should lead past it to Damerham, is much too far to the north. There is no Whitsbury Road and no West Street. The map as a whole has many inaccuracies, but these only add to its charm.

Fordingbridge in the 17th Century

Well into the century, at the end of the Commonwealth period in 1660, Fordingbridge would have looked little different from its appearance in Tudor times. Although brick had been increasingly used for new building for some time, the majority of houses were still timber-framed, and many were still thatched. Such buildings were extremely vulnerable to fire damage.

As a result, the face of the town was changed forever by the devastating fires of 1662 and 1672. Within a few years the shops and dwellings that had been destroyed were replaced, largely by brick buildings. Some thatch continued to be used for roofing, but tile, and to some extent slate, became the norm.

Documents from the latter part of the century confirm that the market was still continuing, if on a smaller scale. Undoubtedly the tendency, already seen in the Tudor period, for the replacement of market-stalls by permanent houses and shops had continued. As a result of encroachment by these new buildings, the market-place was greatly reduced in size. In addition, more shops had been opened in different parts of the town.

The old market-place was finally abandoned in the 1670s in favour of a new site at the junction of Provost Street, Shaftesbury Street and High Street. As a result, this area became the focus of trade as more new shops were established nearby. At the same time, there was a steady increase in population as new housing filled gaps in the Church Street area and along the western side of Salisbury Street.

Customs of the Manors

As already mentioned, manorial courts were becoming less effective as time went on. Nevertheless, the three local manors continued to have a significant role in the life of the town for much of the 17th century, so that their surviving documents are an important source for this history.

> Many of the Court Books and Rolls of the period are available for both Burgate and Woodfidley Manors. The corresponding Court Book for the Manor of Fordingbridge was long believed to have been lost. However, that dating from 1654 onwards has been 'rediscovered' very recently, and is now in the Cornwall County Record Office. The information it contains has added greatly to our knowledge of the town in that period.

Each manor had its own 'customs', or rules, which tenants were expected to abide by. These were often recorded in a 'custumal', a formal statement of a manor's most important customs. Such a document is not known for Fordingbridge, but some of the customs of the manor can be inferred from the Court Book; it records 'orders' for tenants to comply with a long established procedure that they have disregarded or blatantly ignored. Non-compliance with a custom was usually punishable by a fine, but by now it was becoming more and more difficult for manorial courts to insist on such payments. Thus the customs were becoming unenforceable.

The following are selected entries from the Fordingbridge Court Book, with comments.

20th April 1654 ... ... no cattle ought to be kept or tyed in the Common-fields or meadows until the same bee rid and lawfully broken, and then to put in one horsebeast or two rudder beasts on one acre in the mead, and in the fields one rudder beast on one acre or one horse beast on two acres, and at the feast of St Michael Tharchangell fowre sheep on one acre, under the penalty of every one doing contrare therunto 6s.8d.

And that under the like penalty there shall not bee anie steer above the age of two years put to pasture in any of the said fields or meadows.

These are sensible grazing regulations for common land; clearly the word 'cattle' is used here to include all farm animals.

24th April 1655 ... ... there is due unto the Lord of this Liberty by an ancient Coustome 6d for every parcell of goods that shall be estrayed belonging unto one man, though the Cattle be after they are estrayed claymed by the right owners, So that the said owner clayms the same within one year and a day after the Estrays are lawfully proclaymed.

Stray animals were proclaimed in the Market Place by the hayward.

continued ....

They present that no dung ought to be layd in the streets upon paine of everyone makeing default 5 shillings.
30th April 1657 ... *That no person within this Liberty do take in or receive any under tenant into his howse or tenement before sufficient security be given for discharge of the parish, under Penalty of forfeiting to the Lord of the Mannor for every one making default herein 40 shillings.*
20th October 1658 ... ... *John Treus ought to find a Tythingman for his customary tenement for one year next ensueing, or until another shall be lawfully sworne in the office. Wherefore it is ordered that the said John Treus do at his owne charge procure a sufficient person to be sworne to execute the said office accordingly by the 10th November next upon payment of 40 shillings.*
It is ordered that the Casway from the Vicaridge Ground to Shabridge Style be sufficiently repaired by William Pope, Richard Hall and William Gosse by the 5th day of November next under the penalty of 10 shillings for every of them making default.
17th October 1661 ... *They present Robert Addams for suffering his howse to bee in decay for want of thatching. Therefore hee is ordered sufficiently to thatch his howse between this and the next Court under penalty of 10 shillings.*

The fear was that the tenant would be too poor to support his family, and would apply for relief under the Poor Law Acts.

On some manors the duty of providing the various officers fell to each tenant in turn. On others, one of the tenants was appointed by the jury at the Court. If he did not wish to carry out the duties himself he was obliged to find a deputy.

These will have been the tenants who used the causeway (*Casway*) to gain access to their ground.

At the manorial court, the Lord of the Manor annually collected three shillings 'Measure Money' from all the innholders and alehouse keepers of the Manor. In 1655 these were listed as *'the keeper of the Signe of the Black Boy, the keeper of the Redd Lyon, Gyles Sandover keeper of the Taverne, and the keeper of the Great George.'*

The Great George was next to the Bridge on the same site as today's George Inn. The Black Boy was on the west side of Church Street, but the sites of the *Taverne* and of the *Redd Lyon* cannot now be identified. These were the four inns on Fordingbridge Manor; there were also other hostelries belonging to other manors. At Horseport there was the Little George, and within a few years the Greyhound was built on the edge of the then Market Place in Salisbury Street. Following rebuilding after the 1672 fire it was renamed the White Horse, and a new Greyhound was opened in Fore Street (the lower end of the present High Street). During the following century the Greyhound name returned to its original site.

Bulkeleys and Dodingtons reconciled?

In 1607, seven years after Dodington's suicide, John Bulkeley died and left possession of the Manor of Burgate to his wife. She granted it to her four brothers, but the male line soon regained it and the Bulkeleys and the Coventrys retained the title till well into the 20th century.

The rift between the two families seems to have been healed in 1637, with the marriage of John Bulkeley and Anna Dodington, grandchildren of the original disputants. (Old John would not have been amused, we feel sure.) Young John had just returned from a mysterious trip overseas. In 1634, he had obtained a licence for a journey abroad for three years – no reason for his trip appears in the records. Anna Dodington was 20 years old at the time that he left and John probably in his thirties.

In the romantic realms of pure speculation, we imagine a love affair between the two young people, with the total disapproval of their two families. The foreign trip could have been instigated by John's parents, in the hope that the love between him and Anna would have died by his return. If so, the ploy clearly failed, the wedding went ahead – and hopefully old enmities were put aside.

Burgate Manor House

As already mentioned, the Bulkeleys' manor house at Burgate probably stood a little to the north of the present-day Burgate Manor (built in1810, reputedly following a fire - and shown on page 124). We can imagine it to have been a late medieval or early Tudor structure, built by an earlier member of the Bulkeley family. We do not know whether it was half-timbered or built of brick or stone, and this despite the survival of an extensive Bulkeley family archive.

The archive includes an inventory dated 1693, during the ownership of Sir Dewy Bulkeley, great-great-grandson of the original John. The following extracts from the inventory vividly illustrate the high living standards of the family, particularly when compared to the possessions of more humble townsfolk recorded above.

In the Best Chamber

1 mohair blew bed, curtains, bace and vallance
1 fether bed and bolster
5 blanketts, 1 silke quilte
5 mohair little chars, 1 chare with arms
3 large pictures with gilt frames
1 chest of drawers, 1 table and stands
1 large looking Glas, 1 pare of bras and iron doggs, shovell and
*   tongues, 1 pair of bras bellowes*
3 callicoe window curtains, 3 wooden chares
1 sett work carpet under the bed
4 peecis of tapestry hangings

On the Great Staire Case

14 pictures being maps of several countrys
1 clocke

In the Parlour

1 secutare
1 large turkey work couche, 2 turkey worke Chares
1 square side table, 3 callico curtains
1 parre of bras andirons, 1 parr of doggs with bras heads
1 parre of princess mettle candlesticks

In the Hall

1 large round table, 1 little round table
6 turkey worke chaires, 1 paire Iron Doggs

As the inventory lists the contents of the house room-by-room, it gives us clues to its extent and layout. It did not compare in size with Breamore House, being a typical small manor house, probably built on three floors including the attics. On the ground floor were the Hall, Parlour, Kitchen and Buttery. The Great Staircase led up to the Best Chamber, the Red Chamber, the Kitchen Chamber and the Master's Chamber. The latter would have been Sir Dewy Bulkeley's bedroom. At the top were Mr Bulkeley's Chamber, used by Sir Dewy's son James, the Maids' Chamber and the Men's Chamber, the latter two both having garrets next to them. The evidence suggests that there were three chimneys.

Local and National Taxation

Local taxation consisted of Church Rates and Poor Law Rates, while national taxes included Poll Tax and Hearth Tax. Both local rates were levied on householders and on other landowners. The scale of payments was related to the value of their property, with the poorer classes generally being exempt.

Church Rates were administered and collected by the Churchwardens. As we saw in the previous chapter, the proceeds were used primarily for the upkeep of the church, while maintenance of the church house, of the churchyard and of the town's two bridges was also the Churchwardens' responsibility. Rates were usually raised annually, but it was quite common for a special rate to be announced for a particular purpose such as urgent repairs to the Great Bridge. If an unusually high expenditure was required, perhaps for repairs to the church, the rate was levied at double or treble the usual amount. In rare instances it could even be higher than this – on such occasions, the ratepayers, reluctant at the best of times, were not amused.

Under the Poor Law legislation of 1597 and 1601 each parish was empowered to levy rates in order to support the local poor. Two officials known as the Overseers of the Poor were elected annually to collect the rates on a similar basis to the Church Rate. Poor Law and the role of the Overseers eventually became a very important part of local administration, as we shall see later.

Until the Civil War, taxes collected for Parliament or Crown were known as Lay Subsidies. Payment was based on the wealth of individuals, measured in both land and goods. In the main, as with local rates, only the better-off were required to pay, but occasionally the net stretched further down the social scale. In 1641 the first of an occasional series of Poll Taxes was introduced, from which only the very poorest were exempt. Where records survive, the taxation lists include all other males over the age of 16. A return of this date exists for Breamore, but sadly nothing is known for Fordingbridge.

In 1662 Parliament attempted to supplement Crown income by introducing a Hearth Tax. In theory, Hearth Tax returns list the heads of all households with the numbers of their hearths and ovens. Each was taxed at a standard rate of 2 shillings per year – clearly the amounts paid were closely linked to the size and grandeur of a house. From 1663, the returns even list those poorer families who were exempted on the basis that they did not pay Church or Poor Rates.

The return of 1665 is the best for Fordingbridge, listing 50 householders for the town as well as 21 for the Woodfidley lands. Twenty-three of the former, and nine of the latter, were exempted. A further 116 names are listed for Burgate, of which perhaps ten were in the town. A total of 174 hearths are recorded, with a further 244 in Burgate.

The Hearth Taxes were never as lucrative as parliament expected and, after frequent administrative amendments, were abolished in 1689. The first of many Land Taxes was introduced four years later.

The Militia and the Civil War

The militia continued its activities through the 17th century. A muster roll that survives from 1637 records Sir William Dodington of Breamore House as Colonel of the local troop, with his son John as Captain. (Sir William was the son of the William Dodington who committed suicide.) The names of a Lieutenant, an Ensign, two Sergeants and two Drummers are also given. The men of the Hundred possessed a total of 47 corselets and 84 muskets. The day of the bow and arrow was gone. Fordingbridge itself seems to have provided only four corselets and four muskets, continuing its poor record of service. One of the corselets was furnished by the vicar and one corselet and one musket by the Tithing. The others were provided privately.

It is not clear whether any of these men and arms saw action during the Civil War of the 1640s, nor whether they were inclined to take sides in the conflict. The Dodington family supported Parliament, but there is no evidence that any members of the family were involved in more than a political and fund-raising capacity. Nevertheless, one can assume that Sir William, as Colonel, and John as Captain, might well have attempted to make the local militia available to serve their cause.

There is no evidence for military activity in the immediate vicinity of Fordingbridge, but Hampshire generally was said, in 1644, to be practically ruined by the ravages of war. With Winchester largely supporting the King, with Southampton sympathetic to Parliament, and with the county's noble families divided between the two causes, clashes were inevitable. The defeat of the Royalists at the battle of Cheriton, the sieges of Basing House, and eventually the imprisonment of Charles I in Hurst Castle must all have been major talking points locally.

Population

We have seen how difficult it is for modern historians to estimate population totals in medieval times. Perhaps surprisingly, the task is only a little easier for the 17th century, despite the fact that records are both more numerous and much more informative. However, no single record exists which attempts to record the entire population.

Several classes of documents tabulate householders' names, but none is reliably complete. A considerable number of lists of local ratepayers exist, but inevitably these omit the poorer families Fifty-five property owners were expected to pay local rates in 1604. To these must be added about ten from Burgate, making a total of 65. Later rolls show a gradual, but slight, increase with totals in the mid-seventies.

As noted above, the 1665 Hearth Tax suggests that there were at least 81 householders in Fordingbridge (50, town manor + 21, Woodfidley + about 10, Burgate). The papers of the Quarter Sessions, held following the extensive fire of 1672, record the highest total given anywhere. The heads of no less than 102 households are named; and of course there must have been quite a number who were unaffected by the fire.

There is no reason to doubt the accuracy of either list, although it is probable that limited evasion of the Hearth Tax did occur. Some of the 81 dwellings, although treated as a single unit for Hearth Tax purposes, are very likely to have been sub-divided, with rooms rented out to other families. This may at least partially account for the discrepancy between the figures of 81 and 102.

The next problem is that there is no local evidence concerning the size of families or the numbers in each household. Nationally, average figures as low as 4.5 and as high as 6.8 have been suggested. If, for argument's sake, we assume that there were actually 120 households in the town, and use the two suggested averages, we arrive at an estimate of between 540 and 816 people living in Fordingbridge in the second half of the 17th century.

Our only other evidence comes from the Compton Ecclesiastical Census of 1676, which in theory included everyone, male and female, over the age of 16 years. In Fordingbridge, taking the whole parish rather than just the town, 800 members of the Church of England were recorded, plus another 143 who were non-conformists. To obtain a total, we then have to estimate how many under-16s there may have been. Again using a likely estimate, an additional 30 or 40% must be added to the 943 over-16s. This gives a total of between 1226 and 1320 for the parish – perhaps as many as a half of these would have lived in the outlying villages.

The inadequacy of the various sets of figures means that any overall estimate of the town's population is little more than guesswork. A total of between 500 and 700 is the best that can be suggested.

There can, however, be little doubt that numbers increased during the 17th century as the town expanded. The Parish Registers show that there were over 250 more baptisms than burials for the period from the 1640s to the end of the century, suggesting a population expansion. But there is no record of mobility – no evidence to show how many people left the town or how many moved here from the surrounding villages or from further afield.

The Fires

Two disastrous fires occurred in 1662 and 1672 (with another in 1702 which is discussed in the next chapter). Almost the entire housing stock was replaced within these four decades, and this enforced rebuilding was largely responsible for the layout and appearance of the historic core of the town as we see it today.

The devastation caused by these fires is now hard to envisage, as are the panic, helplessness and despair that must have accompanied such terrifying events. The widespread use of timber and thatch enabled a fire to spread quickly once it had established itself in a densely packed urban environment. Not only could fires expand rapidly, but the means to extinguish them were almost entirely lacking. Fire brigades and fire-engines would not exist for many years to come. The only equipment available consisted of leather buckets and long-handled hooks and irons for removing burning thatch from roofs. The effects of buckets of water on a blazing building were minimal, even if a convenient water supply could be found.

> Many English towns suffered large scale damage due to extensive fires during the 17th and 18th centuries. Nationally, the most famous example is the Great Fire of London of September 2nd 1666. Nearer Fordingbridge, at Blandford Forum in 1731, the destruction of 350 houses and of the church resulted in the construction of the Georgian town centre. Salisbury is a rare example of a town which had no major fires, as the water-courses which formerly ran down each street provided ready means to extinguish flames before they took hold.

The first fire, that of Wednesday 2nd July 1662, seems to have largely affected Salisbury Street, perhaps reaching as far down as the north end of Roundhill. We know from Quarter Sessions papers that 15 households were destroyed, causing damage to the value of £1,552, as well as the loss of £506.6s.8d worth of goods.

Almost ten years later, on Sunday 23rd June 1672, an even more devastating fire swept through the town. No detailed description of the fire or of the damage caused is on record. However, we can gauge its effects by the lists of householders suffering loss, and from numerous individual property records which relate to later rebuilding. Virtually the entire town seems to have been affected, from the Vicarage near the church to the top end of Salisbury Street, and we can only conclude that a strong southerly wind must have been blowing for damage on that scale to have resulted. Clearing up the debris and rebuilding was clearly a formidable task, and a considerable number of properties were still not completed more than two years later.

In all, 102 households were destroyed or partly destroyed, with the cost estimated at the enormous sum of £6,751.8s.8d. Goods and possessions lost were valued at a further £6,882. Fire Insurance was not yet available, and those affected were often dependant on the charity of others to resurrect their homes, and in many cases their livelihoods. Collections known as 'briefs' were made at parish churches, some as far away as Oxfordshire, and the money received was apparently distributed amongst those least able to continue to support themselves.

There is no evidence of loss of life from either fire. There may well have been injuries, but no surviving records contain this type of information.

> What is the equivalent value at the present day of this loss of over £13,600 due to the fire in the year 1672? Any calculation must be based on all sorts of approximations and assumptions and can never be considered accurate. In addition, there is very little correspondence between the 'goods and possessions' in a modern house and those to be found in a 17th-century household. However, taking as a starting point the fact that a building labourer was paid around 12 pence per day in 1672, we calculate that the cost of rebuilding alone would have been the equivalent of, at the very least, ten million pounds in today's values.

Street Names

Several of our present day street names were already in use during the 17th century. In fact, the origins of 'Horseport' and 'Provost Street' can be traced back to the 14th century, as described on pages 20 and 35 respectively. For obvious reasons, the name 'Church Street' had also long been in use.

With the name 'Market Place' transferred to the new site (see opposite), the area near the west end of Bridge Street became known as the Old Market Place by the later 1670s. Continued encroachment onto the open space here soon produced the names 'Fore Street' for the northern end of the present High Street and 'Back Street' for present-day Roundhill.

Confusingly, the name 'Back Street' was also often used in the past to refer to today's West Street; but in the 17th century it had a more intriguing name, 'Jiggins Street', the origin of which is unknown.

Shaftesbury Street is mentioned in the Parish Registers. The area around the stream here, including present-day West Street, is referred to in one document as the 'inferior' part of the town. This probably implied 'lower lying' rather than 'of poorer quality'.

There seems to be no clear record of the origin of the name 'High Street'. Although the name is not used in a 17th century context, there is some evidence of development, or at least infilling, taking place there after 1670. 'St Ives' (no.27 High Street) has *1679* inscribed on a date-plaque, while *1685* is just visible on no.58 (Bath Travel).

Nor is 'Salisbury Street' met with at an early date. It is possible that the name was not used until the direct link with Salisbury Road was made past the Old Manor Court House in the 1770s. The section beyond the town, through what was later to become Burgate Park, was already known as Salisbury Lane.

The Two Market Places

In the early part of the century, the old market cross was still in regular use – it is referred to in numerous records. By now, however, only a small open area remained around it for the sale of produce from the surrounding farms and smallholdings. The cross probably stood on the site of the present-day chemist's shop at 1, Salisbury Street, or close by this spot. Friday

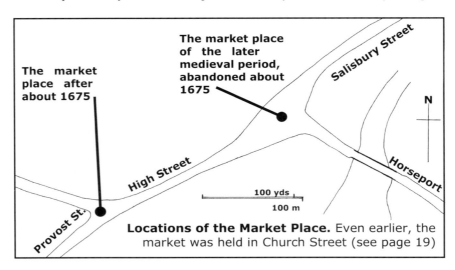

Locations of the Market Place. Even earlier, the market was held in Church Street (see page 19)

seems most likely to have been the regular weekly market day, but evidence for this comes from documents later than the 17th century.

As already mentioned, the site of the market was moved to the further end of the High Street. This seems to have happened during the 1670s, as by the end of this decade there are mentions of *'the late Market Cross'* at the old site. The earliest actual reference to the new market-place, again an indirect one, occurs in 1691.

In the middle of the three-way junction, where a conglomeration of traffic signs stands today, a market-house was constructed. It had an open arcaded area underneath for traders to display their wares, and an upstairs room which could be used for meetings and possibly for the courts of the manor. We can assume that the market-house was built soon after the move, as by the turn of the century it was already in need of repair. It did not take long for enterprising locals to establish new alehouses close by, the first apparently being the Crown Inn, opened by Timothy Coles in, or perhaps even before, 1693.

Titchfield's Market House, now restored at the Open-air Museum at Singleton in West Sussex. Fordingbridge Market House was probably a very similar structure, built soon after 1675 and demolished in 1828

The reasons for this change of site are unknown, but we can speculate that a prime consideration might have been that of traffic congestion. The bridge carried a great deal of local and through traffic – horses, pedestrians and carts of all kinds – and all of it had to pass the old market site. On busy market days, stalls and produce must have spilled out onto the roads, creating a considerable nuisance. However, the timing of the move must surely have been a direct consequence of the 1672 fire.

The Old Manor Court House

The Burgate Court House at the top end of Salisbury Street is undoubtedly one of Fordingbridge's most attractive properties. It contains some of the oldest surviving workmanship in the town, and in the 1990s was restored externally to its early 18th-century appearance. In the earliest record, dated 1657, this site was occupied by a property described as a cottage, garden and orchard. The copyhold tenant was a widow, Jane Grugge, and she paid an annual rent of two shillings and one pound of sugar. Two years later the property came into the

possession of John Mitchell, a local builder, although Jane Grugge was still living there. By 1665 John Mitchell had moved in, and he was still there at the time of the fire which destroyed the building.

After the 1672 fire, John built a new and larger house of brick, incorporating some parts of the original cottage, which can still be detected in the structure today. A condition of the new tenancy agreement was that the Lord of the Manor would be allowed access, when required, to hold manorial courts in one of the upstairs rooms. Thus it became known as the Court House. (Prior to this, courts had presumably been held at the Burgate Manor House, just to the north of the present day Burgate House.) The upstairs room continued to be used for the Burgate courts for more than two centuries.

In 1705, John Tarrant, Gentleman, took possession of the house. He was probably responsible for enlarging it and for adding the bay windows to the front, creating the appearance that exists today.

The Vicars of Fordingbridge – Henson and Clifford

Five vicars served Fordingbridge parish during the 17th century. **William Henson** began his incumbency in 1579 and continued until 1626 - an impressive 47 years in the office.

He was succeeded by **Philip Clifford**, who was even more affluent than most Fordingbridge vicars. The incumbency was a relatively lucrative one, in a large and prosperous parish, and most of the previous vicars had been wealthy by local standards. The inventory of Philip's possessions, taken after his death in 1639, showed him to own goods to the value of £412.11s.3d, which made him far richer than anyone else in the town at the time, apart from the Bulkeleys at Burgate House. Probably his wealth was partly a result of his family background. The Cliffords had been an important landowning family nationally, from medieval times onwards. Philip's ancestry included Sir Robert Clifford; Henry, 1st Earl of Cumberland; and Thomas, 1st Baron Chudleigh.

A fascinating picture of the contemporary vicarage, and of Philip's lifestyle, emerges from the detail recorded in the inventory. The extracts opposite provide an evocative insight into his standard of living.

The vicarage consisted of twelve rooms as well as a brewery, a milk house and a

larder-house. The various chambers were used either as bedrooms or for storage. The Inner Study Chamber contained a *looking glass* [mirror] and an hour glass, while the chamber over the hall held hops and butter as well as a woman's saddle, saddle-cloth and pillion. There were thirteen beer barrels in the buttery, plus two cupboards, including one for glasses, and a meat or food safe.

His farm stock consisted of four cows, six young beasts, four swine and six *horsebeasts*. As well as these he had a *game* [flock] of swans upon the River Avon, a traditional perk of the office.

The colourful memorial to Philip Clifford, vicar of Fordingbridge (died 1639) on the south wall of the chancel in the Parish Church

Philip Clifford's Inventory (extracts)

In his lodging Chamber
All his wearing Apparrell ....£20.
One featherbed Three bolsters One payre of blanketts, a greene
  Rugg, Vallence & Curtaines, Curtaine Rodds Matt & Coarde £7. 2s.
One trucklebed, a matt and Coard and one blankett ....8s. 1d.
An old joyn'd bedsteed, one tableboard & two formes .... £1.10s.
One syde table, fower chayres, two stooles, an old Chest, one box,
  Curtaines & a rodd for the windowe, one windowe Cushion,
  one Carpett ....£5. 3s. 4d.
One payre of Andyrons, fire panne & tongs,
  One payre of bellowes ....£1. 0. 0d.
Eyght pictures, & vyoll glasses...13s.4d.

In the Studdy
One presse of bookes...£20. 10s. 3d.
One pallett bedsteed eyght Coffers & Chests & boxes,
  one glasse Cupboard One bedpan....................................£1. 3s. 4d.

In the Parlour
In moneyes plate and Rings..£36.10s.
One bedsteed, one Cupboord and a trucklebed..........................£1. 3s. 8d.
One Featherbedd, Two coverleds, one bolster, two pillowes,
  Curtaines and vallens, one windowe Curtaine & Rodd...........£1.10s.
One tableboard, one forme, one deske, one looking glasse ....13s. 4d.

In the Hawle
Two tableboards, Two frames & Two forme.....................................13s. 4d.
Eyght joyne stooles, Nyne Chayres, Fower little stooles, Tenne
  Cushions, Two Carpetts & Three pictures ....£4. 13s. 4d.
One payre of Andyrons, One Iron to bear up the fire, One payre
  of tongs, fire pan & bellowes ....6s. 8d.

In the Kitching
One Furnace, the brasse potts, kettles, The Pumpe & Two brasse
  Candlestickes ....£9. 0s. 0d.
One payre of Rackes, Five Spitts, Three Cotterells, an iron barre,
  a fender, a fire panne & tongs, Two Trivetts, a gridyron,
  a Cleaver, a Ronding knife a skimmer & basting ladle,
  One jacke to turne spitt, an iron dripping panne,
  two payre of pot hookes, a fleashooke ....£3. 0s. 0d.
A muskett compleat (except the sword) a coslett, & pike,
  a Fowling peece ....£2.10s.
One Table bord, a Coope, Three shelves, a racke for bacon,
  one benche ....6s. 8d.

**A 'joyne stoole' (joined stool),
perhaps of a similar style to the
eight which Philip Clifford had in
his Hall**

The Vicars of Fordingbridge – Cuffe, Buntlett and Hall

In June 1639 Philip Clifford was succeeded by **John Cuffe**, who was a Professor of Sacred Theology – like all the vicars, he was a scholar of King's College, Cambridge. He was unfortunate in succeeding to the post during the ascendancy of Puritanism and shortly before the turmoil of the Civil War. John clearly did not sympathise with the religious views of the Parliamentary leaders. As a result he was soon removed from office and replaced by **Henry Buntlett**, a good Puritan. Following the Restoration of the monarchy in 1660, however, John was restored as incumbent of Fordingbridge parish and spent over five additional years in the office.

At his death, an Inventory of John's goods was prepared, and his obvious lack of wealth contrasts so starkly with that of his predecessor that it is hard to believe that he was living in the same vicarage. His entire possessions were assessed at only £27.1s.6d, and more than half of this was accounted for by cash and by debts owed to him. While we gave only extracts from Philip Clifford's extensive inventory, this is the list of John Cuffe's entire possessions in March 1666:

His wearing apparrell	*£5. 0s. 0d.*
His books	*£3. 0s. 0d.*
One bed and the appurtenances belonging to it	*£3. 0s. 0d.*
halfe a dozen of stooles and 2 chayres	*10s. 0d.*
Pewter and brasse	*£1. 0s. 0d.*
One Trunke and Chest	*5s. 0d.*
One bedpan	*1s. 0d.*
Andirons tongs and broaches	*5s. 0d.*
in moneys	*£8.15s. 6d.*
in desperate debts	*£5. 0s. 0d.*
in Lumber	*5s. 0d.*
Total	*£27. 1s. 6d.*

It is interesting to speculate whether the contrast between John's possessions and those of Philip Clifford was an indirect result of the Puritan ethic of the Commonwealth. There is little factual information concerning this period in Fordingbridge. We can imagine that Henry Buntlett, as a Puritan, would have considered the vicarage much too luxurious, selling off much of its contents and perhaps putting parts of the large house to other uses. It is obvious that, when John Cuffe resumed his post, he could not have been occupying all of the rooms. Perhaps only some of the dwelling was made available on his return. Alternatively, or additionally, his possessions may have been lost to him at the time of his ejection from the living, leaving him relatively impoverished.

John's successor was **John Hall**, who continued in office through to the end of the century, dying early in 1701.

Churchwardens' Accounts

Quite a number of 17th-century Churchwardens' Accounts survive among the parish records. These record the day-to-day expenditure of the churchwardens and often provide minute detail of repairs to the church, the churchyard, the parish house and the town's bridges. Other purchases include items needed for daily worship and for the various festivals or feast days, while on occasions there are payments for the relief of poor people. The following extracts are taken from the Account of 1639, a year which in many respects was fairly typical, with no exceptional expenses apart from materials for replacing part of the church roof. Much of this work was done by Edward Biles, his two sons and his 'servants'.

Extracts from the Churchwardens' Accounts for 1639

Layde out for bread and wine at Whitsuntide ....*6s. 0d.*
For a book of Articles ....*6d.*
For oyle for the clock ....*2d.*
For a stick to make a scaffoll to William Tiller ....*1s. 2d.*
Payde to Thomas Godfree for stones ....*5s. 4d.*
For a prayer book for the 5th of November ....*6d.*
To the Ringers 25th November ....*2s. 4d.*
To Thomas Walton, his wife and 2 children ....*4d.*
Payde to the sexton for his wages ....*3s. 4d.*
For oyle for the bells ....*2d.*
For wier for the clock ....*6d.*
For bread and wine at Christmas ....*13s. 1d.*
For a bell rope to Ralph Casbert...*1s. 4d.*
Payde to the glazier for mending the church windows ....*10s. 0d.*
payde to the smith for all his ironworke ....*£1. 8s.10d.*
To the Cortnes for making of the dyall in the south side of the Church ....*4s. 0d.*
For bread for communion ....*2s. 2d.*
For mending the great bell clapper ....*4s. 6d.*
For a baskett for the Church ....*6d.*
*For 4 iron wedges and two penny worth of nayles to mend the great bell.*1s. 6d.*
For 6 bushells of lime which we bought of William Casse.......................*3s. 4d.*
Bought first of all 5 trees and the carriage which made 5 loades........*£5. 7s.8d..*
Bought of Mr John Dodington Esq 4 trees and the carriage ....*£5. 8s.0d.*
For 1 tunn and 2 pounds of new led at three halfpence
farthinge a pound ....*£15.11s.6d.*
For 28 pounds of soder ....*1. 1s.0d.*
For taking away of the old led and laying it again ....*15s. 8d.*

The Quakers

The Society of Friends, or Quakers, had been active in the town in the 1660s, although they were not granted a 'Meetinghouse Certificate' until 1689. All forms of nonconformity were still illegal before this date. With the accession of William III in 1688 attitudes changed, and in the following year the 'Toleration Act' was passed, which allowed Dissenters to worship freely. Where they met during those early years is not clear, but by 1693 one of their number, William Lumber, by occupation an awlblade maker, had purchased a house in Roundhill from William Casbert, a local merchant. The building was established as the community's Meeting House by the early part of 1694, William Lumber having invested it in Trustees, although it was also used as his own home.

The garden at the rear was to serve as the Quakers' cemetery. On December 28th 1696 the first burial took place when Mary, wife of Moses Harris, was interred in a woollen shroud. This was in accordance with an Act of Parliament of 1661, intended to help the ailing woollen industry

Trades and Occupations

The trades and occupations in 17th-century Fordingbridge were largely those that would have been found in any rural market town of the period. Butchers, bakers, carpenters, wheelers, victuallers, blacksmiths, tailors, shoemakers and cobblers are all met with frequently in the surviving documents; they were, of course, following centuries-old traditions. The other leather-related trades of tanners, skinners and glovers were still followed, although possibly not in such large numbers as in the 16th century. Most of these craftsmen were still using mainly local produce and raw materials.

A few new trades begin to be mentioned. There were now a number of awl-blade-makers, edge tool makers and pointmakers, all involved with some aspect of metalworking. Weavers, both in wool and linen, also appear in the record, although undoubtedly some must have existed in earlier times without featuring in the surviving documents. In fact, a fulling mill had been recorded at East Mill from the 15th century, with woollen cloth being produced locally from at least that date. There were also several grist mills, both in the town and in local villages, producing flour and meal from grain.

Shopkeepers were beginning to feature prominently in the life of the town. Some regarded themselves as merchants, dealing in a wide range of goods. In contrast to the work of the local craftsmen, much of their stock was bought in from far and wide.

We must not, of course, disregard the small number of professional men, including the clerics at the parish church, and the stewards of the various manors. By the latter part of the century there may well have been an attorney-at-law, but it is not entirely clear when the first one arrived in the town. (There is no indication in the records of any medical men at this stage.)

Beyond the town, many families lived on small mixed farms consisting of anything from a few acres up to twenty or more. A few 'gentlemen farmers' with larger holdings were beginning to emerge before the end of the century.

By this time, however, the largest single occupational group were the labourers, who had no proper trade and a relatively low income. Those lucky enough to have permanent work on the estates or with the shops or tradesmen were adequately rewarded, but many were only able to find seasonal work on the farms. Poverty abounded in winter time and was an ever present threat, all the more so for those with physical disabilities.

Apprentices

Fordingbridge's parish records for the 17th century include more than forty Apprenticeship Indentures. The Statute of Apprentices had been introduced by Parliament in 1563. This regulation obliged anyone who wished to enter a trade to serve a formal apprenticeship, often for a considerable number of years. Normally a fee was payable to the master from the apprentices' parents, but where pauper families were involved, the parish Overseers of the Poor would often find the money.

The details to be found in the surviving indentures give a revealing insight into the strictly binding contracts between apprentices and masters. Not only did such apprenticeships ensure a ready supply of skilled craftsmen, but they served a secondary function of helping to keep young men under control. As an example, we quote in full an indenture for apprenticeship to a point-maker (opposite). It is well worth attempting to read the often strange spelling, in order to see the incredible amount of control which a master had over his apprentice – no visits to taverns, no dice or card-playing, no engagement to marry. The regulation of *'noe fornicacion'* was qualified by *'in the house of his saied Master'* but this was little help to a lustful young man, as he was not allowed to absent himself *'neyther by daye or by night'*!

Sadly, we do not have any information whether Andrew Leceter, the apprentice, went on to complete his apprenticeship or what happened to him in later life. We do know, however, that his master, Phillip Waterman, started a new business as a chandler within a year or two of this date.

Stocks, Pillory, Prison and Justices of the Peace

Most minor crimes were still dealt with locally. Petty offences, assault and damage to property, which in medieval times had been handled by the manorial court, were now under the jurisdiction of Justices of the Peace. These officials were appointed from members of the local gentry, including the Dodingtons at Breamore and the Bulkeleys at Burgate. The punishments they authorised ranged from fines to a spell in the stocks or pillory, the latter sometimes accompanied by a whipping.

Apprenticeship Indenture of Andrew Leceter to Phillip Waterman, 7th September 1628

This Indenture *Witnesseth that Andrew Leceter the Sonn of Henry Leceter of Fordingbridge in the Countie of Southampton husbandman, hath by the Consent of Anthony Casbert Junior and Phillip Withington, Churchwardens, John Paschue alias Cabell Senior, Thomas Mowland and John Norris, Collectors for the parish of Fordingbridge aforesaied and Countie aforesaied.* *As alsoe by the Consent of the Right worshipfuls Sir John Mill Knight and Barronet and Sir William Dodington Knight, two of the Kings Majesties Justices of the Peace and Quorum for the Countie aforesaied Present the forsaid Andrew Apprentice with Phillip Waterman of Fordingbridge in the Countie aforesaid Poyntmaker. And after the manner of a Prentise with him to dwell from the daye of the date hereof unto and untell the full end and tearme of Nyne yeares then next and ymmediately following fullie to be complete and ended dureing all which saied tearme the saied Andrew unto the saied Phillip as his Master well and trulie shall serve, his seecreetes shall keepe, his Lawful Commandements shall observe, noe fornicacion in the house of his saied Master he shall not Commytt, hurte unto his saied maister he shalnot doe nor Consent to be done, to the value of Twelve Pence by the Yeare or above but he to his power shall let or owen his maister thereof warne, Tavernes or Alehouses of Custome he shalnot haunte nor Frequaynt except yt be about his Maisters busyness there to be done. Att the Dyce, Cardes or any other unlawful games he shalnot play, the goodes of his said maister inordynately he shalnot waste nor then to anie one lend without his leave or lycence first had and obtayned, Matrymony with any one within the sayed tearme he shalnot Contractt nor espouse, nor from his service neyther by daye or by night shall absent or prolonge himselfe. But shall in all things behave himself honestly and truely dureing the saied tearme aswell in words as in deedes.* ***And*** *the saied Phillipp the Master unto the saied Andrew the Apprentice the Artt of a Poyntmaker or in any other Artt the which he useth shall teach and enforme or cause to be taught and enformed as much as to the same Artt or Science belongythor any wyse appertayneth. And in due manner to Chastice him, Fyndinge and allowing unto his sayed Apprentize sufficient wholene Meale, drinke, lennen, wullon, hoose, Schooes, Beading, washing and all other thinges meete and necessarie aswell in Sickness as in health dureing all the tyme and tearme as aforesaied. And att thend and expiracion of the aforesaied tearme the said Phillipp the Master shall give or cause to be given to the saied Andrew thapprentize sufficient duble apparrell, viz., Apparrell for the Holy Dayes and apparrell for the workey dayes meete and decent and one shilling of Lawfull money of England. In true witnesse whereof the partyes here above named to these presente Indentures Enterchangably have put to their handes and Seales yeaven the seaventh daye of September, In the Fowerth yeare of the reigne of our Sovereigne Lord Charles By the grace of God of England, Scotland, France and Ireland, King, Defender of the fayth, Anno Domini 1628.*

While there are no details of them in the 17th century, we know that in later times there were two sets of stocks in the town. One set, which remained in existence till 1860, was near the new Market Place, at the rear of the present-day Royal Arms public house. They were said to stand in Shaftesbury Street, by a cottage that had formerly been a baker's shop. It is probable that they had replaced an earlier set at the old market place. The Manor Court proceedings for 14th April 1687 record that the Lord of the Manor was to provide timber for repairing the pillory and the stocks. Also mentioned was the 'cucking stool', a wooden chair into which scolds were strapped and dipped into the river – its position is not recorded. 'Scolds' were women who continually scolded their neighbours.

While the stocks at Fordingbridge do not survive, those at Breamore may still be seen today, opposite the Bat and Ball Hotel.
When James Coventry took this picture in 1898, with two small boys demonstrating their use, the stocks were within the grounds of the village school.

The second set of stocks was in Church Street, against the animal pound, which was where the house called 'The Leys' now stands. The pillory was also found here, as was the lock-up or 'Bridewell', where vagabonds and other undesirables could be held while their fate was decided. Its other use was to detain more serious criminals who were subsequently removed to the County Jail in Winchester. Once there, they would await trial at the Assizes or Quarter Sessions, which often imposed severe punishments – even theft could lead to the gallows.

There was, of course, no form of police service at this time. The official with a role nearest to that of a modern policeman was the 'Constable'. He was elected at the Manorial Court from amongst the ranks of householders in the town – and was unpaid, probably reluctant, and invariably had little real aptitude for the job. It was one thing to punish convicted criminals severely, quite another to catch them in the first place. Much crime went undetected.

In effect the Justices of the Peace ran local government. Their widely varying duties included responsibility for overseeing collection of the Poor Rates, the state of the roads, and the good conduct of inns and alehouses. Meeting their county colleagues at Winchester Quarter Sessions, they ordered repairs to be made to bridges, kept an eye on apprenticeship regulations, licensed the ale-houses, and much more.

They also attended the Assizes, where the Circuit Judge advised and updated them on government policy, while pronouncing on any shortcomings he saw in their work. They were then left to see that the parishes put these policies into practice.

Canalisation of the Avon

In the 1670s an ambitious scheme to canalise the River Avon was begun. The aim was to enable barges to travel from Christchurch to Salisbury and back, increasing trade and greatly reducing transport costs. Two major obstacles had to be overcome. Firstly, there were a number of shallow fording points along the river, including one just below the mill at Breamore. Even the barges, with their shallow draughts, could not cope with these in summer when water levels were low. Secondly, the numerous mills and their weirs prevented the free passage of boats over any great distance.

The river was surveyed and work began in the late summer of 1675. The shallows were deepened and attempts were made to by-pass the weirs by building locks or digging new channels for the barges. A lack of funds delayed the scheme, however. A further ten years elapsed before it was possible to bring barges along the whole length of the river, by which time the local mills at Bickton, East Mill, Burgate and Breamore could all be avoided via their new locks and streamlets, some of which can still be seen today.

Some traffic certainly did negotiate the river over the next twenty years or so, but there is no evidence of substantial use, probably due to a number of continuing problems. On the comparable, but somewhat later, Itchen Navigation, there was a towpath from Woodmill in Southampton all the way to Winchester, so that barges could be horse-drawn. The construction of a towpath alongside the Avon had been considered impracticable, so that an already difficult journey was made worse as barges had to use sails. In some cases they had to be winched through the locks.

There were complaints from local landowners about ruination of fisheries and increased growth of weeds in the relatively stagnant cuts. Repeated flooding, particularly in the Christchurch area, caused damage to the banks of the river. Enthusiasm for the scheme waned and so it was never fully completed, being finally abandoned in the 1730s.

The Little Mill

For a time in the middle of the 17th century there was a little mill just beyond the Great Bridge at Horseport. We know little about it, except that it was apparently run by Thomas Kent in the 1660s. There was, until recent years, a small stream crossing under the road here and running back into the main river to the south of the Victoria Rooms. This was undoubtedly the millstream of the Little Mill.

The Contents and Layouts of Houses

We have already quoted from a number of Probate Inventories, documents that were commonly attached to wills. Around 70 exist for the parish of Fordingbridge during the 17th century. Some relate to properties in the villages and hamlets, but the majority relate to properties within the town. When a property owner died, appraisers listed all of his belongings. Usually they worked through the house recording one room at a time, sometimes beginning on the ground floor, but occasionally starting in the deceased's bedchamber.

The result is often a room by room description of the person's possessions, providing us with a glimpse of contemporary standards of living. Such information is also our only source of knowledge of the size and layout of dwellings of the period. The smaller houses are naturally the easiest to reconstruct. In these cases there was often little more than a hall and buttery downstairs, with perhaps two chambers above, reached by a staircase that adjoined a central chimney stack built of brick. As we have already seen, half-timbered houses with wattle and daub infilling were the norm until the fire of 1672, but brick was widely used thereafter.

The larger houses, owned in particular by the merchant class, provide more of a problem, being relatively complex in design. Some, such as the vicarage, seem to have been a veritable warren of passages and rooms, impossible to understand fully from the available details. With improved standards of building by the end of the century, any kitchen was more likely to be incorporated into the main body of the house, rather than being detached because of the fire risk, as in earlier times.

John Fulford was a weaver of woollen cloth with a moderately good standard of living. He died in 1672 and his inventory records his possessions with a total value of £54.14s.4d. His house was fairly modest with a hall, buttery and two upstairs chambers, although there was also a loft which apparently served as a third bedroom.

Brian Green was an innkeeper to the west of the Great Bridge, and although we cannot be entirely certain, it is likely that he was the proprietor of the George Inn. Not surprisingly his premises were larger, in order to cater for customers and paying guests. Five chambers are recorded, and both the parlour and little parlour held beds, so that up to nine people could be accommodated at any one time, although one of the rooms must have been for his own family.,

The hall was obviously the main room where customers congregated for food and drink, but by our standards was bare of furniture, with only twelve stools set around the large open fire. There is no mention of a table or cupboards. Meat was cooked over the hall fire, where there was a choice of four spits. Most of the brass pans, kettles, brass pots, brass skillets, pewter platters, porringers, saucers, plates and salts must have been in this room. There was no separate kitchen.

There was, of course, a brewhouse which was detached from the main house. It held a furnace and a mashing vat, as well as the rest of the brewing implements, with four hogsheads full of beer and a number of empty barrels.

Thomas Bownde, Tanner

Thomas Bownde, who died in 1617, had probably lived on the north side of the Great Bridge, opposite the George Inn. His dwelling was a simple one, a hall with a chamber above and a fairly elaborate kitchen, which was presumably detached at the rear.

By occupation he was a tanner, so beyond the kitchen there was a *'Tanne howse'* – its full list of contents was as follows :

All his Barke	£6.
10 Hydes	£6.10s.
4 Hydes	£5.
5 Hydes..	50s.
5 Hydes	£4.
3 Calveskynnes, 1 horsehyde, 2 pooles and the drie leather in all	24s.
1 Hyde in haire	6s.
the woode in the backeside	5s.
the Beame knives, and other tooles, shoehorne and chayne and	
the workinge beame	14d.
the boate and 1 pott	5s.
the Mylle to grinde Barke	2s.

Thomas's tannery must have been right alongside the Avon and it may well have been his premises that were discovered during recent archaeological work. The Trust for Wessex Archaeology excavated a number of tanning pits when digging on the old Albany site in 1998 (see page 19). The tannery continued in use until the mid-18th century.

Thomas Knowles, Merchant

Thomas Knowles was one of the small group of mercers or merchants trading in the town during the first half of the 17th century. His house was a relatively large one at the bottom of Provost Street on the west side. It is not known whether he was a native of Fordingbridge, but his father was Edward Knowles and he had a brother Francis and a son James.

We first meet him in 1594 when his life was added to the tenancy of the property, then held by Anna Osborne, who was presumably a relative (see note about lives and tenancies on page 82). He was to remain there for the rest of his days, developing his mercer's business into a prosperous enterprise. By the time of his death in January 1641 he had come to consider himself to be a 'Gentleman', a description which sometimes signified retirement from business. He was clearly a person of some standing within the town. The small bridge adjoining his property, known previously as the 'lesse bridge' came to be called 'Knowles' Bridge', the name that it bears to this day.

His will does not survive, but the Inventory of his goods is of sufficient interest to reproduce here in full, in order to exemplify the way of life of one of the town's wealthier

Knowles Bridge takes its name from Thomas Knowles, a prominent citizen in the 17th century, who owned a property approximately where the houses now stand, on the left of this modern photograph. It was formerly known as the Lesse, Lesser or Lytch Bridge (see page 54). Sweatfords Water and Ashford Water flow together just upstream of this bridge.

inhabitants. Although the equipment in his shop is listed, there is no mention of any stock, which again suggests that he had retired. The lease of the copyhold, mentioned near the end, may indicate that the shop was let out to a tenant who was the owner of any stock present. The lease of the Mills must relate to the Town Mills, just a little way downstream from his house, although there is no further record of his involvement with them.

His Lodging Chamber the greater chamber over the haule

All his wearing apparell...[illegible]
One stand, a bedsted, a matt, a bedcoord, a Curtin ....6s.
One Featherbed, a boulster, two pillowes, One payre of blanketts & one Rugge................£2.10s.
One Trundle bedsteed, a matt and Coard, one Fetherbed, One payre of blanketts,
    a Coverlet, a bolster ....£1.15s.
Three great Chests, one deske, three coffers, one box, one table booord
    and frame..£1. 5s.
One Reeden Chayre, fower Cushions, two little stooles ....2s. 4d.
His Linning viz. Tenne payre of bedsheets, Thirteene Table Cloathes, Two dozen
    & three ordinarie table napkins, Fower Cupboord Cloathes, Three long
    towells, Twelve pillowetyes.. £6.
One suite of Dieper viz. One Table Cloathe, One dozen of Napkins,
    One Towell & One Cupbord Cloath .... £2.13s. 4d.
One little bedsheet..4s.

In the Lesser chamber over the haule

One standing bedsteed, one bedmatt & Coard, One fetherbed, One Rugge,
    one payre of blanchetts, Two Feather bolsters, two pillowes, Curtins
    and Curtinrods ....£3. 10s.
One trundle bedsteed, coard & matt, One featherbed, one bolster, one Coverlett,
    One payre of blanchets..£1.15s.
One Liverie Cupbord Cloath and Cushion ....6s. 8d.
One Chest, two Coffers, one small tableboord, one fram'd Chayre ....6s. 8d.
One Pewter still, one bedpanne, One bason & Ewre, One lookinglasse ....10s.
One payre of Tonges, one payre of Iron Andyrons, one firepanne ....2s. 4d.
One windowe Curtaine & Curtaine Rodd, fower feather Cushions, one old sword.................6s. 8d.
Certen bookes..8s.

In the Chamber over the Shopp

One standing bedsteed, Curtins & Curtin Rods, one bedcoard & matt............................£2.13s. 4d.
One Chest, three Coffers, one olde Chayre, a closestoole ....5s. 4d.
One windowe Curin & rodd ....1s. 2d.

continued ....

In the Haule
One long Tableboard & frame, Six joyn'd stooles & two lesser tableboords,
　　　one joyn'd Cupbord, two Chayres, one stoole ....£2.
In Plate One great guilt salt, one lesser Trencher guilt salt, One nut? n. - - - bowle,
　　　one silver drinking bowle, one silver beaker, seaven silver spoones,
　　　Three gould Rings ....£11. 6s.
One payre of Iron Andyrons, one payre of tonges & firepanne, one Iron Fender,
　　　two payre of Cottrells, two old Corslets, a tosting Iron, fower
　　　vyoll glasses, two brushes, one payre of bellowes ....£1. 3s. 6d.

In the great Butterie
Pewter, viz. tenne broade platters, Nyne lesser platters, one dozen & one
　　　Sawcers, Two Basons, Two Porringers, Two Salts, three Pewter
　　　Candlestickes, two brasse Candlestickes, One pewter plate, One
　　　pewter Tankerd, two Chamber potts ....£1.13s. 4d.
Fower brasse potts, two bellskillets, Three? brasse skilletts, Three brasse
　　　kettles, two brasse - - - , (one) Alimbicke, one dripping pan,
　　　(one) panne, ...?9.10s.10d.
One side board, two - - -, two Trendles, One Keeve, One searche ....6s. 6d.

In the little Butterie
Two barrels, One saffe, three Shelves ....6s.

In the Shopp
One Pestell & Morter, two payre of Skales, a nest of boxes, a Shop hatchett,
　　　all the Shelves & Chests, a payre of Iron wayt beames - Waytes,
　　　viz. One Quarterne, one fowre-teene Pownds & two seaven Pownds,
　　　One brasse Chaffing-dishe, five small boxes, one tubb, one quarter
　　　of a pint measure. One Tunnill ....£3.

In the Warehouse
three Tubbs, One willowe, two old bedmatts, One Covell, one Linturne,
　　　a great Trendle, a cheese Racke, a bagg of feathers ....10s.

In the Counting house
One little Table boord, a nest of boxes, with other little boxes, a little Coffer,
　　　a deske, a little Iron chayne, two measures, a pint & a half pint,
　　　one Sledge & old Iron ....10s.

In the Kitching
One great yoating fawte, One silt, One Cheesepresse, two stands, One
　　　Powdring Tubb, One Table-boord, two old formes, three shelves,
　　　one brasse Furnace, one payre of iron Rackes, two payre of potthookes,
　　　three Iron spitts, a payre of Fetters ....£2.

In the Chamber over the Kitchin
One flocke bed, one Coverled, one cheese Racke, One borden Bedsteed,
　　　One bolster, one old Chest, a planke with hookes to hang Bacon on.
　　　And more one flocke-bed, one Coverled, One Blankett,
　　　One feather bolster...£1. 8s.

in the Barne & stable & out houses
Hay ....£1. 6s. 8d.
wood & Turfe ....3s. 4d.
a saddle & bridle & two prangs..5s.
two horsebeasts ....£2.15s.
soyle in the backesyde...3s. 4d.
Lent abroade a Trundle bedsteed, a matt & cord ....4s.
another benshe, a smothing Iron, two Cushions, with other small things ....2s. 6d.
One Chattle lease of the Mills in Fordingbridge ....[illegible]
One lease of the fee farme of the Coppie houlde in Fordingbridge belonging
　　　to the King's College in Fordingbridge ....£50.
Debts due to him ....£4.10s.

Total...£226. 14s.6d. [altered and not clear]
Funeral expenses..£15.0. 0d.

CHAPTER 8 – THE EIGHTEENTH CENTURY

Queen Anne came to the throne in 1702 and reigned for 12 years. From her 17 pregnancies, only one child survived as long as eleven years, so she died without a natural heir. The 54-year-old German-speaking Elector of Hanover, whose mother was a granddaughter of James I, came to the throne as George I.

The reigns of George I, George II and the immensely long one of George III covered the rest of the 18th century and well into the 19th. In this period, the Industrial and Agricultural Revolutions got underway, Britain gained colonies in various parts of the world (while losing those which became the young U.S.A.) and most of the power of the king was transferred to a prime minister and cabinet.

Sir Edward Hulse, physician both to Anne and to George I, purchased Breamore House in 1748, the male line of the Dodingtons having died out almost a century earlier. The Hulse family has lived at Breamore ever since and, as local landowners, have had continuing influence on the area, including the town of Fordingbridge.

Fordingbridge's Third Fire

For Fordingbridge, the century opened badly, with yet another serious fire. Available records are imprecise, but it probably occurred during the second half of 1702, and it seems that the area worst affected was Roundhill and the High Street. Fortunately, the damage was much less widespread than in 1672. However, it was locally severe – and many of the buildings destroyed were only about thirty years old, having been built after that previous fire. At least eight houses of the Fordingbridge Manor had to be rebuilt over the following few years, as well as several belonging to Burgate Manor and a number of freeholds, but it is impossible to tell exactly how many houses were destroyed.

The total financial loss is known, however, from a surprising source. The parishioners of Hadstock in Essex made a collection towards the relief of Fordingbridge residents – and the parish records there quote the total loss as £5,059.19s.0d.

Several members of the Society of Friends or Quakers owned property in Roundhill and High Street. Their losses alone amounted to £939, almost a fifth of the total. One of the worst affected was Moses Harris, a Quaker merchant who apparently lived at the property now occupied by Harrison's stationery shop – 23 High Street. He lost property and goods to the value of £400.

It seems strange to us today that such a major event should be so poorly recorded. Casual perusal of the few surviving documents could give the impression that life went on as usual around the wreckage. This cannot have been the case, as not only were homes destroyed, but businesses and livelihoods as well. Records of the rebuilding, surviving in the Fordingbridge Court Books, show that some houses were replaced with little delay while others remained in ruins for several years.

The date-plaque on this building at 47-49 High Street, occupied by Forbuoys in 2001, shows that it was built very soon after Fordingbridge's third major fire in 1702.

In the Roundhill area, a number of replacement buildings date from the following year, 1703.

One damaged property, belonging to Richard Waterman, was surrendered back into the hands of the Lord of the Manor, as late as 1705, presumably because Richard could not afford the building costs. Those that did rebuild were usually given permission by the Lord to add an extra life to the tenancy without charge.

Most properties were held for the lives of three named people, a long-established system which became more common in the 18th century. For example, if a male tenant died, the tenancy automatically descended to his widow, and on her death it could pass to a named son or daughter. But on the third death, the tenancy would end. In normal circumstances the addition of an extra person necessitated a large payment to the Lord. Thus some families attempted to save money, eventually to be used to keep the property in the family after the third death. The Lord's concession was therefore a financial benefit to such families when bearing the costs of rebuilding after the fire.

Fire-fighting and Fire Insurance

The older inhabitants of the town had now witnessed three major conflagrations in forty years. Minds were doubtless concentrated on how to prevent similar tragedies in the future. Discussions, and probably arguments, must have continued for months, if not for years. Unfortunately, there are no records of local events at the time, but improvements in fire-fighting were soon possible, and insurance was soon available to help alleviate the financial consequences of future damage.

The first Fire Insurance companies were established in the early part of the 18th century, as a direct consequence of the large number of serious fires occurring across the country over many years. One of the first companies, Sun Fire of London, was issuing policies for London properties by 1710. Within a few years, provincial property owners were able to take advantage of the service. Among the first policyholders in Fordingbridge were Timothy Coles of the New Inn and William Hellier of the Crown, both in 1718. In the same year, the Reverend John Horsnell of Fordingbridge insured the Vicarage. Within the next decade many of the town's tradesmen followed suit, some using other developing companies such as London Assurance and Royal Exchange Assurance. As it happened, there were no more major conflagrations across large swathes of the town, but individual buildings were destroyed from time to time. On such occasions, those without insurance were left to suffer considerable hardship.

A Sun Insurance symbol on a thatched house in Church Street

The actual document for Sun Insurance Policy Number 339172 survives at the Guildhall Library, London. Unfortunately, the volume containing it is in such a fragile condition that it cannot even be examined in order to find the name of the policyholder. It is probably of 19th century date

Simple water-pumps on wheels were now available for fire-fighting, and there was an enthusiastic response to the 1707 Act of Parliament which required every parish to have its own engine. Fordingbridge's 'water-engine' was in use by 1711, or maybe a little before this. It was kept in a brick shed at the junction of Roundhill and High Street, outside No 20 High Street (currently a baker's shop). The churchwardens' accounts reveal that the shed was kept locked, but we do not know who kept the key.

There was, however, no fire brigade. The engine could be collected from this point by anyone who needed it. Clearly, this was better than nothing, but it is easy to imagine how unsatisfactory the arrangement was. If there was a fire on the outskirts of the town, or even beyond, someone had to run or ride to the shed, find the keyholder to unlock it, pull the engine to the scene of the fire, then find a water supply and willing hands to help with the pumping. In practice the small quantity of water that could be pumped probably had little or no effect on a major fire, even if the machine arrived in time.

Within two or three decades, two more engines had been obtained and a new shed had been erected at the north end of Church Street. In his *Fordingbridge and Neighbourhood* (first published 1883), Reginald Hannen stated that a third shed existed at the north end of Salisbury Street, but there seems to be no record of exactly where this was.

Some insurance companies provided fire-engines, strictly for their own policyholders, but there is no evidence of this happening in Fordingbridge during the 18th century.

Maintenance of the Parish Fire Engines

Maintenance was the responsibility of the churchwardens, the engines having been purchased by them in the first place. Numerous churchwardens' documents relate to repair of the engines. The earliest, dated June 1741-2, mentions work on all three, including *'mending the Engins after the fire att Friery* [Fryern] *Court in 1742'*. Other items purchased for their repair included leather, cork, solder and iron. In 1755 Thomas Lawes was paid 8 shillings for *'ringen of a paier Engen wheells and 4 spooks and binden of them'*.

The most detailed information on repair is found in an account submitted by Edmund Dale, a local blacksmith, in 1757. We quote it here in full.

May 13th	
To one day Self and William in mending the Great Engin..........................4s.0d.	
To 5½ lbs of Soder...4s.7d.	
To haveing out 2 of the Engins to clean and work them	
and see them in order...2s.0d.	
July 10th	
To ½ a day in mending the Great Engin ....2s.0d.	
To 2 lbs of Soder ....1s.8d.	
To haveing out Newshams Engin to see in order ....1s.0d.	
	15s.3d.

It is interesting to see that so much care was taken in maintaining the engines in good working order at this time, as in Victorian times there were frequent complaints of neglect, and of engines not working properly when needed.

There are at least two entries in 18th-century documents mentioning the *'Indian House'*; which at first sight is rather puzzling. A closer look reveals that the reference is really to the 'Engine House', and that local dialect has intervened. Spelling was, of course, still notoriously inconsistent at this time. By far the commonest version in the surviving documents is *'engin'*, with other spellings including *'engen'* and *'ingen'* – and just occasionally *'engine'*.

Dwellings, Population and Employment

A considerable number of the buildings existing today in the historic core of Fordingbridge have 18th-century work in them. As we have seen, some were built to replace dwellings lost in the fire. In the first few decades, there was also some infilling of previously open spaces around Church Street and along the west side of Salisbury Street, mostly on land of the Fordingbridge Manor. More houses were constructed during the middle part of the century, the most notable being the large brick town house at 33-39 High Street (see next page), which replaced the earlier Swan Inn. Also of this date, although with later alterations, is the Manse at the rear of the United Reformed Church in Salisbury Street.

A large mid-18th-century brick town-house in Fordingbridge High Street (housing the hairdressing premises of Carl Hillwood in this 2001 photograph)

This building work resulted in only limited physical expansion of the town during the 18th century. Nevertheless, the population was now beginning to expand rapidly.

The rising population could be supported only by increased employment opportunities. Farming was still a major employer in the district, but it could not absorb substantially larger numbers of workers. In any case, much of the work was seasonal, so it could not provide full-time employment. The resulting pool of spare labour was, at least partly, absorbed by new occupations which came to the fore at this time. There was an expansion in the output from weaving and spinning. At first this was largely a cottage industry, but soon new commercial enterprises were producing bleached cloth. By the end of the century, several businesses had established small factories for printing elaborate patterns onto calico. In 1788 Thomas Shepherd opened the Stuckton Iron Works.

While most men were employed in one way or another, there were certainly others who were not able to earn a living, perhaps because of illness or disability. Widows, particularly those with children, were also likely to be impoverished, unless they had better-off relatives to assist them financially. The care of the poor features strongly in parish documents of the time. The opening of a smallpox house at Blissford and of a workhouse in the town reflects the growing involvement of the church in attempts to alleviate poverty and disease.

The Overseers of the Poor

As we have seen, the churchwardens collected parish rates for the care of the poor. The majority of the contributions inevitably came from the landowners, craftsmen, traders, professional men and other better-off householders. At the annual Vestry meeting, attended by the vicar, churchwardens and some leading parishioners, four Overseers of the Poor were appointed, together with other parish officials. By the 18th century, the job of Overseer was a considerable burden, with wide responsibilities that were most likely to be shouldered effectively by the more able members of the community.

> If we assemble a sort of **'job description' for Overseer of the Poor**, it would include :
> collecting money from numerous ratepayers – and justifying any increases;
> determining exactly who qualified for poor relief;
> arranging payments for those who did qualify;
> dealing with those poor people whose claims were rejected;
> arranging for maintenance of the roads in the parish, including the smaller bridges
>   (that is, those other than the Great Bridge and Knowles Bridge);
> supervising the constable's expenses;
> balancing their books *and* taking personal responsibility for any amount overspent;
> annual salary – zero.

Difficult decisions had to be made on a regular basis, with resulting unpopularity and even open hostility, from both ends of the community. Poor people often thought they should be due greater help, while better-off ratepayers were reluctant to pay increased rates – the universal conflict between the desire for public services and the reluctance to pay taxes.

It is hardly surprising that it was not a job that many welcomed enthusiastically, and there was probably not much point in insisting that a reluctant, incompetent individual took up the post. Although the appointment was theoretically for one year, with parishioners serving in rotation, some Overseers served much longer than this. Perhaps some people, once in the position, liked to maintain the official status that it gave them

Under the Poor Law system, each parish was legally bound only to support those who were settled there. Poor families were expected to return to their home parishes to obtain relief. If a Fordingbridge man had settled in a different part of the country, after his death Fordingbridge parish would have been responsible for his widow and children if they fell on hard times, even though they might never have visited the town. Thus, while most payments by the Fordingbridge Overseers would have been made to local people, there were often cases of strangers suffering severe hardship. Some were provided with transport to take them home, but others were simply paid to go away (see page 90).

During the first half of the century, the poorer members of the parish were supported within their own homes wherever possible. As many as 43 poor persons were being paid regular monthly sums by 1738. Their house rents were often paid for them and clothes, shoes, fuel and food were frequently provided. In the main, relief was restricted to the disabled, the elderly, widows – particularly those with young children – and the sick.

> Fordingbridge is fortunate in having many surviving 18th-century records relating to the administration of the care of its poor, although the 1740s and 1750s are better documented than some other decades. There are many overseers' vouchers, which deal with expenditure in minute detail, most of them receipted by traders who had supplied goods and carried out work.

The Smallpox House

People's thoughts and conversations were undoubtedly dominated by concern about the sick – or rather about the spread of disease. For many years, smallpox had been rampant throughout the country, and a more virulent form spread during the 18th century. Fordingbridge and its surrounding villages did not escape this highly contagious infection.

In 1741 the Vestry took the decision to obtain a remote house on the edge of the New Forest at Blissford, where infected people from the town could be housed, away from their relations and neighbours. The lease of a cottage was acquired from Simon Seager and the building was soon extended to make it into a 'Smallpox House' – effectively a primitive 'isolation hospital'. The following account is for bricks supplied for the extension :

Account of Bricks delivered to Beeld the Smallpox hous 1741/2
November the 3.........................2 thousand - 6 hundred
the 5th.....................................2 thousand - 4 hundred
the 8th ....7 hundred & 50
the total Sum is 5 thousand ....7 hundred & 50
which Coms to ....£3. 9s.0d at 12 shillings the thousand
March the 6 1741/2 received the Contence of this Bill of Andrew Admes on the
paresh a Count received infull by me -- John Compton

Running costs of the smallpox house were entirely paid for from the Parish Rates. Food and medicine was supplied, and local surgeons and apothecaries were paid to attend (referred to as *'a Tendance'* or *'Tending'* in the account below). There are numerous notes of the provisions sent there, and the overwhelming impression is that the patients ate and drank well, with a much wider variety of foodstuffs than most would have had at home.

1741 Acount What Sillys famely Cost in the Smalpox
July
Necesserys sent with Sillis Daughter to the smalpox house
To Baken Chees Shugger Currants Nutmeg Bread Biskeet Candls oatmal and Ale and Buttor
and John Martons helping her up to the house
20 July
to the old woman Chees Bread and Buttor and oatmeal ....5s .9½d.
to Beakon Shuger Nutmags Candls Curants & Bear ....4s. 3d.
to a pint Seak a pound of Lentfeigs a pound of Currants, Suger ....*Rice and Reasons*..2s.11d.
to Saferan and a peck malt 3 pounds Beakon monny and salt ....5s. 0½d.
to Buttor and Shuger Soup and Frinch Beans Biscake ....1s. 3d.
to Buttor and monny..4½d.
to the Removeing the old man paid Will Hewlet ....1s. 6d.
John Marton 1s. hors and Cart 1s.6d...2s. 6d.
To a pint Seak and Shuger and Nutmeg ....1s.11d.
To mutton and veal and Galon Bear Lentfigs and Ressons ....4s. 0d.
To prewans Ressons a pint seak and veal 2 Gallons Bear......................5s. 6d.
To 3 pounds Beakon Buttor a Gallon Bear Shuger & Cabage ....4s. 2d.
To Candls Shuger Cabage and frinch Beans and Buttar ....1s. 5d.
To Beakon and Cabage and yard Cloath the old womans leg Thred ...2s.11½d.
Paid Sarah Taylor Going uo and down and her a Tendance 5 weeks .....7s. 0d.
Phanny Elphs 5 weeks Tending 5 shillings per week........................£1. 5s. 0d.
John Collins Bill..£1. 1s. 1d.
£5. 7s. 8d.

Edward Chapman was the apothecary employed to look after the residents of the Smallpox House in 1741. His account for medicines supplied during that year makes fascinating reading. As might be expected bleeding, presumably using either leeches or the technique of cupping, was a routine treatment. Medicines included: *electuaries* [medicines mixed with honey], *cathartic potions* [purgatives], stomach infusions, *vessicatories* [substances to treat blisters], purgative powders, salves [ointments], *cerates* [paste or ointment containing wax], *jalaps* [root of *Ipomoea* - a purgative], and *boluses* [pills]. Other substances provided included Saffron, Flowers of Brimstone, Camphorated Wine, Lavender Drops, Poppy Heads, Cochineal, oil of almonds, liquorish and Hungary Water [oil of rosemary distilled with alcohol].

The Workhouse

As we have seen, poor families were encouraged to remain in their own homes and were supported there. All of this changed in 1754, when the Vestry decided to provide accommodation at a Workhouse for those who did not have the means to support themselves.

June 16th 1754 Memorandum *that att Vestry this day held it was unanimously agreed that the Churchwardens and overseers of the poor shall forthwith have an Estimate taken by the different workman (sic) for Compleatly Setting up the house and premises now in possession of William Kidner, and lately purchased of King's Colliedge for a house for the Reception of the poor of the said Parish and that Such person who will do the same upon the best and Ea(s)iest termes shall be forthwith Employed to do the same.*

A cottage and garden on the south side of Shaftesbury Street, part of the King's College lands, was purchased from the previous copyhold tenant Mary Windover. (For no obvious reason, the actual purchase was made by Thomas Pope of Redbrook, tanner, who then sub-let the property to the Overseers.) The cottage was adapted for use by February 1755. The few records which exist from the early years suggest that about 50 inhabitants were catered for.

More and more space was needed, and in 1789 a Vestry meeting was held to *consider the utility of Erecting and Building additional buildings to the parish Workhouse'*. During the early years of the following century pressure on accommodation increased still further and expansion was again necessary, so that a string of parish-owned buildings soon existed along the south side of Shaftesbury Street (see map on page 109).

The Quakers and their Meeting House

The Quakers' first Meeting House, as we saw in the previous chapter, was also the home of one of their leading members, William Lumber. It was badly damaged in the 1702 fire. This disaster was followed in the next year by the death of William himself, who was interred in his own garden on 5th October 1703.

The decision was taken to build a new Meeting House and this seems to have been completed in 1705 at a total cost of £55. 4s.1d. – and to have continued in use for 130 years (see 19th century). While little is known about the style or appearance of this building, the building accounts of 1705 list in minute detail the materials used, and the wages paid for its construction. From these we can tell that it was built of brick, although it may have been half-timbered. Much of the roof was tiled, but there is also a payment to a thatcher, possibly for an outhouse. The doors and windows were probably painted white as there are entries for white lead and linseed oil, while the floors were made of wooden boards. John Stevens was paid 3d for sweeping the chimney.

Thomas Elliott seems to have been in charge of at least the carpentry work and he was the most highly paid worker, at two shillings a day. He also kept accounts, for which he was paid 6d in beer. Some of the bricks were laid by Master (John?) Mitchell, who also supplied a variety of materials. The wages of labourers varied from 8d to 1s. 6d a day. There is an entry for 6d for beer *'when the sumer was put up'*. The summer-beam was the main beam of the ceiling and must have required considerable effort to put in place – presumably the beer was a reward for the workmen.

The Manorial Court

By the start of the 18th century, the Brune family had become the Prideaux-Brunes and they had owned the manor of Fordingbridge for well over 400 years. This was only one of their estates in Hampshire and Dorset. Their home was Plumber Manor, near Sturminster Newton in Dorset, where many of the Fordingbridge leases of the time were drawn up.

The Prideaux-Brunes visited the town only rarely. Day-to-day management, including presiding over the courts, was in the hands of a Steward, assisted by a Bailiff. In 1753, Mathew Merefield, Gent., was the Steward of the Manor; in 1772 Nicholas Humphrey, Gent., held this post. During Matthew's term, on 8th February 1753, the usual manorial officers were elected by the 'homage' or jury. The names of the Tythingman and of the Hayward for the following year were both recorded as John Day. Could this have been father and son, or was this the same man doing both jobs? John Cleaves and John Gould were appointed as Searchers and Sealers of leather, and the same two men were to be the Ale Tasters. Perhaps this duplication of responsibilities reflects the growing difficulty of cajoling tenants into time-consuming jobs that brought little or no reward.

The Court Books are now known to survive through the century up until 1772, after which date they are apparently lost. We have already mentioned the decline in the power of the Manorial Courts, a process that continued. Even at the beginning of the century, the Steward was desperately trying to enforce the Court's pronouncements. For example, William Barter had demolished parts of the Market House, and his reluctance to rebuild as instructed turned into defiance over many years, as he simply ignored threat after threat.

Much of the Court's time was taken up administering the ancient copyhold tenancies and dealing with their transfer from tenant to tenant. Increasingly, however, copyholds were being turned into long-term leaseholds, although even then tenants were expected to attend the Courts. Attempting to force everyone to be present was becoming harder, as some now viewed the court proceedings as an irrelevance. On 6th June 1734, the following copyholders were 'presented' for non-attendance: Arthur Oats, Joseph Gifford, Thomas Early, Thomas Browning, John Teak, Henry Trippock and John Scovell; as well as ten leaseholders: James Tulk, John Gilbert, Richard Toomer, John West, William Newman, John Stainer, George Stevens, Frances Alexander, Joseph Trusler and Richard Fulford,.

Most of the presentments relating to pasturage, stray animals, ditch cleaning and other aspects of farm life, originally recorded because of someone's failure to observe a specific ancient custom, were now simply repeated year after year as a general instruction. Following these are individual presentments with the fines recorded for various breaches. Most are fairly mundane, but it is worth quoting three of the more interesting entries, as before with our comments.

25th October 1705 *We present That noe person shall have any boards or stuffe to make standings in the faire of any person whatsoever except of the Bayliffe on the paine of 6s.8d every one makeing default.*	The importance of these records is that they confirm that annual fairs were still being held, something which had almost certainly continued since medieval times (see next section).
26th October 1721 *We present the new Pillory to be coloared by the Tenants.*	Later documents show that the pillory stood in Church Street next to the lock-up. Reginald Hannen stated that it was not used after 1801.
19th June 1764 *We present that no person shall thro Ashes over the end of the Bridge against the Town but carry the same and thro them over the middle of the said Bridge on Penalty of 10 shillings each person making default.*	It was, apparently, perfectly acceptable to throw rubbish, in this case ash from the hearth, over the middle of the bridge, where currents would sweep it away. Lazier people were simply going to the nearest point, where wood-ash no doubt blew back to nearby properties.

The Annual Fair

The entry about the fair is particularly interesting. The presentment that *'stuffe to make standings in the faire'* (i.e. materials for constructing stalls) should be obtained only from the Bailiff was repeated in the following two courts but with additions. In the first, *'noe person'* was qualified by *'except a Townes man'*. In other words, the rule now applied only to those from outside the town. At the next court, it was changed again to *'noe person except a Townes man with a tenement'*.

Sadly, these records tell us little about what must have been one of the most important annual events in the town. We do know its location, thanks to one of the references to a shed for a fire engine, which says that it was *'at the north end of the Fairground in Church Street'*.

The Constable

Reginald Hannen's *Fordingbridge and Neighbourhood* contains an excellent description of the duties of the Constable which is worth quoting in full.

> *... the Constable of the Parish was elected,* [at the Hundred Court] *and after having taken the oath he received the Staff of Office.*
> *In former days the duties of this official were very onerous. He was responsible for the peace of the Town; arrested, lodged in jail and boarded prisoners; summoned and set the watch during the 'fence month'.* [See next section] *The mode of summoning was crude in the extreme, the Constable went round during the day and with a piece of chalk made a mark resembling a 2 and 4 in one figure, upon the doors of the houses occupied by the four persons selected to form the watch for the night. The setting of the watch was discontinued in 1840. It was also his duty to examine weights and measures of various kinds ...*
> *The Constable, when it was necessary, conveyed prisoners to Winchester for trial, and carried up to that city yearly the "County money" or rates. On Sundays it was customary for him together with the Churchwardens to leave Church during Divine Service and visit the various Public Houses in the Town and note the persons found there, engaged in drinking.'*

The constable's expenses were paid for by the parish, and consisted mainly of the costs incurred in holding prisoners and in carrying them to Winchester [Winton] – for example :

3rd and 4th October 1742
Charges Disbursed by the Constable of the Hundred of Fordingbridge on Account of Robinson
Pd Charges at New Inn for two Nights .... *11s.4d.*
Expenses at Rogborn .... *1s.8d.*
Expenses with Gaurds at Winton .... *11s.0d.*
Pd Goaler [Gaoler] .... *4d.*
Horsehires 4 to Winton .... *14s.0d.*
Expenses on the Road .... *1s. 2½d.*
Expenses home .... *1s.0d.*
pd two Men to Gaurd .... *3s.0d.*
£2. 3. 6½d

April 4th 1743
received of Mr Vinson Pinhorne two pound three shillings and sixpence in full by Austin Wiggins Constable

---

In the previous year, the then Constable, James Cox, had claimed £2.14s.11d *'for sending James Silly to Gaole and Jane Wats to the hows of Correction',* both prisons being at Winchester. He was also paid ten shillings *'for sending Elizabeth Silly to the hows of corection'* and a further 1s.6d which he *'Gave her to buie Victuels'.* Were James and Elizabeth Silly members of the same family who had been provided for in the smallpox house during the same year? We know that Elizabeth Silly was sent to the House of Correction because she had given birth to *'a female bastard child.'*

The Fordingbridge 'Fence Month' Pike

The 'fence month', mentioned in the quotation above, referred to an ancient New Forest regulation. For two weeks on either side of Midsummer's Day, the period when most young deer are born, commoners had to keep their stock within their fenced holdings. Exits from the Forest, like the Great Bridge, were guarded against poaching; it was for this purpose that the Constable had to 'set a watch'.

According to Morley Hewitt's history of Fordingbridge, a hooked pike with an eight-foot-long handle, the property of the Lords of the Manor, was used as a barrier across the bridge during fence month. This 1966 account also stated that this fascinating ancient artefact was, at that time, still in the possession of the Prideaux-Brune family in Padstow. Unfortunately, we have been unable to confirm the continued survival of this pike.

Saving Money on Sickness and Death

Constable Cox also claimed one shilling which he had given to *'a Sick woman with a childe to go out of town'*. This shows the lengths to which the Vestry would go, in order to reduce expenditure from the Poor Rate. Sometimes, however, events conspired to prevent strangers being moved on and there was no escaping the expense. In the summer of 1741, a man from Warminster was taken ill, and died at the Greyhound Inn. The landlord reclaimed his costs from the parish, but had to wait twenty months and even then did not receive the full amount.

> ### Joseph Birt his bill of Expenses for the poor man that dyed att his house in August 1741
>
> for his Eating & beer & orther thinges 11 days   11s. 0d.
> payd the nurse ....12.s 0d.
> payd men for setting up 7 nights ....7s. 0d.
> for there Eating & bear fiar and Candols ....4s. 6d.
> payd for a Coffen ....7s. 0d.
> payd for a Shroud & blacke clorth ....2s. 6d.
> payd the pason & Clack & Saxton ....6s. 0d.
> payd for washing the badclorthes ....3s. 0d.
> payd men for Cariing the Corpes ....6s. 0d.
> for horse hiar to Worminter and Expences ....   8s. 0d .
>   £3. 7s. 0d.
>
> the 4th Aaprel 1743 Recd for this bill the sume of two pounds tenn shillings in full by me Joseph Birt

Constables and the Militia

In 1757 Parish Constables were given extra responsibilities under the Militia Act of that year. With memories of the Jacobite rebellion in 1745 and with the constant fear of invasion by France, Parliament was determined to provide the country with a strong military capability. Constables were expected to draw up lists of all local able-bodied men, between the ages of 18 and 50; five years later the upper age limit was reduced to 45. The men required to serve were then selected by ballot, the only escape being to persuade, and to pay, someone else to attend as a substitute; this was a common procedure. There are a number of papers in the Parish Records, like that on the left, which refer to such arrangements.

One drawback, from the parish point of view, was that some men who joined their units, in the South Battalion of the Hampshire Militia, left behind families who were unable to support themselves, thus putting an additional burden on the Poor Rate. In due course, attempts were made to amend the regulations, in order to exempt men from vulnerable families. Before this happened, at least one such

A 17th-century Militia Substitute Paper.
Anthony Hayward had agreed to join the Militia, leaving Joseph Stevens free to remain a civilian. As Joseph could not afford to pay Anthony for this favour, the churchwardens paid Joseph £2.10.0d for him to pass on to Anthony.

case was recorded in Fordingbridge, with the parish being reimbursed by the County. We can guess that the 'Sealey' family, whose problem was dealt with in the document below, was one and the same as the 'Silly' or 'Silley' family, whom we have already 'met' on pages 86 and 89.

To the Churchwardens and Overseers of the Poor of the Parish of Fordingbridge in the County of Southampton

Whereas application hath been this day made unto me (one of his Majesty's Justices of the Peace for the said County) by Ann the wife of James Sealey a Militia Man in the South Battalion of the Hampshire Militia now embodied and in actual Service. That she is left with three Children under the Age of ten Years in the Parish of Fordingbridge aforesaid not of Ability to support themselves during his absence. These are therefore to require you to allow to Ann the wife of the said James Sealy the Sum of one Shilling and two pence a Week being the price of one days Labour in Husbandry And the sum of three Shillings and Six pence a Week for the said Children being the price of three days Labour in Husbandry which Money is to be reimbursed to you out of the County stock by the Treasurer of the County who will be allowed the same in his Accounts Given under my Hand and Seal this Twenty first day of July 1760.   John Burrard

---

The militia battalions continued to exist well into the next century, until after the Napoleonic Wars, and until the threat of invasion from France had passed, but none of them ever saw active service.

Smugglers and Murders

Smuggling was rife along the south coast at this time and the New Forest area was a regular haunt. There is at least one recorded instance of a Fordingbridge connection, though there are several versions of the story of 'Captain Diamond' and the murder of Daniel Chater (a.k.a. David Smith).

Let us start with a summary of the authentic story, though no doubt told from the authorities' point of view, published at great length in 1749.

John Diamond and his fellow smugglers were based around Chichester and Arundel. In September 1747 they were sailing from Guernsey in their cutter, the *'Three Brothers'*, laden with an illegal cargo of tea, brandy and rum, with a small bag of coffee. They intended landing at *'... Bonny house near the Sea side which is situate between Ringwood and Limington'*. This was not to be, however, as a privateer, Capt William Johnson, intercepted them and seized the cargo, which was placed in store at Poole Customs House.

The smugglers had evaded capture and were determined to retrieve their cargo. Diamond and his friends enlisted the help of seven members of the infamous Hawkhurst Gang of Kent. Together, they broke into the Customs House on the night of 6th October and recovered the tea.

The next Morning, they returned with their Booty thro' Fordingbridge in Hampshire, where some Hundreds of People were assembled to view the Cavalcade. Among the spectators was Daniel Chater, a Shoemaker, ... known to Diamond, one of the Gang then passing, as having formerly worked together in Harvest Time. Diamond shook hands with him as he passed along, and threw him a bag of tea.

Diamond was arrested on suspicion of involvement in the Poole raid. A reward was offered for information and Chater, who had told his tale to many, was pressed to give evidence. Escorted by William Galley, an elderly customs official from the Port of Southampton, he set off for Chichester, where Diamond was imprisoned. They seem, stupidly, to have bragged of their mission in pubs along the way. The landlady of the White Hart at Rowlands Castle was sympathetic to the smugglers and sent for some members of the gang. Daniel Chater and William Galley then suffered a horrifying and lengthy ordeal at the hands of these men; both were cruelly mistreated and eventually killed. Six of the gang were convicted of the murders and, apart from one of their number who died shortly after being sentenced, were duly hanged.

Now for the embellishments to the story, to be found in the tale *'Captain Diamond, the Smuggler King',* one of the *'Tales of the Hundred of Ford'* (see our comments on this book in the Appendix, page 160).

On reaching Fordingbridge, the gang gathered in the yard of the George Inn and used wool scales to divide the booty of tea, each smuggler getting about a hundredweight. Customs men and soldiers arrived on the scene …

> A terrible encounter ensued in Bridge Street and the George yard. Blood ran in stream, no quarter was asked or given, and many on both sides breathed their last in the quiet streets of Fordingbridge.

A writer on the Hawkhurst gang comments : *'...the Fordingbridge Battle seems to be in great doubt ... I guess it might have been a punch-up after the pubs turned out!'.* [John Dawes, pers. comm.]

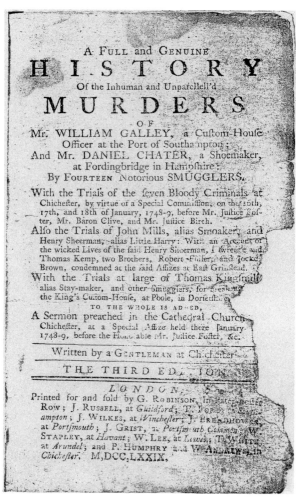

In the fictional version, Daniel Chater was unaccountably referred to as David Smith; Diamond and his men, with the connivance of a local farmer, fooled the pursuing customs men by hiding the bags of tea in a wagon-load of hay; the murders took place on the heathland beyond Godshill; Diamond was captured in the Black Boy pub in Church Square, Fordingbridge; and some of the hangings took place on Gallows Hill at Breamore. In fact, the last three events all occurred in, or well on the way to, Chichester.

The notorious smuggler is rather incongruously commemorated in the names of Diamond Close and Diamond Court, off Church Street.

The title page of the third edition, 1779, of 'A Full and Genuine History of the ... ... Murders of Mr William Galley ... ... and Mr Daniel Chater, a Shoemaker at Fordingbridge ... ...'

Parish Visitations and Questionnaires

Three times during the 18th century, in 1725, 1765 and 1788, Vicars were required to complete Diocesan returns, giving information about the state of the parish, the church and its people. The first and last of these dealt with the parish as a whole, while that of 1765 was rather more concerned with the actual church and the nature of worship.

Between 1725 and 1788 the size of the population of the parish was said to have risen from about 1,700 to about 2,500. At the earlier date, about 377 were said to be Dissenters and 3 Papists, while the 1788 return states that there were only about 120 Presbyterians and 30 Quakers. The number of Papists is illegible. In 1765 it was reported that

> *the most numerous class of dissenter is that of the Presbyterians. Besides them are many Independents, and a few Anabaptists. They all assemble at the same place for divine worship. There are 5 families of Quakers.*

There was no endowed school at the time of either enquiry, but in 1788 there was *'one common school for reading and writing'*. This must have been Mr Beale's school, which was held in the upper part of the Market House.

In 1725, the Vicar, Gregory Doughty, was assisted by a Lecturer, the Reverend John Berjew, curate. In 1765, William Barford was only resident for four months of every year, due to an office which he held at Cambridge University. Much of his pastoral work was carried out by *'2 constantly resident curates'*. The return of that date stated that *'Divine service is performed in the church twice every Sunday'*, and that *'The Sacrament is administered at the 3 great festivals, and on the Sunday after Michaelmas each year'*. The Vicar in 1788, Reverend John Hawes, had no lecturer or curate.

The Town in 1792

The earliest complete, and largely reliable, list of the traders and professional men of the town was issued by the British Universal Directory in 1792. It was reproduced in full in A. T. Morley Hewitt's 1966 book, *The Story of Fordingbridge in Fact and Fancy.*

From this list we can, for the first time, clearly build up a picture of the composition and nature of contemporary shops, trades and businesses. As might be expected, the ubiquitous butchers, bakers, brewers and maltsters feature strongly, as do tallow chandlers [candle-makers]. There were six traders referred to simply as 'shopkeepers', probably all selling a range of general goods. Two of them, John Honeywell in the High Street, and William Withers, on the corner of Bridge Street and the High Street, were also dealing in glass and Staffordshire pottery.

Another major group were involved with the manufacture and sale of clothes. Four tailors and six shoemakers are listed, as are two peruke [wig] makers and two stay-makers. A dyer is mentioned, as is a fellmonger [preparer of animal skins], but there is no tanner. The leather trade, so important in earlier centuries, seems to have virtually disappeared. However, the collar-maker may well have been making horse-collars, rather than shirt collars.

The Directory seems to be defective with regard to the inns of the town. Only the Greyhound, the Crown and the Rose and Crown are listed, although the George and the New Inn were both open at the time (see next section).

The building trade is represented by carpenters, bricklayers, a plumber [a worker in lead] and a glazier and painter. The four local millers are described as 'mealmen', while William and James Neave are working as wool-staplers [dealers].

The largest number of entries is for 'manufacturers of Tick' [linen for mattress covers]. This was a major industry in the area in the later part of the 18th century, with flax being grown locally, particularly in the Stuckton area. The spinning of the fibre was undertaken as a cottage industry, much of it by the members of the poorest households. The linen-cloth was then mostly manufactured in the twelve or more small workshops scattered around the town. The Directory states that *'nearly 500 looms were constantly employed'* in the trade.

The only other factory of any size was Day and Reads' calico [cotton cloth] printing works in Church Street. We have no details of the number of people employed but the Directory records that the volume of trade was *'pretty considerable'*.

The relatively small number of professional men included the vicar, the Reverend John Howes. William Beale was listed as a schoolmaster. The Governor of the Poor House was a Mr Ward. He was relatively new to the job, having replaced William Hannen who was dismissed in 1790 after only two years in office. The two attorneys, Richard Strickland and Stephen Turner, were in constant demand for drawing up deeds and wills, arranging mortgages and dealing with a multitude of other legal matters.

The surgeons and apothecaries, John Gay Attwater and John Mulcott, were in effect the General Practitioners of the time, dispensing medicines and carrying out small operations. They also acted as *'man-midwives'*.

There were two excise-officers, Francis Lambe and a Mr Audridge, who were employed by the government. It was their task to collect duties payable on certain alcoholic drinks produced locally, and on occasion to hunt out any illegal stills of which they had heard rumours.

Of the few women in the list, Mary Absolem was a 'Milliner and Mantua-maker', Mrs Hall was a baker, Martha Kelleway was a farmer and Mrs Read a shoemaker.

INNS AND PUBLIC HOUSES OF THE 18TH CENTURY

The Greyhound

Built in the early 1660s in Salisbury Street, its name was changed to the White Horse after it was rebuilt following the 1672 fire. Exactly when it reverted to the Greyhound is unclear, but it was certainly before 1745 when Joseph Birt was the tenant. During the 18th century the Greyhound became one of the town's main coaching inns. The property belonged to King's College, Cambridge as part of the Manor of Woodfidley.

postcard from early 20th century

The George

By far the oldest of the town's surviving inns, with a history dating back to at least the mid-15th century. Indeed, it may well have originated even earlier given its prime site against the bridge, on the edge of the then market place. The earliest record is of 'Le George' and the name was probably a reference to Saint George and the Dragon, a common medieval inn-sign. In the 18th century, it was, in effect, renamed after King George III.

photographed 2001

The Crown

The Crown Inn is first recorded in 1698 and was probably then relatively new, having been put up to take advantage of the trade from the new market-place. It quickly became one of the town's main coaching inns, and later in the century, the innkeeper James Sturt, was also the postmaster. It survives largely unaltered to this day.

postcard from early 20th century, with The Royal Arms (opened late 1850s) in the background

The New Inn

The New Inn was a small house in the Market-place, probably having opened at much the same time as the Crown. The earliest record seems to be in 1718 when the landlord was Timothy Coles. It adjoined the present-day Ship Inn, which was itself known as the New Inn for much of the 20th century.

from a James Coventry photograph, 1897

The Swan and The Three Lyons

The Swan Inn in the High Street first enters the records in May 1702, when it was owned by William Barter. It closed in 1752 and the adjoining cottage was opened as the **Three Lyons** by Joseph Birt who had previously been at the Greyhound. Both properties were demolished after the Three Lyons closed in 1757, and were replaced by the present large town house at no. 37-39 High Street.

> However, according to one of the *'Tales of the Hundred of Ford'*, the closure of the Three Lyons followed a murder in 1684, the landlord having been convicted of killing a stranger who was carrying moneybags. The discrepancy in dates only serves to underline the unreliability of the afore-mentioned book (see Appendix, page 160).

The Black Boy

For much of the 18th century this was the only public house at the southern end of the town. It is first mentioned in 1676 and seems to have closed in about 1790. It was approached by a long dark alley, and was certainly the 'roughest' of the town's pubs.

Other inns and public houses open in the town during the 18th century included the **Half Moon** in Back Street (1783), the **Rose and Crown** in the High Street (1794), and the **White Hart** at Horseport from at least 1739 until after 1764.

CHAPTER 9 – THE NINETEENTH CENTURY

At the start of the century, George III was still on the throne. His son, George IV, was to be king from 1820 till 1830, having already ruled as Prince Regent for nine years. William IV reigned for only seven years before Victoria became queen in 1837 at the age of 18. Thus the 19th century, while it included the Regency period, was dominated by the styles and values that we now think of as Victorian.

The early years saw conflict with, and the eventual defeat of, Napoleonic France. A series of reforms eventually improved the lot of the growing numbers of industrial workers and strengthened parliamentary democracy. Britain became the richest nation in the world and by the end of Victoria's reign in 1901, the British Empire held sway over a quarter of all the land and of all the people on Earth.

Sources

In earlier centuries, the number of surviving documents limits the information available to the local historian. In general, the reverse problem arises in the 19th century, with so much information available that the difficulty is deciding what to include and what to leave out. (The Sources section at the end of this book lists documents used, as well as some classes of documents whose information has had to be omitted from this chapter, or referred to only in passing.)

Three major new sources become available during the 19th century, greatly enlivening our view of life at the time – accurate maps, reports in local newspapers and photography. Although photographs were being taken in the 1840s, no view of Fordingbridge is known earlier than 1871. The newspaper for this area was the *Salisbury and Winchester Journal*, forerunner of the present-day *Salisbury Journal* and *Forest Journal*. (We refer to it as *S & W Journal* in further quotations.)

Not surprisingly, other documents have apparently been lost. The Court Books of the Manor of Fordingbridge for the period are missing, as are most of the other administrative documents produced and used by the stewards. Others that cannot be traced include the Day Books kept by the Master of the Workhouse, and the Log Books of the British School.

Fordingbridge in the 19th Century

With the appearance of the first detailed maps of the town, we can see that the street layout of the town had changed little between the late17th century and 1840. The Tithe Apportionment of the latter date was the first large scale map to depict the whole town accurately, providing a great deal of information about owners and occupiers. Descriptions of the properties shown on the map were recorded in the accompanying Schedule. The earliest Ordnance Survey Maps of the area had been produced in 1811, and the first edition of the 1:2500 series of 1871 provides a wealth of minute detail of all properties and lands. A reduced facsimile of the second edition of 1897 has been published in recent years and is now widely available in bookshops.

The housing stock was, of course, relatively modern with almost every building having been altered or completely rebuilt after the major fires discussed in earlier chapters. Even those earlier

Part of the Tithe Apportionment Map of Fordingbridge, 1840

structures that survived destruction were now gradually being replaced, as wear and tear took its toll. By the end of the 19th century there were many new houses, shops and business premises and the overall appearance of the town was beginning to change substantially.

By the early years of the century, markets had declined almost to the point of extinction. The market-house was demolished in 1828, and attempts to revive trade in 1844 were unsuccessful. Fordingbridge could no longer sustain markets against competition from Salisbury and Ringwood.

Administration

The pace of change was quickening, and some aspects of daily life were transformed during the century. The manorial estates continued to be farmed largely as they had been for centuries, but difficulties in maintaining them were beginning to build up, and this was accentuated by the agricultural depression of the last quarter of the century. In 1898 the huge Burgate estate was almost entirely dispersed, as the Coventry family ran into financial difficulties. The last few decades also saw the beginning of the break up of Woodfidley Manor as individual properties and lands were sold off.

The manorial courts, already largely impotent, disappeared for good. The parish Vestry meetings (together with the churchwardens, Overseers and other officials) had long acquired a number of civil as well as ecclesiastical functions, but in 1835, their responsibilities for roads were transferred to new Highways Boards (see page 113). County Councils were first established in 1888, with District Councils and Parish Councils formed by the Local Government Act of 1894, thus completing the three-tier form of local administration with which we are familiar today. Church functions remained with the Vestry.

The first civil parish meeting in Fordingbridge was held at the Victoria Rooms on December 8th 1894 under the chairmanship of Mr Reginald Hannen. Although attempts were made to elect the councillors at the actual meeting with a show of hands, a poll was demanded by Mr Alexander. The election for both the District and Parish councils was held a week later.

The first Parish Council Meeting was held on January 12th 1895 with all the councillors present. Mr Thomson was unanimously appointed chairman, with Mr Baxter as vice-chairman. Mr F Gatrell was to be clerk and Mr Gane, treasurer.

The meetings of Fordingbridge Rural District Council were held at the Board Room of the Workhouse. The Clerk's Minute Books contain a wealth of detail relating to the repair and maintenance of roads and bridges, lighting, council houses, water supply, and the abatement of nuisances. Four excerpts follow.

> *In accordance with your request I inspected the water supply to Mr W Chubb's cottages in Back Street. I found that all the cottages drew their water supply from one or other of the streams that run by the property. There appears to be no well on the premises at all and I am very doubtful indeed if one would be of any use in such a low position.*
>
> *The majority of the cottages draw their water from the stream which runs past the Wesleyan Chapel and there is a dipping place above some of the cottages so that the brook water is not contaminated by sewage, but on examination the water is not good for drinking purposes unless boiled. Others of the cottages near the bridge in the middle of Back Street draw their water supply from the stream running under the bridge which is very nearly stagnant and of a very inferior description on examination although I cannot find that any sewage or other serious contamination exists. The alternative water supply is from the Artesian Well at the Gas House and this water is of good quality and fit for domestic purposes, although it contains a large amount of iron.*
>
> *In conclusion I beg to observe that thanks to the Gas Company a thoroughly good water supply is available in Back Street, but that most of the cottagers at the*

Wesleyan Chapel end refuse to get water from this well on account of the distance from their houses and the presence of iron in it, and further that I consider the drinking of water straight from the brook as liable at any time to become highly injurious to health and likely to cause diarrhoea and allied diseases, and should cholera appear, to be a source of heavy mortality from that disease. – report by Dr H N Rake, Medical Officer of Health, 30th August 1895

Fordingbridge Police Station - A complaint has been received that when emptying the cesspool containing the sewage from the police station the liquid had been poured into the Brook on the opposite side of the road. ..... written to Mr Shering the contractor requesting him to convey it elsewhere and not into the Brook. - RDC Minutes, 16th December 1898

Resolved that this Council do bring before the notice of the County Council the great pace at which Motor Cars run, and that the maximum ought to be reduced to eight miles an hour. - RDC Minutes, 5th May 1899

In face of the report of the Medical Officer of Health and the Inspector of Nuisances on the need of a system of refuse, sewage in a solid form etc. in the town of Fordingbridge, we (the refuse committee) beg to suggest that a Dust Cart perambulate the Town twice a week between the hours of 7 and 10am for the collection of such refuse. - RDC Minutes, 28th July 1899

The Fordingbridge Volunteer Cavalry

During the last decade of the 18th century, local volunteer cavalry units had been formed in many parts of the country, in response to the fear of invasion and the general unease following the French Revolution. In contrast to the 'foot-soldiers' of the militia, all members of these units were mounted on horseback. Inevitably, membership was confined to the gentry and the merchant or professional classes. The Fordingbridge Troop, formed in 1798 under the command of Captain Hulse of Breamore House, formalised its Rules on 30th September 1803.

1.   THAT the Volunteers composing this Troop shall, at their own Expence, find Horses, Cloathing, and Accoutrements, Government finding Arms.
2.   THAT every Man who shall quit the Troop without a Cause satisfactory to the Majority, shall forfeit the Sum of Five Guineas.
3.   THAT every Man absent during the Debate of any Question concerning the Troop, shall submit to whatever is resolved on by the Majority present.
4.   THAT every Man shall attend at such Times and Places as shall be appointed by the Commanding Officer, in order to be trained and exercised.
5.   THAT every man who comes after the Roll Call on the Parade is over, shall forfeit the Sum of One Shilling.
6.   THAT the Troop shall be marched off to the Exercising Ground at precisely Half an Hour after the appointed Time of meeting on the Parade, the Officer, Serjeant, or Corporal, of highest Rank present, taking the Command. Any Man coming after the Troop shall have arrived on the Exercising Ground, shall forfeit the sum of Half a Crown.
7.   THAT every Man, in case of Non-attendance, without sufficient Cause, on the Days appointed for training and exercising, shall forfeit Five Shillings.
8.   THAT Sickness in Man or Horse shall be the only sufficient Excuse for Non-attendance at Exercise.
9.   THAT every Man who appears at Exercise not properly dressed, or not completely equipped, as to Arms, Accoutrements, and Horse, shall forfeit the Sum of Five Shillings.
10.   THAT the Sums forfeited shall be paid into the Hands of the Treasurer, to be applied as shall afterwards be determined by a Majority of the Troop.
11.   THAT in all doubtful Questions which may arise, the Majority of the Troop shall decide.

The troop continued to meet for some years after the end of the Napoleonic Wars, but was eventually disbanded in 1827, by which time peace was well established and the French were no longer perceived as a threat. However, the shock of the anti-machinery riots of 1830 led to its re-establishment, this time under the command of Captain Eyre Coote of West Park, succeeded after a few years by Lord Normanton of Somerley.

John Hannen Jnr (see page 125) recorded details of many of the troop's activities, in this later period, in a small hand-written notebook which has fortunately survived. The following entries cover a few months in 1831.

> **March 18th** *To Spittles Field - Did Sword Excercise on horseback first time.*
>
> **April 4th Easter Monday** *- First time of assembling at Fordingbridge in full uniform - marching through the streets to a Field at Marl, to Excercise in the presence of a great number of spectators - after which we dined together at the Crown Inn. Dinner given by Capt Coote. Spent a very pleasant evening.*
>
> **April 8th** *The Troop Marched to Salisbury - Theatre*
>
> **May 27th** *Parade at Capt Coote's Lodge - To Soldiers Ring between Damerham and Martin to excercise.*
>
> **June 27th** *- Pistol Excercise in Kings Arms Garden - Marched into the Market Place (Headed by the Amateur Brass Band) fired Three Volleys and walked on to Withers's and did the same - marched back to Kings Arms again in Line and spent a very pleasant evening in Honour of his majesty's accession to the Throne.* [Withers's shop is now Rose and Alexander.]
>
> **July 1st** *In Burgate park - most of the gentry in the neighbourhood there and members of other troops. At 5 o'clock we sat down at entertainment prepared in a large Tent in the Paddock being the treat of the Privates to the officers - The Band in attendance - great number of people in the field. Band paraded the Town in Evening - Broke up at 11 after spending a very pleasant day.*
>
> **Sept 5th** *first time of fireing on horseback - fired 3 rounds and gave the Cheers for the King and flourish with swords. A few horsemen and Gigs present and about 50 other persons.*
>
> **Sept 8th** *Coronation Day - Mett at 11 o'clock - Sword Excercise in Fields - back to Paddock - fired 3 volleys and marched round the Streets and on horseback. Some dined at the Crown Inn. Bands attended - cannons fired - Bread and Cheese and Beer given away. Dinner to the School Children - great concourse of people.*
>
> **Nov 10th** *Sword Excercise at the New Schoolroom.*

The Fordingbridge Troop of Yeomanry Cavalry was finally disbanded in April 1838 and their *'Arms, Ammunition and Accoutrements'* were returned to the Ordnance Store Portsmouth. A few items seem to have gone missing; there were 67 men in the troop and while 67 swords were returned, only 59 sword-belts and 65 pistols were accounted for. A single bugle and over 1500 ball cartridges were among the items returned.

A troop of the Hampshire Yeomanry (Carabiniers) riding along Bridge Street in about 1900.

These were, of course, professional soldiers, unlike the Fordingbridge Volunteer Cavalry

Population and Employment

The population was increasing rapidly, as it was across the whole country. For the first time there are reliable figures throughout the century, with the first ten-year Census held in 1801. The following census figures are for the whole parish, including the villages and hamlets as well as the town.

Year	1801	1811	1821	1831	1841	1851	1861	1871	1881	1891
Population	2727	2747	2602	2822	3073	3178	2925	3053	2962	3222

For most places the surviving records of the first four censuses provide only total numbers, with the names of inhabitants recorded only from 1841. Fordingbridge is unusual, and indeed fortunate, that the original surveys have survived among its parish records, with heads of households and other details listed for all four of the early returns.

Increasing population meant a consequent increase in the potential work-force. Up to 200 men, women and children were employed at Samuel Thompson's factory at East Mill, where hemp was spun and made into sacks. After the railway arrived in 1866 he opened a further factory at West Mills to take advantage of the proximity of the new station at Ashford. By the 1890s, the Neaves' family business employed around 180. They had been millers at Bickton for generations, but they also took over the lease of the Town Mills and built a new factory near the station once the railway opened. Their main product was *'NEAVE'S FARINACEOUS FOOD, a Staple Article of Diet for Babies ... ... promotive of the action of the bowels'*, which was widely advertised and on sale throughout the country.

Both the Neaves and the Thompsons were Quaker families, with, for their day, enlightened and benevolent attitudes to their employees. Smaller employers in the area tended to follow suit, with the result that employer-employee relations seem generally to have been good in Fordingbridge. Working hours were, nevertheless, very long by today's standards, whether for workers in the factories, for agricultural and general labourers, for young men working as shop assistants or apprentices, or for young women in domestic service.

Anti-Machinery Riots of 1830

The autumn of 1830 saw civil unrest on an unprecedented scale across the southern half of England. Fordingbridge was the focus of some of the worst disturbances. Agricultural labourers rose up in protest at inadequate wages and miserable living conditions, which had been exacerbated by a string of poor harvests and harsh winter weather. The immediate stimulus to action was the introduction of threshing machines on large farms and estates. Previously, laborious methods of threshing with hand tools had been one of the largest employment opportunities for labourers during the winter months.

Initially, mobs of labourers roamed the countryside intent on destroying the threshing machines which they regarded as threats to their livelihoods. As time went on, almost any machinery was attacked, and intimidation and extortion became commonplace. The first attacks began in Kent at the end of August 1830, spreading quickly as support grew.

The buildings of East Mill

This rather picturesque view, across the Avon from Criddlestyle, was on sale as a picture postcard in around 1905

They were commonly known as the 'Captain Swing riots' from the name given to their fictitious leader.

Locally, the East Mill factory and the iron works at Stuckton (which made threshing-engines) were both attacked by a mob of up to 300 men. Although only a few of the rioters were local, the shock felt by the townspeople was to be remembered for many years to come.

A contemporary report in the *Salisbury and Winchester Journal* reveals the drama of the occasion and the extent of the intimidation suffered by local people. The troubles reached Fordingbridge on Tuesday 23rd November.

Fordingbridge has been in a state of great agitation all day today. A number of labourers gathered in the town this morning. Their leader appears to have been a man they called 'Captain Hunt'; he rode ahead of them on a white horse. Witnesses estimated that at its height the mob numbered around 300, it seems that many were forced to join them against their will. From Fordingbridge the men moved on to William Shepherd's threshing machine factory at Stuckton. When they arrived at the factory one of the mob, Charles Read, asked for Mr Shepherd. On being told that he was not at home he turned to the mob and said, "come on lads, we will break the house down, and Mr Shepherd in the middle of it". Short work was made of destroying the machinery and wrecking the building, and the men refreshed themselves with eight or nine buckets of cider in the process.

It was just after two this afternoon that John Fulford and his son arrived at the Greyhound Inn at Fordingbridge. Fulford had a piece of bread and cheese in his hand and said to Michael Lyster Street, the innkeeper, "Master, bring me a pot of beer in a minute at your expense". Mr Street brought him the beer. Fulford went on to tell the innkeeper that he had been out all day and night breaking threshing machines and was now on his way to East Mill to destroy the factory there. .... The mob arrived at the Greyhound at around half past two. Hunt ordered £1 worth of beer and some of the men rushed into the house and took out everything edible. The majority of the men then went off in the direction of East Mill, a few remained drinking at the inn.

As the mob passed William Mercer's house two of the men, George Clarke and Edmund Nutbean, came to the door demanding food and drink. Mr Mercer gave them food but said that he had no drink to give them. They said they would have money instead and if he did not give it to them they would set fire to his house. When Mr Mercer refused to hand over any money they called after the mob, "Here, here, come back". It appeared that some of the mob might indeed come back so Mr Mercer handed over 3d and told Clarke and Nutbean to order themselves some beer at the Greyhound and he would pay for it.

On hearing that a mob was approaching the factory Jonah Thompson, brother of Samuel Thompson who owns the mill, went out to meet them. Hunt was at the head of the men and Thompson spoke to him. "My friend, may I ask what you are going to do?" "We are going to the factory to destroy the machinery," was Hunt's reply. Hunt quietened the mob and said they should listen to Mr Thompson. Mr Thompson spoke to them for five minutes and tried to dissuade them from their intended actions. He told them that the factory, which spins hemp and weaves sacks, employs between 50 and 60 poor people. The mob became noisy again and clamoured to go on. "Attend to me," shouted Hunt as he waved his hand, "let every man stand to his colours and go on".

Many of the men went into the mill and started breaking the windows and machinery. It was said that the noise of the machinery being broken could be heard from outside. Hunt left the scene after about 20 minutes and went off over the bridge, many of the men going with him.

Others remained and began throwing the broken machinery outside. Having completed their task they went off in all directions as they had arrived, some going across the fields. Among those recognised were Henry Eldridge, Joseph Arney (a journeyman carpenter), Samuel Quinton, Charles Read and George Clarke. Mr Thompson estimated that around £1000 worth of damage had been done.

Other houses were visited and money was extorted from their owners. Some of the mob, including Hunt, returned to the Greyhound and finding it locked, broke open the gates. The newspaper went on to report the capture of some of the men on the following day.

> Early this morning many of the townspeople of Fordingbridge were sworn in as special constables. Already they have succeeded in capturing several of the men who were so active at East Mill and Stuckton. Among them is Hunt who, it seems, is actually a man called James Thomas Cooper from Grimstead ………
> He was taken at an inn in Damerham. The men who had captured him had to hold pistols to the windows of the chaise they carried him in as they passed through Fordingbridge and Ringwood in order to prevent the inhabitants of these towns from attacking him, they were so incensed at the damage he and his followers had done to their properties.
> This evening a detachment of the 3rd Dragoon Guards, under the command of Cornet Kelson, arrived in the town and it seems that peace has been restored.

As a result of rioting in various parts of Hampshire, including that at Fordingbridge, 345 men were brought before the Assizes at Winchester. Most of them were given a prison sentence or were bound over to keep the peace; 67 were acquitted. James Cooper and five others were executed. Three local men, Henry Eldridge and Joseph Arney from Fordingbridge and Charles Read from Breamore, were transported to Australia, the latter being pardoned in 1836. (In the country as a whole, ten men were executed and 450 transported.)

The Churches

Strict Sunday observance was the norm throughout the 19th century. Although attitudes were slowly changing, it was still a brave, or stubborn, person who did not, at least occasionally, attend services. The parish church regularly held congregations of between 300 and 500, perhaps even more on special occasions. By present-day standards churches of all denominations were full to bursting point.

In the Victorian era, if not before, the churches demanded of society a high moral tone with great emphasis on prayer and Bible reading. In this way, it was argued, each individual could improve not only himself, but those about him. The churches also played a major social role, organising meetings, fund-raising events and other activities beyond the purely ecclesiastical. This common approach enabled the different congregations to work together, and sometimes even managed to mask their wide differences in the matter of church ritual.

Improvements to the Parish Church

In 1840, it was decided that St Mary's Church was in need of renovation, both internally and externally. This refurbishment was started at the beginning of August 1841, and was so comprehensive that it necessitated the closure of the building for very nearly a year. (Circumstantial evidence suggests that services were held, in the meantime, in the uncomfortable conditions of the National School.) The removal of the old pews and galleries was followed by work on roofs, floors, windows and doors at a final cost of £1,227, compared to the original estimate of £1,100.

The various workmen have commenced their operations in the parish church of Fordingbridge, preparatory to its being re-pewed and perfectly restored; and we are gratified to be able to add, notwithstanding the plan adopted by the Churchwardens and Committee of Management appointed with them to carry it into effect, includes the removal of several private and public galleries which have heretofore accommodated a considerable proportion of the congregation, that these gentlemen confidently state to the parishioners, that their arrangements on the ground floor will not only compensate for the loss so occasioned but will give from 200 to 250 additional sittings - a very desirable object in this large and populous parish, more particularly so when it is known that at present there are many persons unprovided with Church accommodation.
– S & W Journal, Aug 2nd 1841

THE CHURCH OF SAINT MARY, FORDINGBRIDGE, having been completely Re-pewed and Restored, will be RE-OPENED for DIVINE SERVICE on Friday, the 8th of July, 1842. – The Morning Service will commence at Half-past Eleven o'Clock. The Sermon will be preached by The Hon. and Rev. S. Best, M.A., Vicar of Abbots Anne, Hants. On this occasion the MORNING SERVICE will be CHANTED, and the ANTHEM will be sung by the CHORISTERS of the SALISBURY CATHEDRAL.

In the Evening there will be a Grand Performance of SACRED MUSIC (Vocal and Instrumental, with a full Band and Chorus) at the Church, commencing at Six o'Clock, under the immediate and very kind Patronage of the Ladies of the Neighbourhood.
– advertisement, *S & W Journal*, July 2nd 1842

The vicar at the time of the 1841-2 restoration was Charles Hatch M.A., then only recently appointed by the Provost and Scholars. He occupied the large Vicarage (now flats - picture on page 58), which had been built opposite the church some twenty years previously by Reverend Joah Furey. The church had new bells in 1857 and a fine new organ installed in 1887.

The churchwardens kept detailed records of the numbers attending morning and evening services at St Mary's on each Easter Sunday from 1856 till 1864. The table below shows the results for the first of these years. The overall total would be somewhat less than 871, as there would undoubtedly be some who attended both services. What is perhaps surprising is that only 56 of these parishioners were Communicants.

	Morning Service	Evening Service
Chancel	50	52
Nave, etc.	154	210
Free Seats	44	118
Gallery	19	25
Choir	14	14
School Boys	58	55
Girls	32	26
Totals	371	500

The Churchyards and Burial Grounds

The Parish Church and each of the other denominations (see next page) had its own cemetery, but by 1895 all were overcrowded and in need of extension.

> **THE BURIAL GROUND QUESTION** *On Wednesday last a Commissioner visited Fordingbridge to make enquiries respecting the condition of the various burial grounds, and as a result of his visit the Churchyard of St Mary will probably be closed on Oct 31st 1896. The burial grounds of the various dissenting places of worship will be closed on the same date. The question of providing a burial ground had received great consideration at the hands of the Parish Council without any definite results, but when the Commissioner has made his report to the Home Secretary an order will doubtless follow to provide a new burial ground.* – S & W Journal, Oct 26th 1895

After detailed and lengthy consideration by the recently-formed Parish Council, an interdenominational cemetery was agreed upon, with separate sections for the Church of England and the Non-Conformists.

Sir Edward Hulse of Breamore House offered land in Stuckton Lane. This was gladly taken up, and work began almost immediately. Although the Non-Conformists saw no need for a chapel on the site, the Church of England decided to construct one on their section. It was consecrated at the end of January 1897. The total cost of £500 included £200 for fencing and shrub planting, as well as £300 for the chapel. More than £270 towards this was raised within a week, by a house to house collection throughout the parish.

The 'Mystery Tombstone'

During the excavations on the 'Albany site' in 1997 (see page 19), a broken tombstone was revealed, which had been rather incongruously used as the cover of a well. The inscription was to one Robert Standfield, who died aged 70 in 1832; no words appears below the breakage. A newspaper report of the time, *'Dig yields mystery stone'* suggested *'perhaps the work was discontinued when the stone was accidentally broken by the stonemason'*.

Corroboration of this idea is provided by the final version of the tombstone, which stands in the churchyard of St Michael's, Verwood, complete with additional inscriptions below the level of the break on the first attempt.

NON-COMFORMIST AND CATHOLIC CHURCHES

The Non-Conformist churches all had major building programmes in the 1830s, while a new Catholic Church was built later in the century. In addition to those churches illustrated on the facing page, there was also a group of **Plymouth Brethren**. They were mentioned in Kelly's Directory and met in an upper room of the old King's Arms in Provost Street, but little is known of their activities.

The Congregational Church in Salisbury Street was rebuilt in 1832. It had originated as the Independent Chapel in about 1665. Following amalgamation of the Congregational and Presbyterian Churches in 1972, it became the **United Reformed Church**. Railings along its frontage, seen in this postcard of about 1905, were removed, like so much other iron-work, during the Second World War. The Manse on the left dates from the middle of the 18th century, although there have been later alterations.

The Wesleyans originally had a meeting place in Provost Street. They built a new Wesleyan Chapel in Back Street in 1836 and enlarged it in 1882. It is now known as the **Methodist Church**, while Back Street has become West Street.

A new Meeting House for the **Society of Friends** (Quakers) was erected in Roundhill in 1835 to replace the former building of 1705 (see page 87). There were influential families among the Friends, including the Neaves and the Thompsons. The congregation here was considerably smaller and eventually declined to the extent that regular services ended in 1905. The building in Roundhill survives. When it was relinquished by the Quakers it became a private school, and after 1947 an auction sale-room. It has now been converted into a private dwelling.

When John Coventry, a devout Catholic, inherited Burgate House in 1871, one of his first actions was to finance the building of a **Catholic Church** on the former cricket ground of Calves Close. Dedicated to Our Lady of Seven Dolours, it was originally intended to be part of a small monastery.

Education

Education became more widely available. The National School was established for Church of England children in a cottage in Provost Street in 1831, but a larger and more convenient building was erected in Shaftesbury Street in 1836 (now part of Avonway Community Centre - *opposite*)). The British School, for Nonconformist children, was opened at Horseport at about the same time, but later moved to Roundhill. School log-books and minute books of the managers provide a great deal of interesting material about the day-to-day affairs of the National Schools from the 1860s onwards. Sadly, there seem to be no similar records from the British School.

In 1856, the stone floor of the National School *'passed under the auctioneer's hammer'* before being replaced by a substantial wooden floor. The *Salisbury and Winchester Journal* reported that *'The stone was purchased principally by the inhabitants of the town, and is being laid down in the streets, much to the comfort of pedestrians'*. This effectively reminds us that prior to this there was no form of paving in the streets – the re-use of the old floor was an ingenious way of providing one of the first lengths of dry pavement. (It was probably the section of pavement outside Arnold's Post Office, seen in the 1871 photograph on page 129.)

Eventually the 'British' and the 'National' amalgamated into a single school. By the end of the century, education was compulsory, at least in theory, for all children until they had reached their thirteenth birthday.

The following notes are extracts from the minutes of a meeting of subscribers to the National Schools, held in the schoolroom on July 2nd 1879.

Present The Vicar, Mr Reeves, Mrs Boys, Miss Venables, Rev. A. Child, Mr Aldridge, Mrs Venables, Mr Hannen, Mr Applin, Mr A. Venables

[The Vicar said that the work of reorganising the schools was the first work he wished to do on coming to the place. The recent report of H. M. Inspectors and the grant earned had been most unfavourable; the present Master and Mistress were to leave and the time had come to make fresh arrangements.]

The present Infant room 22ft by 15ft was wholly inadequate for its purpose. His plan was to build a new Boys Schoolroom and classroom and to divide the existing building by a partition wall so making separate schools for the girls and infants.

The New Boys' School should be large enough to contain one hundred boys. After the first outlay for the new premises he did not think the expenditure would be much increased over the present. He would not promise that such would be the case, but that was his opinion formed by the results of his experience in former parishes. Still if the cost were to be greater than it had been it would be still their duty to face it. They ought to have a good school in a town like Fordingbridge and the Church of England ought to take in hand the work of Education.

He had had conversation with Mr H. Thompson who was sorry not to be able to come to the meeting but agreed with all that it was proposed to do. Mr Thompson had had much experience in building matters and could give valuable advice in the matter. The estimate for the new building was put at about £350.

The Vicar added that it would be a good plan at once to divide the present schoolroom and try and build the new Boys' room before the winter; then they could engage their new staff of teachers for the new arrangement of the schools and so obtain a superior class of teachers than they would be likely to get for the present unsatisfactory state of things. Perhaps some day the British School might be closed, and they should bear that contingency in mind in building so as to be able some day to accommodate the whole of the children of the parish.

These plans evidently went ahead. The partition wall had been built by November by Mr J. W. Shering at a cost of £19.13s.0d. The new staff, Miss Laura Reynolds, Miss Elizabeth Reynolds and Mr J. Brown, were engaged in August. Mr Brown may have been one of a *'superior class of teachers'*, but he was dismissed in the following year for running up personal debts of more than £100.

Four years after the vicar had anticipated the possible closure of the British School, this occurred at Christmas 1893. Its 36 boys, 50 girls and 34 infants were transferred to the National School, bringing the numbers on the roll to 120 boys, 123 girls and 126 infants. The Log-Books of the newly combined and re-organised school are now held by the present-day Fordingbridge Junior School.

Excerpts from the Log-Book of the National School

The Boys School

1883 Sept 28th	*New scholar admitted whose parents were fined last week for not having sent him regularly to school. The boy has been working 12 months.*
1887 May 13th	*Gave lessons to Standard V in Practise. Standard III Simple Long Division - Standard II learned eight and nine times tables - Infants and Girls departments closed through epidemic of measles.*
May 30th	*Boys School closed - measles.*
June 21st	*The children assembled this morning but as it was the day for celebrating the Queen's Jubilee the scholars from the three departments marched through the town halting in the Market Place and sang the National Anthem.*
1888 Sept 12th	*Roman Catholic School was opened on Monday [10th] causing 4 withdrawals from the School.*
1891 Jan 9th	*So very cold in the school that lessons were much interfered with, writing and arithmetic being quite out of the question.*

George Parberry was the master in charge of this group, Standard I of the Boys' School (National School) in 1896

The Girls School

1879 Oct 3rd	*There has been a fresh supply of books, slates, etc... every class has now two sets of reading books.*
Oct 10th	*The children in Standard I require much attention. Have taught some of them to knit and the whole class can do "Position Drill".*
Nov. 7th	*We have begun fires this week and on Thursday morning the stove smoked so much that a great part of the Scripture time was wasted in attending to it.*
Nov. 28th	*Thursday afternoon a holiday was given by Reverend W. J. Boys who paid for all regular children to go to the Circus.*
1880 July 16th	*The children of Standards III and IV require much attention in Arithmetic. The boys went into their new school on Monday and the infants into their own room, we have therefore the use of the Class room.*
1881 Jan 17th	*On account of very heavy snow storms it has been necessary to close the school for a fortnight.*
July 15th	*Several of the garments made by the children for examination have been sold this week.*
1882 Nov 17th	*Children learnt words of a new song on Friday. They could not learn the tune as the harmonium was out of order.*
1883 Apr 21st	*The girls have been allowed no playtime this week as a punishment for rudeness in the play ground. They have had physical exercises between the lessons.*
1884 Jun 27th	*Sent some children home for being dirty.*

At the beginning of the autumn term 1891, free education was introduced nationally. Pupils no longer had to bring their weekly fees – but the change had no immediate effect on the rate of attendance.

There were also private schools in the town, with two or three generally in operation at any one time. Most of them took only an handful of children, with the commercial proprietor also being the sole teacher. While teachers at the British and National Schools all had a basic form of teacher training, those in private schools were often completely untrained. In the 1840s, Alexander Joyce in the High Street took ten pupils at a fee of 22 guineas a year, while Miss Emma Hicks' fee of 13 guineas included not only instruction in grammar, geography, history, arithmetic, needlework and dancing, but also her pupils' washing. Later in the Victorian era, Miss Sophia Bland ran a 'Seminary for Young Ladies' in the building now occupied by Harrison's stationers shop.

Poverty and the Workhouse

Poverty was rife throughout the period. As in previous centuries, much agricultural and building work was seasonal, with many unemployed in the winter months. One means of helping poor people to survive the colder weather without entering the workhouse was the town's regular Coal Fund. In December 1860, the *S & W Journal* reported that '... *the Fuel Society Committee are about to resume operation; coals and wood will be distributed to the poor before Christmas*'. Subscriptions were solicited from landowners and other more prosperous townspeople.

Some of those who could not find work no doubt moved to the growing industrial cities or took the even more drastic step of emigration overseas. The *S & W Journal* recorded in April 1871: '...*about forty persons left the town and neighbourhood for Liverpool, from which port they will embark for America*'. Among them was 54-year-old John Edsall, formerly schoolmaster at Breamore, and his wife and children. He quickly became a pillar of the community in Thamesville, Ontario and his descendants still live in North America today.

The Workhouse was financed by payments to the Fordingbridge Union from all of the property-holders in the parish, based on a rateable value for their property. This receipt is for the sum of £1.7s.0d, paid by the Misses Riles in 1871

Of Thompson's 200 workers at East Mill, between 50 and 60 were classed as 'poor'. Without their factory jobs they would have been dependant on relief from the parish – which generally meant being admitted to the workhouse in Shaftesbury Street. The Vestry Committee Minute Book of 1813-15 records applications for relief and the decisions of the committee and many other matters. It appears that there was concern about both the Workhouse and the Smallpox House. Mr Trowbridge was the Master of the Workhouse at this time.

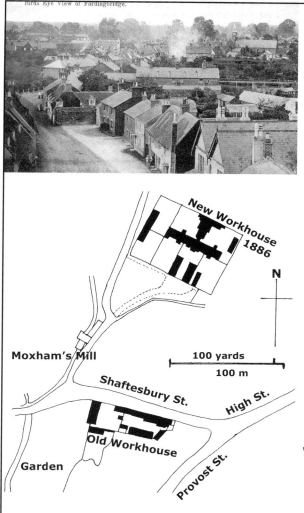

TOP LEFT: Some of the rather haphazard buildings that comprised the Workhouse from 1755 to 1886 can just be discerned in the top-left-hand corner of the view from the top of the church tower *(picture postcard, c1910-1915)*

TOP RIGHT: The 'new' Workhouse of 1886 now forms the premises of the Fordingbridge Hospital

LEFT Location of the two Workhouses, pre- and post-1886

> **July 16th 1813**
> John Philpott's daughter applies for relief being ill - to come into the House
> William Savage applied for relief - to have 8 shillings this week but if not able to keep himself to come into the House himself Wife and Family
> William Sargeant to have 5 shillings this week, but to be admitted into the House if he cannot do without further relief.
>
> **July 23rd 1813**
> Sarah Hannan applies to go out of the House and to be allowed some weekly pay - to go without any allowance.
> The House used as a small Pox House at Blissford appears to be in a improper situation for that purpose and it is therefore necessary for the Committee to look out for another House.
> That a General Meeting of the Inhabitants be held on Thursday next at the Church at 5 o'clock in the afternoon, to take into consideration the state of the Workhouse being inadequate for the accommodation for the numbers that are now in it and on other business.
>
> **July 30th 1813**
> Mr Trowbridge having stated to the Committee that many of the Old Men who go out on Sundays under pretence of attending Divine Service, do not go to Church. Mr Trowbridge is therefore requested to inform them that if they continue that practice they will be deprived of their dinner and severely reprimanded.

Legislation passed in 1834 divided the country into Poor Law Unions. As a result, the Fordingbridge Workhouse, occupied by townspeople alone, became the Fordingbridge 'Union House' available to the poor from all the parishes around. By 1841, its inmates included 18 men, 22 women and 27 children. It was administered by the Guardians of the Poor of the Union; the following extracts are taken from their Minute Books.

> **Aug 27th 1841** - William Hunt having been allowed to go to work for Mr Thompson was brought home last evening in a shameful state of intoxication. The Board have therefore thought it advisable to direct the Master not to allow Hunt to go out of the House in future unless any person chooses to employ him and pay him sufficient wages to enable him to support himself.
> That John Philpott be employed to whitewash the Able Bodied Women's apartments, Hospitals, Hall, Old Women's and Old Men's Bed Rooms, Old Men's Sitting Room, Wash House, Kitchen and Parler.
>
> **March 31st 1843** - That in consequence of a complaint having been made by the Master of the Workhouse that Henry Moyle the Porter had made statements to the women in the Workhouse which were prejudicial to his character and untrue, the Board have strictly investigated the case, and find that the statements made by Henry Moyle to Mary Gray and Jane Noyce respecting the conduct of the Master to be without the slightest foundation, the Board are therefore of the opinion that the said Henry Moyle should be immediately deprived of his office as Porter of the Union Workhouse.
>
> **March 6th 1846** - The Guardians having fully investigated the complaint made by the Able Bodied Paupers (Thomas Green, Charles Kenchington and James Tiller, who absconded from the Workhouse and afterwards returned) of not having a sufficient allowance of food are unanimously of the opinion that inasmuch as they refused to obey the Master by doing the necessary work of the House in carrying water, he was fully justified under Article 36 of Workhouse Rules and acted perfectly right in witholding the Broth from their Breakfast, and offering Bread only, and there is no cause whatever of complaints against the said Master.
> continued ....

> ***March 13th 1846*** - *That James Welch acknowledges having 'wrung up his fist' at the Master, and used insulting language because he was not allowed to go out of the House, the Board sentence him to 24 hours confinement.*
>
> ***Feb 28th 1848*** - *That the original dietary be adopted in lieu of the present one, with the difference that one ounce of bread more be allowed for the Breakfasts and Dinners, viz. 7 ozs Men and 6 ozs Women and that the Thursday's Dinner be 4 ozs bacon and 5 ozs Cooked Meat.*
>
> ***May 25th 1849*** - *The inmates of the Workhouse to be allowed to go out of the Workhouse on Whit Tuesday at 10 o'clock and to return to the Workhouse at 7 o'clock in the evening.*
>
> ***Aug 17th 1849*** - *The Dinners for the following week to be Mutton and Rice daily in lieu of the correct dietary in consequence of Cholera having taken place in the Workhouse.*
>
> ***Aug 24th 1849*** - *The Board to purchase the property of Benjamin Witt adjoining the present Union Workhouse.*
>
> ***Feb 1st 1850*** - *It is desirable that a Schoolmistress should be appointed to the Union Workhouse.* [Until then the 'workhouse children' had been educated at the National School on the other side of the road.]
>
> ***Mar 8th 1850*** - *That the present cottages lately purchased by the Union be converted into a Male and Female Infirmary and that the Clerk is to obtain plans and an estimate of expenses.*

The so-called Union House was actually a ramshackle and rather dilapidated collection of buildings along the south side of Shaftesbury Street. Additional houses had been pressed into service as needed over the years. In 1884 the whole site was condemned as unfit for habitation. After much argument as to whether the Fordingbridge and Ringwood Unions should be merged to save costs, it was eventually decided that Fordingbridge would borrow sufficient funds to construct a new Workhouse in the Bartons. Plans were drawn up and work began in 1885, with the inmates being transferred from the old House on 22nd January 1887.

Health Care

For most people, rich and poor, health care was steadily improving. Indeed, the rise in population was largely due to reduced infant mortality and increased longevity. James Clifton and Herbert Rake were doctors who served the needs of several generations of local residents in the later Victorian era. They were also joint honorary medical officers to the Cottage Hospital which was opened on the corner of Frog Lane in 1871. Sadly, it closed due to lack of funds in 1880; the building is now a private house. To commemorate Queen Victoria's Golden Jubilee in 1897, a Nursing Home was built to the rear of the old King's Arms Public House in Provost Street.

Earlier in the century, Robert Budd, Humphrey Pinhorn and Henry Pargeter were all practising as 'surgeons' in 1840, although the latter unfortunate gentleman died of lock-jaw [tetanus] only five years later, following a fall from a horse. Many still died from conditions which are easily treated today. Medicines and no doubt quack potions could be bought from the town's druggists and apothecaries; Joseph Gatrell was running such a business in Bridge Street in 1840. The 'Smallpox House' (see page 85) was clearly still in use in 1813, but had closed some time between then and 1840.

All surgeons' consultations and medicines had, of course, to be paid for and the cost of an illness could be crippling even for those families in the middle ranks of society. The parish often paid medical fees for the poorest people, while those who could afford the regular payments often contributed to Friendly Societies as a type of medical insurance.

BELOW LEFT: Mr Frank Gulliver and his daughter with the Greyhound Inn's 'station omnibus' outside of the Ashburn Hotel in Station Road in the declining years of horse-drawn transport

BELOW RIGHT: Sir Edward Hulse, 6th Baronet, of Breamore House, portrayed in a photographer's studio on a firmly-clamped bicycle – a reminder of the rise of this form of transport in the latter years of the 19th century

Means of Transport

In the final decades of the 19th century, the motor-car made its appearance, no doubt infrequent and sensational at first. We have already recorded (page 98), the District Council's request of May 1899 for a reduction in the speed limit from 12 to 8mph. A bicycle accident in Fordingbridge was reported in the local newspaper as early as 1885. But for most of the century, 'traffic' had meant horse-drawn vehicles, while for the majority of people walking long distances in all weathers was an accepted part of everyday life.

Inevitably, there were many carts, of various sizes and types, in the town and surrounding countryside – they were essential possessions of every farmer and of most shopkeepers, craftsmen and traders. In general, working class people only had the opportunity to ride if this was part of their employment, or if they could afford an occasional journey by carrier's cart. Many things changed with the arrival of the railway in 1866.

Small gigs, the more elegant carriages and the larger coaches were the preserve of the well-to-do, although they must have been a common sight on the streets and roads of the district. None of these horse-drawn vehicles were immune to dangerous accidents.

> *Mr Robert Oates, accompanied by Mr Attrim and another person, was returning in his gig from the Breamore cricket match, on approaching the town, the horse started into a gallop, resisted every effort to impede his progress, and became quite unmanageable, proceeding at a fearful rate, when in turning the corner at the entrance to the town, about thirty yards from the Star Hotel, the horse ran against a rail fence, throwing the whole party out with much violence. Mr Attrim received a severe contusion on the head ... ... no hopes are entertained of his recovery. – S & W Journal,* August 1849

Maintaining the Roads

The roads were generally poor, with ruts, pot-holes and deep puddles in wet weather. They were perhaps a little better in the actual town, but were often covered with a mixture of mud and manure. In dry summers, dust clouds often blew from one end of the street to the other; in later years water-carts were hired to damp the roads down. As time went on there were considerable improvements.

In 1832 the Cranborne Chase and New Forest Turnpike Trust took over responsibility for the route from Brook to Cann St Rumbold near Shaftesbury. The turnpike passed through the town, so Horseport, Bridge St, the High Street and Shaftesbury Street were provided with new gravel surfaces, which the turnpike company was obliged to maintain. The nearest toll-gates were at Bramshaw Telegraph and at Sandleheath, so travel beyond either of these points required payment. After the abolition of turnpikes in 1878, about ten miles of road, in and out of the town, reverted to the responsibility of the parish.

Under parish administration, care of the roads had been administered by Surveyors of the Highways appointed by the Vestry or churchwardens. In 1835, this rather unsatisfactory system was replaced by the formation of Highways Boards. The Fordingbridge Board had control, not only of the town roads, but of those in adjoining parishes, only excluding those which were part of the turnpike system. The members of the Highways Board were local men, and had powers to levy rates for the maintenance and repair of highways and associated drains.

The following extracts are from the Minute Book of the Highways Board dated 1863-1877. The 'Surveyor' mentioned was not a holder of the ancient parish office but an official appointed by the local Justice of the Peace, and employed to carry out road repairs as required by the Highways Board.

3rd August 1863
Resolved that the Surveyor purchase one patent road Scraper for the common use of the parishes in the district and the cost of the same be charged to the Common Fund. (£2.15s.0d from Messrs Brown and Harris.)

3rd October 1863
Resolved that the Surveyor give notice to owners and occupiers of the several lands etc. adjacent to the roads to cut and trim their hedges and fences and scour the ditches, and that in default proceedings would be taken.

10th January 1868
Mr John Witt and Mr M. A. Manning occupying houses of J. Brymer Esq. complain that there being no street drain in Roundhill they are prevented draining the premises they occupy, and the Dead Well so overflows that it is become a Nuisance dangerous to their health, and ask the Highway Board to place a public drain in the street. Resolved that Mr Brymer be permitted (at his own expense) to lay a drain from the premises in Roundhill by Messrs Witt and Manning to the Town drain near John Russels (18 High St.) by relaying and repairing the road to the satisfaction of the Surveyor.

24th January 1868
The Surveyor to have the Church wall, which formerly was repaired by the different tithings in the Parish of Fordingbridge, (a part of which has recently fallen down) repaired forthwith.

23rd July 1868
Mr Rake having written to the board complaining of the stench arising from the town drains and advising that such drains should be efficiently trapped.

Resolved that the Surveyor take the necessary steps to effectually trap the Town drains, 14 of them, the remaining three to be stopped altogether.

22nd September 1870
The Surveyor gave notice to every Tradesman in the town of Fordingbridge that he must not place his goods on the footpath and that if they persist in doing so after such notice he will summon them before the justices.

Coaches and Carriers' Carts

Until the railway opened in December 1866, all goods entering or leaving the town were carried by horse and cart. Some carriers operated from the town and provided regular services to Salisbury in particular. Others passed through and picked up goods, and sometimes passengers, on their way to and from Poole and Christchurch. There had no doubt been similar services since medieval times, but it is not until the later 18th century and through the 19th that we start to find timetables and advertisements.

The Universal British Directory (of 1792) recorded that there were two or three carriages for conveying passengers and small parcels to and from Fordingbridge and Salisbury. These were clearly intended for visits to Salisbury Market, as they operated only on Tuesdays and Saturdays. One of these probably belonged to a Mr Chater who a few years later was terminating his journey at the Spreadeagle Inn at Salisbury.

Two other carts passed through Fordingbridge; William Witcher's stage wagon from Poole apparently called at 2am every Wednesday on its way to the Goat Inn at Salisbury, returning the same afternoon. William Watkins's cart from Ringwood reached Fordingbridge at 8am on Tuesdays and Fridays, returning from the Lamb Inn at Salisbury on the same evenings.

Brookman's wagon arrived from London every Monday afternoon at 4pm, and left Fordingbridge on the following day at 2pm. Carriage cost four shillings per hundredweight.

Pigot's Hampshire Directory of 1831-2 provides more information on the various services and their departure points from Fordingbridge inns.

Coach –
Thomas Fagg & Co (London - Poole) calls at the **Star**, *Mondays, Wednesdays and Fridays, going to London, and on the following days for the journey to Poole.*
Carriers-
To London; William Burnett's wagon from the **Crown** *every Tuesday at 2pm (via Winchester); John Woolcott (from Poole) calls at the* **George** *once or twice a week (via Salisbury)*
To Christchurch; George Drew from the **George**, *James Newman from the* **Star**, *every Tuesday and Saturday at 12 noon (via Ringwood)*
To Poole - John Whicher (from Salisbury) calls at the **Star** *every Tuesday, Wednesday and Friday morning (via Ringwood)*
To Salisbury - John Rouse from the **George**, *Tuesday, Thursday and Saturday*
To Southampton - William Manning from the **Crown** *every Friday at 12 noon.*

By 1857 William Dove was running a daily coach to Salisbury from the Greyhound. In June of the same year, the landlord of the Greyhound, George Sworn, advertised omnibus trips to *'that delightful WATERING-PLACE BOURNEMOUTH'* every Thursday, leaving at 7.45am and arriving at 11.00am, with seven hours at the seaside before the return journey. From a later advert we know that the carriage was a *'PAIR-HORSE OMNIBUS, on Collinge's patent axles'*. Whether the trips were a success is not recorded, but by the end of September Mr Sworn had left the Greyhound and moved to Wareham.

With the arrival of the railway, the heyday of the long distance coaches was over. Local carriers' carts still had a significant part to play, however, and they could be seen wending their way to Salisbury through to the end of the century and well beyond. A few survived long enough to make the transfer from horse to petrol engine.

The Coming of the Railway

After numerous delays, arguments and false starts, the railway line through Fordingbridge finally opened in 1866, 22 years after one was initially planned. The original intention had been that the Fordingbridge line would be the Poole branch of the Manchester and Southampton Railway, but the necessary parliamentary bill failed and the project was abandoned.

SALISBURY, FORDINGBRIDGE, WARMINSTER, FROME,
AND LONDON WAGGONS,
REMOVED FROM THE ANGEL, FLEET MARKET,
TO THE
SALISBURY ARMS, COW LANE, SNOW HILL, LONDON.

WILLIAM SUTTON, for the better Accommodation of his Friends and the Public, has removed his Waggons from the *Angel, Fleet Market,* to the *Salisbury Arms, Cow Lane, Snow Hill;* where Goods are taken in for, and with the greatest Attention and Regularity forwarded to the under-mentioned Places. The utmost Care will be paid to the Delivery of Goods immediately as they arrive in Town, and at the respective Places of Destination.

Set out from Salisbury	Arrive in London	Set out from London	Arrive in Salisbury
Tuesday Morn. at 12	Thursday Morn. at 6	Thursday Morn. at 12	Monday Morn. at 6
Thursday Even. - 10	Monday ditto - 6	Monday ditto - 12	Thursday ditto - 11
Saturday ditto - 10	Tuesday ditto - 6	Tuesday ditto - 12	Saturday ditto - 6

Also regularly to and from Wilton, Codford, Heytesbury, Warminster, Frome, Crewkerne, Yeovil, Ilminster, Honiton, Axminster, Chard, Blandford, Shafton, Fordingbridge, Downton, Wareham, Poole, Weymouth, Sherborne, Somerton, Stockbridge, and all adjacent Places. They call at the Old White Horse Cellar, and Black and White Bears, Piccadilly, going in and coming out of London.

*** Will not be accountable for Money, Plate, Jewels, or Glass, above the Value of five Pounds, unless booked and paid for accordingly.

S. Gosnell, Printer, Little Queen Street.

William Sutton was a carrier in the early part of the 19th century, prepared to transport goods between London and a number of towns in the south of England, including Fordingbridge

Note that goods leaving Salisbury at noon on Tuesday did not arrive in London till 6 o'clock on Thursday morning - and this was the fastest time achieved in his timetable

In 1860, the plans were resurrected by the newly formed Salisbury and Dorset Junction Railway Company, intent on connecting Salisbury to Poole and Bournemouth by constructing a link from Alderbury (on the existing Salisbury-Romsey line) to West Moors (on the Ringwood –Wimborne line). As the largest town along the route, Fordingbridge was inevitably the focus of much of the pre-building activity and publicity, with meetings of promoters and interested parties held at the Greyhound Hotel.

The following three years proved frustrating, as attempts were made to raise the required finance through the sale of shares. Local landowners and businessmen eventually contributed substantial amounts but there was considerable irritation at the apparent lack of interest in Salisbury. Eventually, sufficient shares were sold for the project to go ahead, but meanwhile an increasingly acrimonious debate was underway concerning the best site for Fordingbridge Station. No part of the proposed line was to be within half a mile of the town, and neither of the possible sites, at Sweatford or Ashford, had ideal access. In due course the company directors chose Ashford, but in order to mollify the residents of some of the outlying villages they agreed to build further stations at both Breamore and Alderholt.

Fordingbridge Railway Station from the south.

This postcard was posted in 1904, but there had been few changes since the construction of the station nearly forty years previously

The 'Station omnibus' leaving the station yard on its way back into the town
(Postcard, about 1908)

Meanwhile work had started at Three Legged Cross in April 1864, and by the end of May there were navvies moving earth at Alderholt. The southern part of the line was to be completed first so that materials and equipment could be brought up from the port at Poole. Progress was steady but unspectacular during the following year, as gravel, to be used as ballast, was removed in enormous quantities from the Fordingbridge Station site. By December 1865 the Ashford cutting was nearly complete, as were the road 'arches' on the Sandleheath road and at Burgate, allowing greater activity along the northern section of the route. In the middle of June 1866 it was reported that the line was complete, and that only the visit of the Government Inspector was awaited before the grand opening could take place.

Frustrations continued as the Inspector demanded alterations at a number of places, some of them substantial. Gangs of men were set to work, but it was December before all was ready. The first trains ran on Thursday December 20th 1866. To start with there were four a day in each direction. A small celebration was headed by Barter's Garibaldi Band, but as the railway company had only given a few days notice of the actual opening, the event was less elaborate than originally envisaged.

The local railway became a major news story again in June 1884, even making the cover of the *Illustrated London News*, when a southbound train was derailed just south of Downton. Many people were injured and five were killed, including 14-year-old Lilian Kate Chandler, daughter of the Fordingbridge station-master. It was the worst accident to occur on Britain's railways up to that time. Many passengers claimed that the train had been driven recklessly but the official explanation blamed poor track maintenance by the railway company.

These present-day buildings, the Augustus John public house and the industrial premises behind it, owe their positions to the opening of the railway station at Ashford in 1866.

Mr and Mrs Alfred Hood had established the public house, as the Station Hotel, a few months before the first trains ran, while the Neave family, already milling at Bickton and the Town Mills, opened a new factory here (now Corintech) to take advantage of the new means of transport.

Celebrations and Entertainment

If much of the material in this 19th-century chapter has given the impression of dour Victorians, working hard all week, praying hard on Sundays, some of them in the depths of poverty and suffering the indignity of the workhouse ... they did know how to enjoy themselves. Leisure time was minimal, but there were some evening entertainments and also celebrations involving the whole town and locality on special days.

Perhaps there had always been processions through the town on important occasions, but they do not seem to be recorded before the 19th century. As time went on they became larger and more elaborate, particularly with the participation of the Friendly Society, founded in 1823, and of the Ancient Order of Oddfellows, formed in 1844. Whit Tuesdays saw the major annual celebrations as churches and schools joined in, and everyone processed to Church, dressed for the occasion and bearing appropriate banners (see page 118). Significant royal events, including the Coronations of William IV and of Victoria, were celebrated with extravagant displays. The town was decorated on a scale not equalled in recent times, and there was music, dancing and sports events, with food and drink provided for virtually the entire population.

> *The event of his most gracious Majesty King William the Fourth having succeeded to the throne of these realms was proclaimed here, on Thursday last, in the most loyal and patriotic manner. The bells, at an early hour, rang a merry peal, and every face indicated a desire to be foremost in the doings of the day. At two o'clock the High Constable, preceded by trumpets, accompanied by the principal inhabitants and a full band of music, with appropriate flags, moved towards the Church, where they were joined by the worthy Vicar, the Minister of the Independent Chapel, and a large party of the gentry and clergy of the town and neighbourhood. The proclamation was then read, and the hearty cheers of all present were succeeded by the band striking up "God Save the King". The procession then proceeded to other parts of the town, where the same ceremonies were repeated, and at length returned to the Church, when our national anthem was sung by the assembled multitude in a way that at once evinced how sacred they held the person of their King, and how entirely he possessed their affections. An adjournment then took place to a field near the town, where the populace were liberally regaled with strong beer; and to those who, by old age and infirmity, were prevented from attending, a small gratuity in money was given, to enable them to drink their Sovereign's good health at their respective houses. A large party afterwards met at the Crown Inn, and the evening was spent with that unanimity of feeling which the occasion of their meeting was so highly calculated to produce. – S & W Journal, Monday July 12th 1830*

In 1838, a Mechanics Institute was formed, which attempted to educate a perhaps reluctant populace with lectures such as 'The Intellectual Composition of Man' and 'Mechanical and Chemical Properties of the Atmosphere'. The Institute's most successful enterprise seems to have been an exhibition, inspired by the Great Exhibition, which had good attendance for a week in July 1853. Exhibits provided by local gentry and tradesmen included statues, photographs, paintings, Roman artefacts, stuffed animals, ironmongery, antique china, samples of Thompson's sailcloth, rugs, jewellery, watches, greenhouse flowers and many other items. The Institute closed in 1861, its premises being taken over by the British School; today, they form the core of the Fordingbridge Club buildings in Roundhill.

No celebration seems to have been complete without the attendance of one or more of the local bands. As well as the 'Volunteer and Town Band' shown, there were Barter's Garibaldi Band, the Ashford Band, Edsall's Breamore Band, the Fordingbridge Cornopean Band, Jefferis' South Hants Band, Calkin's Quadrille Band and the Fordingbridge Congregational Sunday School Drum and Fife Band.

FORDINGBRIDGE VOLUNTEER and TOWN BAND BY A.V.B. THOMSON

The Loyal New Forest Lodge of the Ancient Order of Oddfellows initially held its meetings in the Star Inn. In 1878, they built themselves a fine hall in the Market Place.

The *S & W Journal* reported *'This handsome building … … will prove not only an ornamental structure, but of some service to the inhabitants of the town and neighbourhood for entertainments and public meetings'.*

And so it has proved; in 1889 the Oddfellows sold the building to the 'Town Hall Company' for £900, and it has been **Fordingbridge Town Hall** ever since.

James Coventry photograph, 1897

The Victoria Rooms, built in 1875 at the sole expense of Thomas Westlake (see page 127), were soon in frequent use for meetings, lectures and many other events. They remain an asset to the town today. Previously, concerts had often been held in the school-room. In January 1838, for instance, anyone who could afford the quite high ticket price of three shillings, or ten shillings for a family of four, could attend a musical evening at the school, with seven principal soloists and twelve instrumentalists (all the performers being male).

MR W H BIDDLECOMBE'S CONCERT OF VOCAL AND INSTRUMENTAL MUSIC, Consisting of the most popular and admired Songs, Duets, Glees, Madrigals, Choruses, Solo and Concerted Pieces, will commence on THURSDAY EVENING NEXT, Jan. 11 at Seven o'clock.

There was a good attendance at the Victoria Rooms in 1884 for a very unusual concert, given by the Jubilee Singers, *'all freed slaves, from South Carolina'*. Following the singing of genuine slave songs, *'One of the party gave a graphic and interesting account of his fifteen years of slave life, detailing the hardships and the cruelties to which the slaves were subjected ...'*. This must have been a remarkable experience for the Victorian citizens of Fordingbridge.

The gentlemen of the town, including the shop-keepers, found many excuses to meet at the various hostelries for formal dinners. It was frequently reported that *'After dinner, the usual loyal and patriotic toasts were drunk with enthusiasm'* and that *'The speeches were interspersed with songs'*. Reading between the lines of these reports, one imagines highly convivial evenings, with some of the diners weaving their way homewards.

An extensive procession turns the corner from High Street into Bridge Street led by the banners of the Congregational Sunday School. While this may be for some special occasion in about 1905, it is likely to be the annual celebrations which had been held on Whit Tuesday throughout the 19th century.

Almost all of the town's inhabitants had some role to play – it is noticeable that there are few bystanders.

Some events were mainly patronised by the higher echelons of society while others were frowned on as popular with the 'lower orders'. In September 1865, *'A grand ball was held at the Star Hotel Assembly Rooms ... ... A large number of the nobility and gentry of the neighbourhood were present, and it was one of the most fashionable reunions that has taken place for many years'*. Four years previously *'The annual pleasure fair was held here on Friday and Saturday last, and was visited by Bartlett's steam circus and swing boats as well as by several lesser shows. ... we hope that this will be the last "holding of the fair", as it is undoubtedly a nuisance and a disgrace'*. The fair did, however, continue for many years after this.

In the early part of the century, holidays in our modern sense simply did not exist. Days off were still mainly on 'holy-days' as in medieval times. Bank Holidays were introduced by Act of Parliament in 1871. This boosted the idea of holiday trips, greatly aided by the railway, which enabled local people to visit the seaside without a long, bumpy ride in a horse-drawn carriage.

Organised sport probably brought the different levels of society together to some extent. Cricket was being played as early as the 1830s and 1840s, and a football club was formed in 1874. The first of a long series of annual Fordingbridge Regattas was held in August 1889; at one time they were so successful that special trains were run from London.

The activities of the various sports clubs featured prominently in newspaper reports. When the Fordingbridge Turks won the Hampshire Football Challenge Cup Final against Basingstoke Grammar School in April 1881, they were greeted with a heroes' welcome at the railway station. The score was one-nil, but a biased reporter claimed that *'a second goal would have been scored without a doubt, had not the ball pitched on a stray dog'*.

In Phil Anderon's humorous interpretation of the event, below, the top of the goal is shown as a rope. Wooden cross-bars were introduced to the game two years after this match.

Constables, Police and Law and Order

The Hampshire Constabulary was formed in the 1840s, and a police presence then became a permanent feature of the town. The powers of manorial officers – Constables, Tythingmen and Haywards – waned even further and the posts were eventually abolished. (It is worth noting, however, that the honorary position of Hayward, appointed by the Lord of the Manor, is still in existence in Breamore.) A Police Station was built in Shaftesbury Street in 1858-9, intended to provide a home for a married sergeant and an unmarried constable. The building is still the local police station today.

Only a few years later, in June 1862, P.C. Rodaway was involved in a sensational murder case. He was approached one Sunday afternoon by George Gilbert, who reported finding the body of a young woman in a ditch in the meadows to the south of St Mary's Church. The victim proved to be 23-year-old Mary Hall, who had been attacked while walking from her home at Midgham Farm to the church. Suspicion fell on Gilbert and the initial news report of the event described him as

> *...a returned convict, having been transported for a criminal assault upon a female, but set at liberty on a ticket-of-leave before expiration of his sentence ... a native of Fordingbridge ... well-known to the police as a thoroughly bad character, having been imprisoned on many other occasions for minor offences ...a labourer, but lately, he has had no work to do, and consequently has had more leisure time than is at all profitable for men of his character or the public at large.*

Gilbert (*'alias Philpott'*) was convicted of the murder and hanged at Winchester Gaol, the event being witnessed by a crowd of over 10,000 people.

Mary Hall was buried in Breamore Churchyard and is commemorated by a tablet in the church there (*right*). In the following October, her father went to Wilton Fair and *'there encountered one of those disgraceful exhibitions a penny show, representing the Midgham murder, with numerous painted placards thereon depicting different scenes of that dire tragedy'*. He was so shocked by this that he died a few days later.

On rare occasions, Fordingbridge needed a large police presence. At the time of the elections held in December 1885, following a disturbance at the Crown Inn ...

> *The crowd passed down the High-street, smashing the windows as they went, and throwing stones, lumps of coal, and sticks ... upon the public-houses closing ...there were numerous fights ... The next morning the town presented a pitiable appearance, the pavements being literally covered with glass. It was fully anticipated that similar scenes would be enacted on the following night, but a large body of police being stationed in different parts of the town prevented anything of the kind occurring.*

Fordingbridge - Kelly's Directory Entry for 1895

Trade Directories for Hampshire were occasionally published during the first few decades of the century, and after 1850 become much more numerous. Several series were produced regularly, one of the most important being Kelly's, which provided a great deal of detail about trades, administration and other practical matters. The following extracts (often lacking in punctuation and capital letters) give a 'snapshot' of the town near the end of the 19th century.

Post, Money Order and Telegraph Office, Savings Bank, Express Delivery, Parcel Post and Annuity and Insurance Office - Mrs Elizabeth Arnold, sub-postmistress. Letters through Salisbury; box closes for dispatch at 11.10am and 7.15 pm; Sunday 6.20pm. Letters received until 7.20pm if an additional stamp be affixed to each. Mail leaves for Salisbury 7.25pm; delivery takes place at 6.30 am and 2.30 pm. Pillar Letter Boxes at railway station, Alderholt, Godshill, North Gorley and Stuckton. Sub-Post Offices at Burgate and Sandleheath.

County Magistrates for Fordingbridge Sub-Division of Ringwood Petty Sessional Division
Bond William Henry esq. Fryern Court, Fordingbridge
Coote Eyre esq. West Park Rockbourne
Foley Admiral The Hon. Fitzgerald Algernon Charles, Packham
Goff Major Gerald Lionel Joseph, Hale Park
Hulse Sir Edward Bt. BA, DL., Breamore ho.
Hulse Edward Henry esq. Breamore house
Hulse Major Charles Westrow, Breamore house
Neave William Reynolds esq. Elmhurst, Fordingbridge
Thompson Henry esq. Ashburn, Fordingbridge
Viney Thomas Gould esq, Flaxfield, Fordingbridge
Clerk to the Magistrates Arthur Howland Jackson, Ringwood

Petty Sessions are held at the Town Hall monthly, every 2nd friday at 11am. The following places are included in the sub-division :- Ashley Walk Township, Breamore, Damerham, Fordingbridge parish, Hale, Martin, North and South Charford, Rockbourne, Toyd and Allenford, Whitsbury and Woodgreen.

Fordingbridge Rural District Council - Meets at the Boardroom every fourth Friday at 2pm
Clerk, William James Clayton, Salisbury street
Treasurer, George Richard Gane, Wilts and Dorset Bank, Bridge Street
Medical Officer of Health, Herbert Vaughan Rake, High St.
Sanitary Inspector, Arthur Edward Alexander ASI, High Street

Public Establishments -
County Court, His Honor F. A. Philbrick Q.C. judge; Francis Arthur Johns, registrar & high bailiff. The court is held at the Victoria rooms.
For bankruptcy purposes this court is included in that of Salisbury.
County Police Station, Ringwood sub-division, Sergeant Edward Hawkins and 5 constables.
Stamp Office, Mrs Elizabeth Arnold, distributor.
Town Hall, Henry Thomas Brown, sec

Fordingbridge Union
The Union comprises the following places:- Ashley Walk (Township), Breamore, North Charford, South Charford, South Damerham, Fordingbridge, Hale, Rockbourne, Woodgreen, Martin, Toyd Farm with Allenford, Whitsbury.
The population of the Union in 1891 was 6,241; area, 36,210 acres; rateable value in 1893, £27,935.
Board day, every alternate Friday at the Boardroom at 2pm.
Treasurer, George Richard Gane, Wilts & Dorset Bank, Bridge street.
Clerk to the Guardians & Assessment Committee, William James Clayton, Salisbury street.
Relieving Officer for the Union, Walter George Holloway, High street.
Vaccination Officer, Wm. John Fance, Salisbury street.
Medical Officers & Public Vaccinators, No. 1 district, John William Johnston M.D.Edin. The Leys Church street. No. 2 district, Herbert Vaughan Rake, High st.
Superintendent Registrar, William James Clayton, Salisbury st.; deputy, Henry Thos. Brown, High street.
Registrar of Births, Deaths & Marriages, Fordingbridge sub-district, Walter George Holloway, High street.
Workhouse to hold 110 inmates; a new building has been erected at a cost of over £6,000; John Wm. Johnston M. D. Edin. medical officer; William Thornton, master; Mrs Mary Ann Thornton, matron; the children attend the National schools. *continued* ....

School Attendance Committee
Meets at the Board room every six weeks at 3pm. Clerk, William James Clayton, Salisbury street. Attendance Officer, Walter George Holloway, High street.

Public Officers
Assessor & Collector of Taxes, Wm. Targett Chubb, High st.
Assistant Overseer & Collector of Poor Rates, Frank Gatrell, Market place.
Certifying Factory Surgeon, Herbert Vaughan Rake MRCS.Eng. High street
Coroner for Fordingbridge Hundred, John Hannen, High street.
Inland Revenue Officer, Geo. Woodcock, Shaftesbury st.
Town Crier, James M. Fry, Market place.

Places of Worship, with times of services.
St. Mary's Church, Rev. William James Boys M.A. vicar; 8 & 11am & 6.30pm; daily at 7.30am.
Our Lady of Seven Dolours (Catholic), Rev. Stephen Barry OSM priest; holy communion, 8am; mass, 10.30am; compline & benediction, 6pm; daily mass 8am; Fri. rosary & benediction, 6pm.
Friends Meeting House, Roundhill; 10.30am & 6.30pm.
Church Mission room, Godshill; 3.30pm.
Brethren, Provost street; 10.30am & 6.30pm; mon. & thurs. 7.30pm.
Congregational, Rev. Enoch John Hunt; 10.45am & 6.30pm; wed 7.30pm.
Congregational, Stuckton, Rev. Enoch John Hunt; 11am & 3pm; tues 7.30pm.
Wesleyan, 10.30am & 6.30pm; mon. & wed. 7.30pm.
Primitive Methodist, Sandle Heath; 10.30am & 6.30pm

Schools
National, built in 1880, for 120 boys, 160 girls & 120 infants; average attendance, 90 boys, 100 girls & 93 infants. George Parberry, master; Miss Eleanor Knight, mistress; Miss Kate Knight, infants' mistress.
Catholic (mixed), built in 1891, for 50 children; average attendance, 36; Miss Jane Frances Stanmore, mistress.

Railway Station, Isaac Dudley, station master; Omnibus from the 'Greyhound' to meet all trains.

Carrier to Salisbury - John Jubbs, tues. thurs. & sat.

VICTORIAN PHOTOGRAPHERS

Our modern impression of our Victorian ancestors is often based on the many surviving photographs. One of the earliest known photographs of Fordingbridge residents is a daguerreotype of the Hannen family (see page 125).

The portrait of Hannah Westlake (née Neave) is an ambrotype, a method that originated around 1852. Like the daguerreotype, the ambrotype is actually a negative image, mounted to appear positive, with the result that Hannah's wedding ring appears to be on the right hand. We know that a photographer from Salisbury, Mr Pitcher, was based in Fordingbridge for two months in the autumn of 1856; maybe he took Hannah's picture. She married Thomas Westlake, whose picture appears on page 127, in 1854. Her son Ernest was born in 1856 and she died in 1857, aged 24. (Thomas married Hannah's sister, Agnes, six years later.)

In the 1870s, William Hockey was the first professional photographer resident in Fordingbridge. This early carte de visite, taken by him, depicts a young man who may well have posed for this portrait to mark the completion of an apprenticeship. It is quite likely that the photograph of Arnold's post office on page 129 was also taken by Hockey.

Photography was considered a suitable occupation for a woman in Victorian times; by 1890 Jean Herbert was working from the High Street. She had left by 1895, when the town's only photographer was Frederick Eyras Angell of the 'School of Photography' in Provost Street. While Hockey's early prints bore nothing but the photographer's name on the back of the mounts, by the 1890s fashion had dictated very ornate backs. Here, Angell has used a pun on his name to include cherubs in his design.

Amateur photography was rare before the 1880s, when dry plates were introduced. Even then it required ample funds and leisure time, also the space to devote to a darkroom, not only for processing, but also for loading the plates into light-proof carriers. Thus it was the province of the well-to-do, particularly the gentry. James Coventry of Burgate House was such an amateur. Many of his surviving pictures, taken mainly in the 1890s, are of superb technical and artistic quality. This portrait of his elder sister, Mary Flora Coventry, is an example of his work, which has been showcased in an earlier volume by the present authors.

The Coventry Family and the Burgate Estate

James Coventry, the amateur photographer, took the picture (*below*) of his family home, Burgate House, in 1896. John Coventry, James's grandfather, had inherited the extensive Burgate estates, formerly in the hands of the Bulkeleys, in 1829. Although his position made him the leading landowner in the Fordingbridge area, he and his wife Elizabeth spent much of their married life elsewhere. Certainly, from 1836 onwards, the house was leased to a succession of tenants, and it was to be nearly a quarter of a century before John returned permanently (by then with his third wife Ellen).

There must have been occasional visits to the Fordingbridge area, as in 1842 John and Elizabeth's eldest son, John, married Catherine Seton of Brookheath at Fordingbridge Church. The young couple then moved to Cornwall so that John, junior, could pursue his chosen career in the church. His first appointment as Curate at Fowey was followed by others in Cornwall and elsewhere. They also lived near Oxford for a spell, during which time John gained his Master of Arts degree at Magdalen Hall.

Drama followed, however, as John began to question his position in the Church of England. In 1857 he and his wife took the irrevocable decision to join the Catholic Church, earning the utter contempt of his father and other members of the family. With little or no income and few remaining friends, John and Catherine moved to France, where they lived with a like-minded community under the influence of the Servite Fathers near Tours. Here they stayed until the Franco-Prussian War forced them to return to England in 1870.

In the following year, John senior died at Burgate. He had not accepted his son back into the family and would have gladly withheld his inheritance, but was constrained by the terms of his own father's will. Thus John and Catherine could not be prevented from returning to Burgate House with their twelve children. They immediately set about establishing a permanent Catholic community in the town and built a new Catholic Church (see page 105).

All was not well with the Burgate Estate, however. Long-standing annual payments and mortgages were a constant drain on finances during a sustained period of agricultural depression. When John died in 1897, he left a financial crisis which resulted in the final break-up of the estate. The property was split into lots and sold off between 1898 and 1900, although the family retained the house into the 20th century.

Land to the north of the Catholic Church was purchased by Alfred Chafen, a developer from Southampton. He immediately parcelled it up and sold it off as building plots. This resulted in the construction of Park Road and Alexander Road as we know them today; it was the beginning of 'suburban expansion' beyond the historic core of Fordingbridge.

> ### The Seton Family of Brookheath
> Catherine Seton's grandfather had been Governor of the island of St Vincent, but her father had returned to Britain and bought the Brookheath estate. Several generations previously, the family had owned estates in Scotland, but had sold up and moved to the West Indies due to their devotion to the Jacobite cause.
> In 1845, three years after her marriage to John Coventry, Catherine lost a brother in tragic circumstances. John Alexander Seton was shot by a Lieutenant Hawkey at Stokes Bay, Gosport, and died of his wounds, gaining the unenviable distinction of becoming the last person to die as the result of a duel on English soil. His tomb is a prominent one, situated not far from the eastern end of St Mary's Parish Church.

The Hannen Family

In January 1859, the Lord of the Manor of Fordingbridge presented an inscribed gold snuff box to Mr John Hannen *'as a mark of esteem and in recognition of the valued services of himself and his family for a period of 100 years'*. The Hannens had been involved in the administration of the manor for three generations.

The Hannen family (often recorded as 'Henning' or 'Hannan' in early parish records) are traceable in Fordingbridge from at least the later part of the 17th century. From at least 1728 until 1738, William Hannen or Henning was landlord of the Black Boy at Church Street, beginning a long family association with brewing and the town's public houses.

His son William was born at the Black Boy. In 1759, at the age of 25, he became innkeeper of the George by the Great Bridge. In 1757 he had married Mary Moody of Fordingbridge; and their nine children were born over the following 20 years. From December 24th 1758 he took on the additional role of Bailiff of the Manor of Fordingbridge. In 1771 the family moved to the Crown Inn, but their stay there lasted only three or four years. Soon William also took on the New Inn just around the corner, and this was the family home until 1783.

Meanwhile his sons were clearly receiving a good education. James, the eldest, became a divorce judge, and his younger brother William a solicitor. The third son, John, born in 1771, became Steward of the Manor of Fordingbridge at the early age of 20, and retained the position for almost seventy years. Alongside this work he was also developing the auctioneering business which remained in the family into the 20th century.

John's ten children were born to his wife Anne (née Harrison), between 1800 and 1818. Charles, born in 1811, maintained the family's public house tradition as landlord of the King's Arms in Provost Street from the 1830s until it closed in 1869.

His older brother, John, born in 1809, followed in his father's footsteps. As a land agent and auctioneer, he was involved in selling private property, shops, businesses, farms and stock of every description over a wide area of the countryside around Fordingbridge. His wife, Sarah (née Troubridge), was a sister of Rear Admiral Sir Thomas Troubridge, a contemporary of Nelson. As John senior reached old age, the post of Steward of Fordingbridge passed down to the third generation of the Hannen family, resulting, in due course, in the presentation of the snuff box to John junior. From the 1870s, he took on a similar position for the Burgate Estate.

John died in 1898, having enjoyed many years of retirement. He had been succeeded in the auctioneer's business and as steward of the two large local estates by his son, Reginald Hannen, who was also the author of the first known Fordingbridge history (see Appendix, page 160). The dispersal of the Burgate Estate in 1898 provided Reginald with the opportunity to purchase large areas of land in and near Stuckton. In his later years he and his wife Florence (née Heath) spent much of their time at Richmond, Surrey and although the local estate was kept on by the family after his death in 1930, it was finally sold off in 1948.

John Hannen (born 1771), photographed by the daguerreotype method in the late 1850s. His four sons (not necessarily left to right in the picture) were Charles, William, James and John. John senior was Steward of the Manor of Fordingbridge for over seventy years, with the position passing to John junior, who also took on a similar position for the Burgate Estate. His son, Reginald Hannen, took over both roles.

Whereas

AN EWE,

THE PROPERTY OF MR. WILLIAM WING, OF GODSHILL,

HAS LATELY BEEN

STOLEN,

And the Skin and Carcase found (the Legs and Shoulders having been cut out and carried away) in a Well at MUDMORE, near Godshill, on the Morning of Wednesday last:

Whoever will give Information of the Offender or Offenders, shall, on his or their Conviction, receive a Reward of

10 GUINEAS

OF MR. WING,

And a further Reward of Three Guineas

OF MR. HANNEN,

SOLICITOR TO THE FORDINGBRIDGE ASSOCIATION FOR THE PREVENTION OF THEFTS, &c.

FORDINGBRIDGE, August 24, 1818.

TELEPHONE *The first of these useful instruments introduced for use in this town has recently been fixed by Mr. R. Hannen, who now holds communication from his house with his offices at the Auction Mart, a distance of about 300 yards.*
– S & W Journal, Feb 9th 1889

Over several generations, the name of Hannen would have been familiar to all residents of the town and surrounding villages. As auctioneers, solicitors and agents for the local estates, the family name appeared on many notices. This one, kindly loaned by Reginald Hannen's grandson, was issued on behalf of the 'Fordingbridge Association for the Prevention of Thefts, etc'.

It is also clear, from the news item above, that the family readily embraced 'modern technology'.

Other Prominent Local Families

As the Prideaux-Brunes never lived in the town, the role of 'squire' was effectively held by the residents of Burgate House. Between 1836 and 1860, however, even the Coventrys lived elsewhere, leaving their House to a series of tenants, who also took over the social role of the leading land-holder of the area. Most prominent among them was John Brymer, who tenanted the estate from 1836 till 1845 and took part in many of the town's festivities and contributed to its charitable activities.

Other local gentry frequently involved in the town's affairs included the Hulses of Breamore, the Cootes of West Park at Rockbourne, the Normantons of Somerley and the Setons of Brookheath. The occupiers of Packham House, notably the Brices and later the Foleys, were clearly regarded as 'minor gentry' by the locals, but undertook a variety of 'duties' from time to time.

Families who came to prominence through their trading activities included the families of Neave, Thompson and Westlake, all of whom were Quakers with very enlightened views for their day about the care of their employees. Josiah Reynolds Neave, having greatly expanded his milling business, was sufficiently affluent to build his own mansion, called Highfield, at Bowerwood. Samuel Thompson, who had built up his thriving flax spinning and weaving business around the factories at East Mills and later West Mills, lived at Southampton House, Horseport, until 1848, when he moved across the road to Bridge House.

A nephew of Samuel's, Thomas Westlake, had come to Fordingbridge in 1843, at the age of 17, to work in his uncle's business. In 1848 he took over Southampton House, and having become a partner, was, by 1869, able to afford to build his own substantial house called Oaklands in Marl Lane. His all too brief marriage to Hannah Neave (see page 122) produced a son Ernest, who became prominent in many fields, as commemorated by Fordingbridge's only 'blue plaque'.

The brothers Edward, John and Samuel Thompson, photographed in about 1865. Samuel founded the canvas-making and flax-spinning factory at East Mills, with the company continuing at West Mills until long after his death. The company was a major employer in the area for many years.

Thomas Westlake (*above*) was responsible for building the Victoria Rooms in Horseport. **His son Ernest** was born at Southampton House nearby. The initials on the plaque indicate that he was a Fellow both of the Geological Society and of the Royal Anthropological Institute. He purchased the Sandy Balls Estate (still owned by the Westlake family today) in 1919 as a campsite for the Order of Woodcraft Chivalry, of which he was the founder.

The End of an Era

'The end of an era' is an overused phrase, but if it is justified anywhere it is surely in relation to the passing of Queen Victoria. Her death at Osborne House on 22nd January 1901 marked the end of a century of unparalleled industrial, economic and colonial expansion. In Fordingbridge, the sense of the end of an era may have been even stronger than elsewhere. Within a few years before the Queen's passing, the town had lost at least three pillars of the local community - John Coventry in 1897, John Hannen in 1898 and James Reynolds Neave in 1899. As we have seen above, the sale of the Coventry Estate resulted in additions to the street-plan of the town, foreshadowing greater expansion.

FORDINGBRIDGE POST OFFICES, 1784 – 2001

1784 : Robert Blachford at the Greyhound Inn, Salisbury Street was the Postmaster. A post-chaise is recorded as operating from There. This was a four-wheeled carriage driven by a post-boy, but probably with room for a few passengers.

1792 : By now James Sturt, landlord of the Crown Inn at the Market-Place was the postmaster. The post from Salisbury arrived every morning at 10am, Mondays excepted, and left every afternoon at 3.30pm, Saturdays excepted. There was, of course, no Sunday post.

1813 : Mrs Pleaden at the Star Inn, Salisbury Street (*shown in its present-day appearance on the right*) was now appointed as postmistress, a job she was to hold until her death in 1848. In 1840 she had overseen the commencement of pre-paid post, with the introduction of the Penny Black.

1848 : For the first time, the new postmaster, James Chubb, was not an innkeeper. James lived in Provost Street, at the top end of where Nicklen's Garage now stands (*in the picture, the light-coloured building beyond the thatched terrace*). By trade he was a corn dealer, and the local agent for the Sun Fire and Life Office. Letters were now received at 5.30am and dispatched to Salisbury at 7.30pm.

In **1864** James Chubb was succeeded by Mr Thomas Jenkins who is listed as a tailor, bookseller and agent for the the Times Fire Office, in the Market Place. As yet it has not been possible to trace exactly which shop he owned. In **1870** a registered letter was stolen from the post-office by a young boy, and Thomas was suspended for allowing the theft to happen. Within a few weeks he had lost his job.

1870 : The new postmaster was named as Mr Arnold, but it was actually his young wife Elizabeth who took the job, one which she was to carry out successfully for many years. Almost in the week that she arrived, the telegraph wires were being connected from the railway station to her post-office, at what is now 57 High Street.

Details of deliveries and collections in **1895** are recorded in the Directory entry quoted on page 97. By **1903** Mrs Arnold had been succeeded by her daughter Annie.

1871 photograph, probably by William Hockey

After the 1st World War a new post-office was opened at no.16 Salisbury Street, next to May's the butchers. In **1927** the sub-postmistress was Miss Priscilla Rose Quarterman. The front room of one end of a row of cottages was converted into the office and extended out across part of the pavement by a distinctive flat-roofed stone projection. The frontage has since been altered to accommodate Barclay's Bank.

By the **1960s** more space and a more convenient location was needed. A purpose built post-office was constructed on the opposite side of Salisbury Street (no.49). Here, it adjoined the sorting-office which was entered from around the corner in Green Lane.

In January **2001** it was all change again, as the post-office moved within the new One-Stop store on the old Greyhound site at no.10 Salisbury Street.

THE MARKET PLACE GAS LAMP, 1867-2000

Fordingbridge's Victorian gas-lamp, newly restored in September 2000, now stands in Church Street. It originally occupied a central position in the Market Place. It was given by the then Lord of the Manor of Fordingbridge, Mr J Prideaux-Brune, to commemorate the introduction of gas lighting throughout the town in 1867.

LEFT : the gas-lamp in its original position in the centre of the Market Place
CENTRE: the base and pillar, neglected for many years in Church Street
RIGHT: the lamp, newly restored and converted to electricity in 2000

Prior to 1867, the streets had generally been very dark on moon-less nights. These two quotations from the *S & W Journal* indicate the extent of the problem.

[It was hoped] *that next winter some steps may be taken to light up our town with oil-lights, and not let us hear of so many complaints of persons running against each other, and doctors' boys breaking the phials containing medicine for invalids, owing to the very dark state of the town.'* (1847)

A great accommodation has been afforded to those passing over the Great-bridge after dark by Mr. Samuel Thompson, who has caused a lamp to be placed in front of his house. Mr. Henry Thompson has also put one up in front of his house in the High street. (1864)

In the late 1860s, it took a while for some shopkeepers to appreciate that gas and naked flames were not compatible. Some learned their lesson the hard way:

as a workman was endeavouring to discover an escape of gas at the premises of Mr. James Curtis, grocer, a lighted candle caused the gas to ignite, and damage was done to some of the contents of the shop.

CHAPTER 10 – ASPECTS OF THE TWENTIETH CENTURY

Although the first half of the century was characterised by wars and industrial unrest, there was a gradual and sustained improvement in living conditions as new technologies were introduced. The second half saw more peaceful conditions, on the whole, with enormous changes in the lifestyles of most people, linked to growing prosperity and much greater leisure.

Changes have occurred at an ever increasing, and sometimes bewildering, pace. Daily life in the Edwardian household bore only a minimal resemblance to that of the last years of the millennium. Much of the drudgery of housework has been removed by labour-saving devices such as the vacuum cleaner and the washing machine. The list of household conveniences and appliances of the year 2000 would have featured only in the most far-sighted science-fiction of a century earlier.

Electric light, piped water, flushing toilets, central heating, telephones, radios and CD players, fridges and freezers, televisions and video recorders have become the norm in most households, to the extent that all are often considered to be essentials. By the end of the century, the home computer and the mobile phone were rapidly attaining the same status. However, the biggest changes in life-styles and in the physical nature of our towns have resulted from the rapid increase in car ownership, especially since 1945.

Aerial photograph of Fordingbridge in the 1930s. The Great Bridge is near the centre of the picture with Horseport to the right and the parkland around Burgate House beyond. On the other side of Salisbury Road can be seen the streets which were developed in the early part of the century. The High Street runs off to the left, still with open fields between it and Parsonage Farm.

The Expansion of Fordingbridge, 1898-2001

At the end of the 19th century, Fordingbridge had not expanded much beyond its historic core, although a few late Victorian 'villas' had been built around the periphery of the town by some of the more wealthy inhabitants. The first big expansion followed the Burgate

On this postcard of Park Road, posted in 1904, the houses at the furthest end are still under construction

Estate sale of 1898. As already mentioned, a Southampton developer purchased an area to the north of the town, which he divided up and sold on as building plots. Within a few years, construction was well under way in Park Road, Alexandra Road and Whitsbury Road, and over the next few decades estates were springing up as far as Waverley Road.

These were private developments, but during the 1920s and 1930s there was pressure to build council estates. St George's Road had been developed in the 1920s, but by 1931 great efforts were being made to obtain more land for council housing not only in the town but also in Woodgreen, Rockbourne, Damerham and Hale. Sites were selected by council officers and offers were made for the land. Most landowners objected to losing their property, and disputes lasted for some months, with the threat of compulsory purchase in the background. Mr Albert Edward Stallard offered a five-acre site at Waverley Road, Fordingbridge, and this was eventually accepted, with the Gas Company volunteering to lay a gas main and to install meters and cookers free of charge. There were further offers of land at the Bartons Allotments and at Tinkers Cross, but at the time these were rejected.Since then house-building has continued at a steady rate. There are small developments to the south and west of the church and rather larger ones at Ashford. The largest of the housing estates, Parsonage Park, adjoins the old moated Rectory site. The housing between Salisbury Road and the 1970s by-pass was built on a section of the former Burgate Park. It is worth noting that present day Fordingbridge would look very different had the Burgate estate been retained by the Coventry family.

> Burgate House itself continued to be occupied by members of the family until 1939, but was then sold to Imperial Chemical Industries. Its present day owners are the Game Conservancy Trust, who prefer to call it 'Burgate Manor'.

Redevelopment has gradually infilled a number of spaces within the historic core of the town. These include houses on and behind the old Kings Arms site in Provost Street and on two former industrial sites in West Street – the gas-works and Neave's old West Mills buildings. In the last few years some infilling has also taken place to the rear of historic house plots, away from the street frontages.

Not surprisingly, as a result of all this housing development, the population of the town has more than trebled during the 20th century, from around 1500 to about 5500 as the 21st century begins.

In the 1990s, a Hampshire County Council initiative enhanced the urban environment with trees, new paving and traffic-calming measures. For much of that decade, however, a large plot in the centre of the town, the sites of the former Greyhound Inn and Albany Hotel, was occupied by a rather unsightly temporary gravel car-park. The development of this area as Painter's Mews and Riverside Parade in 2000-2001, did much to modernise and improve the appearance of the centre of the town.

Elaborate ceremonial arches were erected in the Market Place to celebrate the Coronation of King Edward VII on 22nd June 1911. Others were constructed at Bank Corner, Church Street and Shaftesbury Street.

The First World War, 1914-1918

Small numbers of men from the district had made the long journey to South Africa for the Boer War of 1899-1902, and several of them did not return. Local recruitment for the Great War was on an altogether larger scale, however.

The Declaration of War between England and Germany was made on 4th August 1914.

> *Two days after War was declared, 35 Recruits from the District came forward; of these, 4 joined the Hants Carbiniers, and 31 the 7th Hants Territorials, on the 7th August. They were the first body of Recruits from the County of Hampshire to join their Regiments, and it is doubtful if any other District in England came forward so promptly.*

Within two months 375 men, some 12% of the male population of the district, were already in uniform. Almost 160 of the men were from Fordingbridge parish, and of these over 60 were new recruits. The remainder were full-time serving soldiers and sailors, in regiments as diverse as the 7th Hants Territorials, the Royal Engineers, the Grenadier Guards, the Argyll and Sutherland Highlanders, Lord Kitchener's Army, the Royal Field Artillery and the Burma

World War I cap badge of the 7th Battalion, Hampshire Regiment
The wreath surrounds a representation of the 'Crown Stirrup', a relic of Forest Law which is retained in the Verderers' Hall at Lyndhurst

Police. Only nine were sailors, two of them being on *H.M.S. Glory*, and the rest on separate vessels. Recruitment continued apace, and many local men died in the trenches.

The Memorial Gates at the Recreation Ground (see pages 134 and 139) list 57 Fordingbridge men who lost their lives, but remarkably, only a few of those who had already enlisted by the autumn of 1914 seem to have been killed in action.

Although the war ended in November 1918, many of the surviving troops did not return home until well into 1919. When they did, a party was held for them.

Ceremony at the gates of the War Memorial Recreation Ground.
It is reasonable to assume that this was the official opening ceremony after the end of World War I

WELCOME HOME - About 200 officers, non-commissioned officers and men were the guests of the Committee of the Fordingbridge War Work Depot at a dinner held in the Drill Hall on Thursday. The hall presented quite a festive appearance with its numerous flags decorating the walls and festoons of small emblems stretching across the room, whilst the tables were profusely decorated with flowers. On the wall at one end of the hall on a white ground in large red letters was the following apt quotation:-

Sublimest thanks to those come back,
Co-equal those whom many a house doth lack,
And yet greater still to those who stayed,
And stayed - to ne'er return.

A substantial repast was provided, to which ample justice was done. There were three tables stretching the length of the room, General Cowie taking the head of one, his son, Major Cowie another, and Captain Davenport the third. After dinner General Cowie gave the only toast, 'The King,' which was received with great enthusiasm. Later Mr R. Mills proposed a vote of thanks to the War Workers' Committee, coupled with the names of the Hon. Mrs Foley and Miss Coventry, after which coffee, cigars and cigarettes were provided, and the remainder of the evening was devoted to music. – S & W Journal, June 21st 1919

After much disagreement among the Allies, a Peace Treaty with Germany was finally signed at the end of June. The nation then set about making preparations for its official celebrations. In common with many other towns and villages, Fordingbridge chose July 19th, which sadly turned out to be a thoroughly wet day. The committee, selected during the first week of July, was charged with hastily preparing the festivities, and these were reported in the *S & W Journal* of July 26th.

Peace festivities were carried out in Fordingbridge on Saturday in most unpropitious weather. A short service of thanksgiving in the Cricket Field was carried out in a drenching rain, which continued until late in the afternoon. The proceedings, however, went on in the best of spirits, but the procession was robbed of much of its brilliance. The thanksgiving service over, the procession, led by the Hyde brass band, proceeded on its course. It consisted of the children, Ancient Order of Foresters, chairmen and officers of the district and parish councils, Comrades of the Great War, and past and present members of H. M. Forces, including members of all women workers' organisations, interspersed with decorated motor cars, horse-drawn vehicles and bicycles, children and young men in fancy dress. *continued ....*

Arriving at the Quadrant a pause was made, and Mr Coventry unveiled a marble tablet with the following inscription:- " Presented by Reginald Hannen to the Parish Council, June 1919 as almshouses in memory of John Hannen and of the glorious peace of 1919". During the pause the flag on the church tower was at half-mast, and the bell tolled in memory of the dead.

The procession then proceeded to the Park where the decorated vehicles were drawn up in line and prizes were awarded. Mrs B. Rake's "Rose Car", a pretty exhibition, was awarded first prize; Mrs Lister Keye's Red Cross car was a very close second, and third was a horse-drawn vehicle representing Britannia and her Allies. This consisted of a number of Messrs Neave's workgirls appropriately dressed to illustrate our Allies. Miss Dorothy Picot was awarded first prize, Miss F. Thomas second prize and Mr F. Colborne third prize for decorated bicycles; Master Jack Hart " the cigarette card" boy, and Miss Margaret Bailey as "Miss America" took first and second prizes respectively for fancy dress.

Tea was served to the children, followed by a tea to all past and present members of H. M. Forces who had served in this war, and their wives and dependants, all widows whose husbands had fallen and all wives whose husbands are still serving. A programme of sports was carried out, and some well contested events were seen. The children's sports were postponed. There was no attempt at organised decorations, but the Committee asked all townspeople to decorate their houses, which was done on an extensive scale, and the town presented a very festive appearance. As it was too wet in the Park for dancing, the Committee hired the Drill Hall for this purpose, and a most enjoyable time was spent. In addition to the Hyde band, the Salvation Army band took part in the procession and played at intervals during the afternoon and evening. The Park was kindly lent for the occasion by Mr Coventry and Mr H. Hullard and the Cricket Field by Mr Hannen. Notwithstanding the weather, the celebration was a great success, reflecting the highest credit upon the Committee.

Between the Wars, 1918-1939

Following the invaluable contribution of women to the war effort, the aim of the pre-war suffragette movement was attained with little further controversy, although only women over 30 were given the right to vote in 1918; the under-30s had to wait another ten years.

The 1920s and the 1930s saw the highs of the 'flapper' era, the celebrations for George V's Silver Jubilee in 1935 and those for George VI's Coronation in 1937. But it also saw the lows of the great Depression and of the General Strike, as well as the crisis of Edward VIII's abdication – and the growing threat of Hitler's Germany.

Fordingbridge joined in the royal celebrations but also suffered at the time of the General Strike. This lasted twelve days in May 1926 but was followed by a lock-out of coal miners which lasted almost seven months and reduced national coal production by 15%. At that time, coal was, of course, the main source of household heating, industrial energy and fuel for the railways.

Fordingbridge District Council established a system of permits, which had to be obtained before any coal could be bought. By June 1st of that year the local stocks were reported as:

Messrs Hanham Brothers......................	22½ tons	
Hood & Son..	44 tons	
Ringwood Co-operative Society.............	3¼ tons	
J. Frowd..	9 tons	
P. Harrington..	½ ton	Total 79¼ tons

FORDINGBRIDGE ALMANAC AND DIRECTORY.

EAT MORE FISH.
Best Quality at Lowest Prices
can be obtained from . . .

A. J. BROWN, Fishmonger and Poulterer,

Phone 3125.   High Street, FORDINGBRIDGE.

Fresh Supplies daily.   Agent for Brown & Sons' Sausages.

Telephone 2148.   Established over 30 years.

H. E. BAILEY

Ladies' and Gentlemen's

HAIRDRESSERS

MEMBER OF THE ABOVE.

**BRIDGE STREET
FORDINGBRIDGE**

We specialise in . . .

Eugène, Wella Rapid, Nestle and Mayfair
Systems of Permanent Waving.
Whole Head from 17/6.

Tinting, Bleaching, Water and Marcel Waving, Eyebrow Shaping
and Manicure.

D. DOYLE

**MARKET   PLACE
FORDINGBRIDGE**

Draper and Wardrobe Dealer

Telephone 2254.

J. MAY & SON

Family
Butchers
and

Licensed
Dealers
in Game

Salisbury Street and Provost Street,
FORDINGBRIDGE.

FAMILIES   WAITED   UPON   DAILY.

High-class Work and Prompt Delivery.

Valet
Service
Depot
at Mr. Buckley's,
High Street.

— THE —
MODEL
LAUNDRY

Agent
for
Achille
Serre, ltd.

Church   Square,   Fordingbridge.

Proprietor—H. WILLITTS.   *Telephone 2260.*

TRY OUR DRY CLEANING—48 hours service.

FORDINGBRIDGE ALMANAC AND DIRECTORY.

Bees, Hives & Appliances
OF EVERY DESCRIPTION.

THE "NATIONAL" HIVE

With SHALLOW ROOF.   With DEEP ROOF.

This Single-walled Hive adopted by the Ministry of
Agriculture.

HONEY   BOTTLES.

STANDARD FRAMES, fitted with Foundation
and Wired.
SHALLOW FRAMES.
SECTIONS.   SMOKERS, etc.

Feed with Medicated Candy to guard against starvation.

D. E. ALEXANDER

Hon. Sec., The Avon Valley Beekeepers' Association

FORDINGBRIDGE

H. & A. J. COLEMAN

High St., FORDINGBRIDGE

Phone 3170.

BUTCHERS and FRUITERERS

Specialising in

PRIME   DAIRY-FED   PORK.

First Grade Canterbury Lamb   ::   Finest Chilled Beef
Wiltshire Bacon a speciality.

Sausages and Cooked Meats and Pies fresh daily.

W. BRINE

Joiner and : :
Cabinet Maker

BROOK TERRACE, CHURCH ST., FORDINGBRIDGE

Household and General
— Carpentry —
Furniture Repairs.
*We make and sell new, and
make the old as good as new*

GENERAL
TURNERY
executed on the premises
at short notice.

FRENCH POLISHING.

All orders neatly and promptly executed.   Estimates given.   CHARGES MODERATE

Personal interviews
any evening after 5 p.m.

A Note or Postcard
will receive prompt attention.

Advertisements taken from the *'Fordingbridge Almanac and Directory'* 1939

Every permit application was considered on its merits, with laundresses given special permits if they were entirely dependent on such work. Within 10 days, a total of 899 permits had been issued, and stocks had dwindled to 38 tons, with Hanhams having 10 and Hoods 25 tons. As summer approached the need for coal dwindled in most households. The impending winter crisis was just averted when the strike ended in November.

Fordingbridge, 1939

A perusal of the lists in the *'Fordingbridge Almanac and Directory 1939'* shows that by this time many of the shops and businesses in the town were the same ones which were familiar a generation later. Some, however, had moved to different premises by the 1950s and 1960s.

In Bridge Street, A. T. Morley Hewitt's estate agent's and auctioneer's business adjoined Lloyds Bank, while next to the Albany was Bailey's hairdressing salon. Opposite, at no.8 Bridge Street, now partly occupied by Rose and Alexander's shop, was East Mills Motor Works, selling Esso petrol. On the third side of 'The Square', at 1 Salisbury Street, was Lock's chemist shop (succeeded now by Lloyds Chemists). Next door Mr Foster was selling fruit and vegetables, and beyond him was Ernest Baines, selling and repairing watches and clocks, and doing eye-tests.

In the High Street, Alexander's ironmonger's shop occupied the present site of the Roman Quay arcade, and further along was a little corner tobacconists' shop run by W. & E. A. Taylor, later taken over by Harrisons (nos.23-25). Next door was another ironmongers, belonging to F. F. Dennis & Son, while 'St. Ives' was occupied by a solicitor, H. G. Beach. Dr. Hamber ran his surgery at 'Lowlands', and the small shop beyond his gateway was a butcher's shop owned by Mr Gilbert. Fred Perry, a well remembered character, had his barber's shop at no.47 High Street, where Forbuoys' is today. Nearby were W. King & Sons, grocers; R. K. Kenchington, cycle agent; A. T. Paxton, wine and spirit merchant; and Eastmans the butchers.

On the opposite side of High Street, on the site of the present Co-op supermarket, was the popular 'fancy bazaar' belonging to Buckley Brothers, and adjoining on the north was Brown's fish shop. The row was completed by Frisby's shoe shop, managed by C. W. Rowlatt, Mr Tubb's theatre sound service, the International Stores, and Jones's drapers shop (right)

At the Market Place, Harry Barrow's Shoe Warehouse, managed by Mr Marshall, adjoined the Town Hall, and further down were a butcher's, run by Mr J. Ings (still a butcher's shop today – Price's), and the town's other chemist's shop owned by W. B. Gaddes.

The small shop next to the Royal Arms was a men's outfitters owned by Mr Eldridge.

Jones' drapers shop, listed in the 1939 Directory, was still thriving over twenty years later when this advertisement appeared in a Rural District Council guide book. It is noticeable that, in the first years of the 1960s, fashion was still stuck in the previous decade!

You will enjoy a visit to

GEO. A. W. JONES

YOU can shop from the newest and most attractive merchandise . . . smart Fashions, Outfitting, Children's Wear, Millinery and all Household Needs, secure in the knowledge that at GEO. A. W. JONES you will always find the soundness of quality and values which are second to none.

Geo. A. W. Jones

HIGH STREET · FORDINGBRIDGE
PHONE 2156

The two shops between the New Inn and the Crown were Edwards and Smith, photographers, and a sweet shop run by Mr. A. McClymont.

Nos.26-30 Salisbury Street (now the premises of Caxton Decor) were the Riverside Hotel run by Mr P. Stanford. Further down the street, next to the then Post Office, was May & Son's butcher's shop, which still operates from the same thatched premises (nos.18-20) today.

In Shaftesbury Street, it is perhaps significant that both M. Tiller and Henry Davenport had confectionery shops, not too far from the Regal Cinema (now the premises of Branksome China). There were more traders in the 'outlying streets' at that time, for example a cabinet maker and a shoemaker in Whitsbury Road, a motor engineer and a builder in Green Lane.

The town's representatives on the Rural District Council were then Mr A. T. Morley Hewitt of the Old Manor House, and Mr A. J. Frampton of the Greyhound Hotel, both of whom had been elected for three years from 15th April 1938. (From the early 1930s, the Fordingbridge RDC was incorporated into the Ringwood and Fordingbridge RDC, a situation which continued till the formation of the New Forest District Council in 1974.) The 1939 Council had its usual Finance, Rating and Valuation, Public Health and Housing, Town Planning and General Purposes Committees. As a sign of the times, it also had an Air Raid Precautions Committee. Mr Morley Hewitt was a member of this, as were Captain Booth-Jones from Hale House, Mr Graham Smith from Furzehill, and Commander Egerton from Hungerford House, among others.

The Parish Councillors from October 1938 were: A. T. Morley Hewitt (Chairman), R. Hanham (Vice-Chairman), H. E. Bailey, F. Chubb, R. Clements, F. G. Garland, H. A. King, H. J. Luffman, S. B. Rake, H. Willits and G. S. Wort. The Clerk was Mr. R. Overill.

The *Directory* gave the population of the parish as 3753, which was actually the 1931 census figure. The Coroner for the Hundred of Ford was Dr F. J. Hamber. The Registrar of Births, Deaths and Marriages, and Vaccination Officer, was Mr C. J. Chaffey of Alexandra Road.

The long list of organisations and clubs included:-

The Avon Valley Beekeepers' Association run by Mr D. E. Alexander

The 'Vale of Avon' Lodge of the Freemasons - Mr H. G. Bryant, Greenbank

The Nursing Association - Mr S. B. Rake, Oaklands

Fordingbridge Badminton Club - Major W. B. Shakespear, Sirmoor, Bowerwood Road

The Cricket Club - Mr M. Crossman, 'Coronna', Station Road.

'Turks' Football Club - Mr C. J. Bailey, The Quadrant

Whitsbury Road Athletic Football Club - Mr R. L. Gould, 11 Albion Road

Fordingbridge Ex-Service Men's Club - Mr W. E. Gilbert, Nyanza Terrace

The Territorial Club - Mr A. E. Dorrell, The Drill Hall

The 5/7 Hampshire Regiment, 14 Platoon, D Company - 2nd Lieut. R. C. Eldridge

The Second World War, 1939-1945

Hundreds of men from the district saw active service during the Second World War, and twenty from the town were killed during the course of hostilities.

The town and district saw a great deal of activity throughout the war, with troops often stationed nearby. The 3rd Tank Corps was here during much of the first half of 1940. After American forces entered the war at the end of 1941, and until the D-day landings of June 1944, their 7th Armoured Brigade was stationed at both Breamore House and West Park House. General George Patton was an illustrious visitor to the town on one occasion, visiting his troops as they passed through the streets on their way to France.

Some women enlisted in the Women's Royal Army Corps or the Women's Royal Air Force. Others joined organisations such as the Women's Voluntary Service or the Land Army, while, as in the First World War, many took on jobs formerly done by men.

> *HOSPITAL SUPPLY STORES WHIST DRIVE - A successful whist drive was held on Monday, at the Welfare Centre, in aid of the local branch of the Central Hospital Supply Stores. Up to date this branch has cut out over four miles of material, making over 6000 garments.*
>
> *W.V.S. NEWS - The knitting party during the past year have despatched a grand total of 554 garments to the Forces, R.A.F., Merchant Navy and Civil Defence. The party has also marked 700 blankets, 300 towels and a large number of small articles for the local rest centres. That the canteen is undoubtedly appreciated is shown by the fact that 30,621 cups of hot drinks have been served in the year. A junior member, Miss Phyllis Tomkins, has organised an active Youth Squad who are doing most useful work.*
>
> -   S & W Journal, March 28th 1941 and January 30th 1942

A squadron of the Air Training Corps was established in the town in February 1941, with the Scouts' Hall as headquarters. Within a few days the names of 15 young men had been received towards a target of 40 to 50 cadets.

The area's major installation relating to the war effort was undoubtedly the bombing range, established at Ashley Walk late in 1939, when some 3,800 acres were fenced off to keep out the New Forest animals. Bomb testing continued from 1940 until 1946, operations being under the control of the Armament Squadron of the A&AEE Boscombe Down. The heaviest bomb of the war, the 22,000 lbs 'Grand Slam', was among the wide range of munitions and devices dropped there. Only incendiary bombs were banned, due to the extremely high fire risk to the forest. Just prior to the 'Dambusters' raids in May 1943, Lancaster bombers of 617 Squadron used the range to practise low level bombing runs, and in August of the same year further experiments were carried out in preparation for other raids.

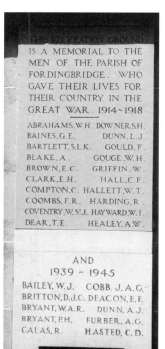

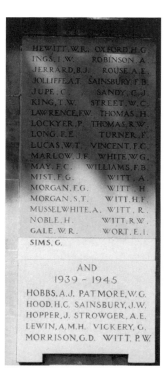

The tablets on the War Memorial gates
(see page 134)
required further sad additions following the Second World War

139

Immediately adjoining the bombing range, on the north side of the Cadnam road from early 1941, was the Armaments Research Department, Millersford, an offshoot of the Ministry of Supply. There up to a hundred people, many of them locals, were employed in testing static explosive devices. Bombs of all sizes and types were detonated and the effects of the explosions filmed for research and development purposes.

Fordingbridge, like other rural towns and villages, received evacuee children from vulnerable urban areas. By February 1940 there were 45 children from Portsmouth in the town, and all had to be housed, fed, schooled and sometimes clothed. The schooling did not at first go well. The District Council could not understand why this relatively small group of children had 14 teachers looking after them. The children could not be accommodated at the School on a full-time basis, but were given two rooms there in the afternoons. To start with they were allowed the use of the upstairs room at the Victoria Rooms in the mornings, but this was unpopular with the locals because of the noise. It was reported that for the first half-hour of each day the children were allowed to play, while the teachers sat round the fire and read newspapers.

They were asked to leave the Victoria Rooms, and were given the use of a room belonging to the Congregational Church for one and a half hours each morning, although attendance was apparently not compulsory. The Council was also concerned that there were no desks and no proper equipment.

Some men were excused from enlisting in the services because of age or because they were in a 'protected occupation' such as food production. Most of them joined the Home Guard, which was formed in 1940 and was initially known as the Local Defence Volunteers (*'Dad's Army'* to most people today). The Fordingbridge Home Guard was based at the Drill Hall, and consisted of a number of sections from various parts of the town and parish. Other villages such as Breamore, Hyde and Rockbourne had their own units.

> *HOME GUARD ROUTE MARCH - The Burgate, Ashford, Sandleheath and Packham sections of the Fordingbridge Home Guard performed a route march of about 5 miles through Fordingbridge on Monday evening, with a view to obtaining more recruits. The volunteers, numbering 30, under the command of Platoon Commander Mr M. Dowson made a good impression as they marched through the streets in a smart and soldierly fashion headed by a piper.* – From the *Salisbury and Winchester Journal*, January 10th 1941

With the threat of invasion over, the Home Guard was disbanded, and the Fordingbridge Platoon held their 'Stand-Down' dinner at the Drill Hall on 19th January 1945. The 150 guests present included Major W. A. D. Edwardes, Commanding Officer, 'C' Company of the Fordingbridge Home Guard, Captain W. B. Shakespear and Lieutenants Dowson, Gilbert, Miles and Farmer.

Health Matters

The workhouse still existed in the early part of the 20th century. By then, the term 'Union House' was preferred officially, but people's perception of it as 'the Workhouse' was hard to remove – even when the buildings were adapted for use as Fordingbridge Infirmary after the introduction of the National Health Service in 1948. Today it is Fordingbridge Hospital, part of Salisbury Healthcare NHS Trust and a much-appreciated part of local facilities, with more serious cases referred to Salisbury.

One of the town's medical practices, led for many years by two Dr Vickerys, father and son, was situated in Samuel Thompson's former home, Bridge House. By the 1980s, accommodation there was extremely cramped. In 1992, the practice moved to modern facilities, converted from the former Children's Block and Schoolrooms of the 1886 workhouse buildings.

Road and Rail, 1920s - 1964

In the first decades of the 20th century, horse-drawn vehicles were still common. Until the 1920s, many of the roads must have been in little better state than they had been in earlier centuries. A horse-drawn water cart was regularly used in dry weather to dampen the road surfaces in the town to prevent dust clouds forming with every passing vehicle. Some roads were 'metalled', that is, they had a firm surface of flint, crushed by a steam-driven road-roller. Then came 'tarmacadam'. The Rural District Council's Minute Book of May 1922 recorded that – *'The County Council to tar the metalled District Roads in Provost Street, Church Street and Green Lane, this council finding the tar and the County Council providing the plant and labour'*. In July 1925 the RDC requested that white lines should be painted on the road at the Bank Corner and at 'Mr John Coventry's Corner', probably the first lines to appear on the recently tarred roads.

For most people the railway was still important, with easy access several times a day to Salisbury (with connections for London and elsewhere) and to the south coast. The line was run by the London and South-Western Railway until 1923, when it became part of Southern Railway, until that was incorporated into British Railways. The line had never proved particularly profitable, but in pre-car days it did transport large numbers of passengers, at least on occasions.

> *DISAPPOINTED HOLIDAY MAKERS - About 100 would-be passengers to Bournemouth repaired to the* [Fordingbridge] *railway station on Monday, but when the train arrived at the station it was already full. Room, however, was found in the guard's van for a number, but the majority had to return home, many with families having come from a distance. – S & W Journal,* June 4th 1919

In the 1950s, the holiday Runabout Ticket was popular, with a quite small fee providing unlimited travel between Salisbury, Christchurch, Bournemouth, Swanage and Weymouth for a week of the summer.

In the 1960s, Dr Beeching wielded his infamous 'axe' in the name of rationalisation and closed many branch lines throughout the country. The last passenger service through Fordingbridge was on May 4th 1964. Increased use of the roads had been part of the reason for closure, but the reduction in rail travel inevitably added still further to road traffic.

The traction engine 'Victor', manufactured by Wallis and Stevens, was owned by Neave and Co.

Here it is seen here being driven past Lloyds Bank by Albert Weaving, en route to the Town Mills.

The Impact of the Car, 1899-2000

At the end of the 20th century, nothing symbolised personal freedom more than car ownership. Many people's life-styles today are entirely dependant upon the ease of individual travel. The cost, however, is high, and not only in financial terms – in pollution, in the volume of traffic, in congestion at busy periods. Sometimes the stress outweighs the advantages.

We know that cars were already seen in the streets of Fordingbridge on occasions before the end of the 19th century, and we have already noted the council's plea for an 8mph speed limit. Although the earliest 'motor-carriages' were on sale before 1900, it was the opening of a Ford Model T factory in Britain in 1909 which really started the trend.

Car owners in Edwardian times were pioneers, with none of the motoring infra-structure that is now taken for granted. Contemporary photographs of Fordingbridge streets show 'Pratt's Motor Spirit' on sale at ironmongers and similar shops, no doubt with very poor safety standards. It was only after WWI, with a steady increase in car ownership, that purpose-built garages were opened. By 1927 there were several businesses within the town catering for the burgeoning motor trade, as shown by these entries extracted from *Kelly's Trade Directory of Hampshire* for that year:

> *Beale and Sons, motor engineers, Horseport*
> *William Henry Crowdy, motor engineers, High Street*
> *Enright Brothers, motor engineers etc, Salisbury Street*
> *Walter George Nicklen and Sons, motor engineers, Provost Street*
> *Pitt and Sons, motor body manufacturers*
> *Arthur Frank Percy Waters, motor car proprietor, Park Road*

Garages have come and gone over the years but Nicklens', which like many others was originally converted from a blacksmith's shop, is still with us. The other main petrol station as the 21st century begins is Southampton Road Garage, just beyond the by-pass. A number of small engineering units also exist around the town and district.

While car owners were very much in the minority in the first half of the 20th century, Fordingbridge today, like any other town, is dominated by the car. It is rare indeed to look out onto an empty street. Road use on the present scale was not envisaged before the 20th century, and a great deal of adaptation has been necessary, here as elsewhere, including the provision of large areas of parking space near the town centre.

A change of era and a change of pace are symbolised by these pictures. On the left, a horse-drawn cart is being driven down the High Street, passing a shop sign advertising 'Motor Spirit' for pioneering motorists. On the right, an early tradesman's van, belonging to Lonnen and Son's Family Butchers business, is parked outside the Old Manor Court House.

The Fordingbridge By-pass on the A338 Salisbury-Ringwood road was opened on January 31st 1975. Thus it has, for almost three decades, protected the town from much of the north-south traffic. (Heavy vehicles using the east-west route through the town have remained a problem and no solution is envisaged.) The value of the by-pass – and the volume of traffic using it – was brought home to all during the floods of Autumn 2000. With the by-pass closed for a long period, the town centre descended into near chaos, producing long queues and the threat of damage to roads, buildings and the medieval bridge.

Modern Travel and Life-styles

In most previous centuries, almost everyone with a job worked within walking distance of their homes. The majority of people did not travel far beyond the towns and villages where they were born. If they did, horses or their own two feet provided the motive power. If men went overseas, it was most probably because they were in the army, in the colonial service or perhaps on business. Only a small minority of women ever left these shores, unless they were accompanying their husbands to the colonies or emigrating. In 1900 the aeroplane had not even been invented, but it has played a major role in the history of the century, both as a weapon of war and as a means of transport for the masses.

In the latter part of the 20th century and now at the start of the 21st, many residents of Fordingbridge are prepared to commute to their daily work in Salisbury, Bournemouth, Southampton or even further afield. Foreign travel by passenger jet is available to many people, thanks to the package holiday industry, and a town the size of Fordingbridge is able to support two travel agents. But travel <u>to</u> Fordingbridge must also be taken into consideration. One of the authors (GP) taught at a Fordingbridge school, commuting 23 miles each way for over five years, and there must be many similar cases. Tourism is of considerable significance to the local economy with many visitors to the New Forest, and especially to the Sandy Balls Holiday Centre, coming to Fordingbridge for shopping. The potential exists to increase the importance of tourist income to the town in the coming years.

The town has regular amateur theatrical productions, which are well supported. Fordingbridge had its own small cinema from 1927 till 1960. But for cinemas, for professional theatre and for other forms of entertainment, local residents must now travel to Bournemouth, Salisbury, Southampton or beyond. While Fordingbridge has a (relatively small) town-centre supermarket and a good range of independent specialist shops, many shoppers prefer to travel to large out-of-town stores, reducing the income of local traders. This is a modern parallel of the inability of Fordingbridge Market, in the 18th century, to compete with the larger markets of Ringwood and Salisbury. However, Fordingbridge does have a significant advantage over some of the larger centres today – free parking. New Forest District Council introduced charges during 1998, but the outcry from traders in Fordingbridge and the other small shopping centres in the District was so vociferous that the ticket machines were soon removed.

A search of the card index of local organisations at Fordingbridge Library, and of relevant pages of the Hampshire County Council web-site, reveals around forty different clubs and societies which meet regularly in the town, or which draw their supporters from both Fordingbridge and Ringwood. Some encompass wide interests, such as the Fordingbridge Society, with its affiliation to the Civic Trust; the Women's Institute; or the Community Association based at Avonway. Others cater to specialist interests, ranging from archaeology to writing, from embroidery to rugby, and from Mother and Toddler clubs to the Evergreen Club for senior citizens. A twinning association maintains close links with Vimoutiers in Normandy. Fordingbridge Show, held in a field at Godshill each summer, is one of the major events of the annual round.

Changes in the Villages

Although this is a history of Fordingbridge town, it is worth noting the changes in the surrounding villages during the 20th century. These have produced a very different social structure in the town's immediate hinterland.

In 1945, the great majority of a village's population was employed, directly or indirectly, in agriculture. Most families had lived in the same village for generations. With the introduction of tractors and other machinery, a smaller labour force was needed and many farm workers moved to jobs in towns. Several of the large estates, now in financial difficulties, placed formerly tenanted properties on the open market. Former city-dwellers moved into the countryside – for retirement, for weekend and holiday homes and for commuting. Labourers' cottages, rarely with 20th-century conveniences, were upgraded into highly desirable residences which are now often beyond the means of local young people.

The centuries-old thatched cottages, internally modernised, remain a photogenic attraction to the area's visitors, but there is still a need for the development of small rural-based industries that would provide local employment.

Augustus John

Fordingbridge's most famous former resident is commemorated by a statue by Ivor Robert-Jones. Augustus John, one of the most notable British painters of his generation, lived and worked at Fryern Court until his death in 1961.

But during this time, *'the legend of John as the last great bohemian artist began to supersede his real achievements'*. Perhaps due to tacit disapproval of his lifestyle, for many years the town showed no great pride in its Augustus John connections and the statue was relegated to a corner of the Recreation Ground. Only with the development of Painter's Mews and Riverside Parade has it been moved to a more prestigious position.

Fordingbridge Museum

John Shering, who has been prominent in many aspects of town life, began a personal collection of 'bygones' in the 1960s, initially for the interest of his own family. The Shering Collection eventually occupied two floors of purpose-built premises off Church Street; part of a gallery is shown left. In 1995, after the loss of the building, the collection was offered to the town. A new Fordingbridge Museum, run by a Trust, opened in Kings Yard in August 2000, thus making parts of the collection again available to the public.

FORDINGBRIDGE SCHOOLS, 1880-2001

The original building of the National School (see page 107) was extended in 1880 by the addition of the 'Boys School' (*left*) and in 1895 by the construction of the 'Girls School'.

The combined premises continued in use as an 'all-age' Elementary School until 1957 and as a Primary School until 1974, after which they gained a new lease of life as the Avonway Community Centre.

In January 1957, 220 pupils aged 11-14 were admitted to the new Fordingbridge Secondary School. It was not long before the informal use of 'the Burgate school' was adopted officially. The more able local pupils were 'creamed off' to attend Grammar Schools in Salisbury or Brockenhurst. This largely came to an end in 1980, when Burgate finally achieved comprehensive status. A series of extensions between 1972 and 2001 included the addition of a Sixth Form Centre in 1995.

This building was originally a part of Fordingbridge Primary School. In May 1968, nine classes remained in the main building in Shaftesbury Street while three classes used this 'Annexe' at the far end of the town. This arrangement continued until 1974 when the Primary School closed and separate Infant and Junior Schools opened. These premises have been Fordingbridge Infants School since that date.

Fordingbridge Junior School opened in 1974 in premises adjacent to the Infants School in Pennys Lane.

At this event in 1988, pupils, parents and existing and former staff of the Infants School celebrated a 20th birthday, marking the opening of the original annexe in their building.

CHAPTER 11 – INTO THE TWENTY-FIRST CENTURY

It is the privilege of few generations to welcome the start of a new millennium.

The start of the First Millennium of the Christian era was obviously not recognised as such at the time. Around 1AD, the Fordingbridge area had a Celtic population, perhaps subservient to chieftains in the local hillforts at Whitsbury and Godshill. Technology was at the Iron Age level – and the Roman invasion was still almost two generations in the future.

At the start of the Second Millennium, Forde, while only a small village, was notable for its river bridge, Hundred-courts and perhaps markets, which had already elevated it above the ordinary. The local population was largely Saxon, although there had undoubtedly been a degree of intermarriage with the descendants of their Celtic predecessors. Administratively, Hampshire ('Hamtunscir') had been in existence for well over two centuries, longer than the Kingdom of England. King Ethelred (known as the 'Unready', meaning ill-advised) had pressing concerns about Danish raiders. His links with Normandy paved the way for invasion in 1066.

As we enter the Third Millennium, Fordingbridge residents are people of many backgrounds. The county of Hampshire provides a continuity of administration, athough its boundaries

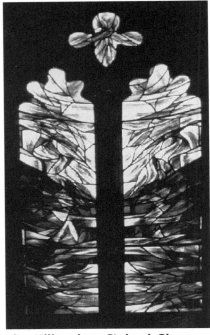

The Millennium Stained Glass Window in St Mary's Parish Church

have fluctuated from time to time. England is part of the United Kingdom and increasingly part of Europe – and we are all, for better or worse, part of a truly global economy.

Many communities have marked the beginning of the Third Millennium with some physical reminder – a village sign, a community hall, an addition to the fabric of the parish church – which will outlast the immediate celebrations. Fordingbridge, like a number of other Hampshire communities, chose to install a Millennium Window in the Parish Church

Although the 21st century is still very new at the time of writing, we have devoted a chapter to it, in order to provide some record of the town as it is today. Previous histories by Reginald Hannen and A. T. Morley Hewitt have been of considerable help in fostering our understanding of the more recent past, and we hope that the following pages will be of equal interest and use to future generations.

Photographs and old postcards, of the Edwardian period in particular, help to bring the past to life almost a century later. The new street scenes in this chapter, photographed during the summer of 2001, have been selected to record the appearance of the town at the beginning of the new millennium. We are also conscious of the interest of such views to the not inconsiderable number of readers who now live far away, with perhaps only childhood memories of their birthplace.

Space does not permit us to include a full list of all the businesses in the town, in the style of the old directories, but we have attempted to list those shops and businesses that exist in the heart of the town in the early summer of 2001.

Shops and Businesses, 2001

Only a small number of businesses still survive in the town from the first half of the 20th century. Jacksons the solicitors, Nicklens Garage and Mays the butchers have traded continuously over many years, but apart from these three, only Lloyds Bank and a few of the Public Houses would be recognisable to pre-Second-World-War residents. However, Rose and Alexander's hardware shop is the successor of Alexander's earlier shop (which was situated on the site of the present-day Roman Quay) and this in turn had developed from a much older plumbing and glazing business run by the same family.

Today there are new types of shops and offices which reflect the major changes in society over recent decades. The Co-op supermarket in the High Street has taken much of the town's trade in a wide variety of products, while the two travel agents capitalise on increasing leisure time and spending power. Although the town has always had at least one fish and chip shop during the past three-quarters of a century, the more recently introduced Indian and Chinese restaurants and take-aways are indicative of the modern taste for a wider choice of foods.

Earlier generations would have been astonished to see a betting shop, a video rental shop and a computer business. Charity shops such as Help the Aged in Salisbury Street and Winged Fellowship in the High Street have become a familiar sight today in almost every town.

The list on the next two pages is intended as a 'snap-shot' of the shops in the town in the summer of 2001, which we hope will prove of interest, especially to those who look back at this book in decades to come. It is not meant to be a comprehensive list of all the town's businesses – we have concentrated on the 'historic core' of the town and wish to make our apologies for any possible omissions.

View of Church Street, looking approximately north-north-east from the top of the church tower. The Town Hall can be distinguished in the background, to the right of the centre of the picture. Taken during the St Mary's Festival, July 8th 2001

Salisbury Street - east side

	unoccupied new shop
10	One Stop - convenience store
12	The Alcove - newsagent
14	Reflections - hairdresser
16	Barclays Bank
18-20	J. May & Son -butchers
22	Meesons - solicitors
24	Animals Voice Trust
26-30	Caxton Decor
34	Scammel's Antiques
38	New Wong's Garden Chinese Restaurant
40	Fox Garden Machinery

Provost Street - west side

(Market Place)

	The Royal Arms Public House
2a	Paragon Hair Design
22	Nicklens Garage + RapidFit
34	John Shering - undertaker
	New Forest District Council Office
	Citizens Advice Bureau

Provost Street - east side

(Market Place)

5	Jacksons solicitors
7	Perkins motor accessories
9	Tale of Bengal take-away
11	Perkins Cycle Shop

Church Street

1	The Wine Cellar

Shaftesbury Street

2	empty shop
5	Design House
7	Sarum Insurance Ltd
	Branksome China
28	I.N.Newman Ltd - funeral directors
36	Avonway Community Centre
75	Raj of India
	Police Station
	Fire Station

Albion Road

4	Albion Road Garage

Salisbury Road

45	Fordingbridge Dental Surgery

Salisbury Street - west side

1-3	Lloyds Pharmacy
5-7	Fox & sons- Estate Agents
	Miles of Value
	15 The Fordingbridge Bookshop
17	Chain Connections - fashion
21	Seconds of Quality - factory shop

Kings' Yard:

	Tourist Information Centre
	Fordingbridge Museum
	A J Bailey – electrical contractor
25	Help the Aged - charity shop
27	empty shop
33	Woolley & Wallis - Estate Agents
37	Whitsbury Autocare
	United Reformed Church
43	China and Gifts
45-47	Bristow & Garland - antiques, books, prints
49	former post-office
51	Versatiles, carpets
	Makuti Hair Design

Roundhill

	Roundhill Mini Market - greengrocers
	The Fordingbridge Club

Green Lane

	Postal Sorting and Delivery Office
Unit 1	Nigel Price - curtain maker and upholsterer
Unit 2	Green Lane Works - motor
Unit 3	Jones Marine and Diving Services
Unit 4	Bob Hann - precision engineer
21	DataKinetics
24	Select Pets and Foods

The Bartons

	Elliotts - builders merchants

Bartons Road

	The Doctors' Surgery
	Fordingbridge Hospital
	The Drill Hall - Army Cadet Force - Air Training Corps
	British Red Cross

High Street - east side

1	Farewise Travel
3	Forest Country Wear and Saddlery
Roman Quay: empty shops	
5	Barry Rickman photography
7	Country Cobbler
17	Tale Ends - bookshop
19	Philpott's Fish and Chips
21	Premier Fish and Game
23-5	Harrison's - stationers
27	National Westminster Bank
29-31	Toad Hall - restaurant
33-39	Carl Hillwood Hairdressing
43	Dixon & Templeton - solicitors
45	Clockwork Yellow - dry cleaners
49	Forbuoys - newsagents
51-3	The Cottage Loaf – bakers
	Corralls Coal Orders
55	Forest Flowers and Forest Pets
57	Audio Vision
59	Jessica - ladies fashions
(Market Place)	
63	Town Hall
69	D.J. Price - butcher
71	Euro Property Network
	Movie Zone
	Cooks' Kitchens
	Chiropractic Clinic

High Street - west side

2	Nationwide Building Society
4	Town and Country Wardrobes
6	H S B C
12	Avon Wines & Wholefoods
14	Lorgnettes - spectacle boutique
16	Coral - betting shop
18	Belinda's Bakery and Tearooms
22	Tribbeck, gold and silversmiths
	I. Newman - undertaker
	The Barber Shop
24a	Adrian Dowding - estate agent
24	Mark Collier Antiques
26	Coffee & Cream - café
28	Jane the Florist
	Fordingbridge Library
32	Sun Salads - greengrocers
36	A. J. Bass - optician
38	Co-op supermarket
52	Winged Fellowship - charity shop
54	South Coast Construction
56-58	Bath Travel
60	Goadsby and Harding - estate agents
(Market Place)	
62	The Crown Inn
64-66	MCS.com computers
68	The Ship Inn

Bridge Street - north side

1	Lloyds TSB Bank
3-5	Doll Museum & Tea Rooms
7-9	Peking Restauant
11	unoccupied new shop

Bridge Street - south side

2-8	Rose & Alexander - hardware
10	empty shop
12	Cricket-Hockey.co.uk
14	The George Inn

Horseport

23	New Forest Restoration Ltd - antique restorers
	The Victoria Rooms

Southampton Road

	Hillwoods Garage and Car Sales
	Southampton Road Garage and Londis Shop
	Pixies Plant Centre

STREET SCENES, FORDINGBRIDGE, 2001

The next five pages are devoted to a series of photographs, taken in June - August 2001 by one of the authors (GP). They are intended to be a straightforward record of the appearance of the town at the start of the 21st century - the kind of views which would have been readily available in picture postcard format in Edwardian time.

[A CD-ROM with the original colour versions of these pictures, and others taken for this book, has been deposited with Fordingbridge Museum.]

Church Street, with the restored gaslamp in the foreground at the entrance to Timbermill Court, built on the site of the former builders' yard and Shering's Museum

1990s development in Provost Street on the site of the old Kings Arms Inn, which closed in 1869

West Street, formerly Back Street or Jiggins Street, was once described as the *'inferior part'* of the town (see p. 68). However, with the 2000-2001 development on the site of the West Mills, it now boasts desirable modern housing.

The Fordingbridge Bookshop in Salisbury Street, with street furniture provided by Hampshire County Council in the 1990s. Roundhill, with access to the main car park, is on the left of the picture.

Bridge Street from 'Bank Corner', with the pedestrian footway attached to the Great Bridge in the background. The modern development of Riverside Parade is on the site of the former Albany Hotel.

Another view from Bank Corner, looking up the High Street. The buildings on the right, extending back to Roundhill, originated as 'market infill' - they occupy the site of the Market Place, prior to about 1675.

The statue of Augustus John stands in Riverside Parade and provides the name for 'Painter's Mews'. This riverside area was occupied by a series of tea-gardens in the 1930s, but excavation in the area has shown that much less salubrious activities once took place here. The tannery (see p.78) must have both polluted the river and given a very distinctive smell to this part of the town!

Horseport, the part of the town to the east of the Great Bridge. The Victoria Rooms are on the left of the picture. The creeper-covered building in the middle distance has been an inn; it was the home of Samuel Thompson, the mill-owner; and for much of the 20th century it was a doctors' surgery.

This picture should be contrasted with that on page 35, as they were taken within a short distance of one another, looking in roughly the same direction. However unsightly the 1970s by-pass, it is a great boon in removing the heavy north-south traffic from the town centre. The Southampton Road Garage can be seen under the road arch.

ABOVE : a third view of Bank Corner; High Street to the left, Salisbury Street to the right, Bridge Street 'behind the camera'.

RIGHT: this view from the Recreation Ground illustrates two of the conservation concerns outlined on pages 155-157. The Great Bridge is a Grade II* Listed Building, while the River Avon and the Valley have numerous wildlife conservation designations.

BELOW: the lower part of the High Street, looking towards Bank Corner. This was once known as Fore Street, to contrast with Roundhill, then called Back Street.

ABOVE : the Market Place, looking down Provost Street. It is interesting to imagine this view when, instead of the collection of road signs, the Victorian gas-lamp (p 130) occupied this spot; or earlier, when the Market House (page 69) stood here.

LEFT : another view of Provost Street, with Nicklen's Garage.

BELOW : Shaftesbury Street, once part of the turnpike road from Brook to Shaftesbury.

Think Globally, Act Locally

Twenty-first-century residents of Fordingbridge cannot fail to be aware of big issues of a world-wide nature. 'Globalisation' has become the important trend in economics but it is not without its vociferous critics. Environmental degradation poses major threats to our way of life and ultimately to the future of the whole human race. Climate change suddenly became a talking point locally during the severe flooding of autumn 2000, when shots of water flowing into the bars of the George Inn were featured on national television news.

Friends of the Earth

International oganisations like Greenpeace and Friends of the Earth campaign on the problems of over-population and world poverty, the depletion of the planet's resources, pollution of rivers, of the air and of the sea, global warming, the loss of natural habitats and endangered species of wildlife – all world-wide conservation problems.

Everyone can help a little in the global problems by using the re-cycling banks, by cutting down on their use of energy and of water, by buying 'green' products when possible and so on. But it is also very important to conserve the local environment, both built and natural.

Fordingbridge and the area around it have many official 'conservation designations', outlined in the following paragraphs.

The whole of the 'historic core' of the town is now a **Conservation Area**, defined as *'an area of special architectural or historic interest, the character or appearance of which it is desirable to preserve or enhance'*. There are over sixty **Listed Buildings** within this area, including St Mary's Church (Grade I); the Great Bridge and the old Manor Court House (both Grade II*); and the Hospital and May's thatched butcher's shop (both Grade II).

ENGLISH HERITAGE

The thatched butchers' shop in Salisbury Street is one of many Listed Buildings within the historic core of the town. It rates English Heritage's Grade II.

The riverside gardens to the south-east of High Street and the remains of the medieval Rectory Moat are within the Conservation Area. The open space by Sweatfords Water and the so-called 'Bishop's Pond', also both within the Area, are managed by the Town Council and volunteers with the assistance and advice of local Officers of **Hampshire Wildlife Trust**.

Fordingbridge is on the edge of the **New Forest Heritage Area**, which is expected to become a **National Park** early in the 21st century. Horseport and the recreation ground are likely to be within the boundary of the Park. A substantial part of the Forest is also a **Site of Special Scientific Interest** (SSSI) and various other designations show that it is internationally recognised as of very special wildlife conservation interest.

To the north-west, Hampshire's 'Western Downland' villages of Damerham, Whitsbury, Rockbourne and Martin are included in the Cranborne Chase and West Wiltshire Downland **Area of Outstanding Natural Beauty**. Martin Down is a **National Nature Reserve**.

The flood-plain of the River Avon, from Netheravon to Christchurch (excluding built-up areas), is designated an **Environmentally Sensitive Area**. This signifies a requirement, instigated by the former Ministry of Agriculture, that farming practices should help in the preservation of the valley's special environment. Much of the area also has SSSI status.

From Bickton to Christchurch, the flood-plain is also a **Special Protection Area** under the European Union wild birds directive, as well as a 'Ramsar' site. This designation is given to **'Wetlands of International Importance'**, Ramsar being a town in Iran where the original conference on this topic was held.

The actual river and its tributaries, from Bickton to Christchurch, is an SSSI because of the very valuable chalk stream habitats; and is also a candidate for designation as a **Special Area of Conservation** by the EU.

The **Avon Valley Long-Distance Footpath** traverses the whole distance from Salisbury to Christchurch, but not always on the valley floor. The path passes through Fordingbridge churchyard on its way from Burgate to Bickton.

Sites of Importance for Nature Conservation - this is a new status to be given to sites of local nature conservation interest not covered by any of the other designations. New Forest District Council may apply it to several small sites around Fordingbridge, including Damerham water meadows.

The **Avon Valley and West Hampshire Project** covers 14 parishes, from Martin and Hale in the north to Sopley and Bransgore in the south, including Fordingbridge. It is a Hampshire Wildlife Trust initiative, working with landowners and communities -

'to maintain and enhance this unique and internationally important part of Hampshire'.

The Great Bridge has long been used as the symbol of Fordingbridge. This engraving from the 1840s once appeared on notes and cheques issued by the Wilts and Dorset Bank, whose local premises are now occupied by Lloyds Bank.

Postscript - Looking Back and Looking Forward

Fordingbridge at the beginning of the 3rd millennium is, like any other historic town, the product of a curious combination of continuity and change over many generations. The historic core which remains today is, however, largely the result of 18th century rebuilding after the great fires, with subsequent enhancement and modernisation. There can be little doubt that the appearance of the town today would be very different if its ancient housing stock had not been destroyed by the fires of the 17th and early 18th centuries.

Change is a continuous process. History is the story of this change, brought about by succeeding generations as they adapt to new situations and fashions. Only those features which are capable of modification and adjustment have survived the centuries. It is only in very recent times that much of our past has been 'artificially' retained through planning controls, such as the regulations on Listed Buildings.

The manorial system, which controlled daily life in Fordingbridge for centuries, has long gone, as have most of the families who administered it. The stately homes of the landed gentry and the large houses of the Victorian nouveau riche either do not survive (e.g. the Eyre Coote family mansion at West Park Rockbourne), or have been adapted to other uses. Only Breamore House is still the home of the same family that lived there in the 18th century.

Burgate House, long-time seat of the Bulkeleys and the Coventrys, forms the headquarters of the Game Conservancy Trust. Packham House, home of the Brices and of the Foleys in Victorian times, is a nursing home. Highfield, the former home of the Neaves, is now in private hands again after spells as the Cottage Hospital and a nursing home. Parsonage Farm survives as a private house, but without its lands, some of which have been developed for housing.

As with buildings there is a degree of continuity with our local families. Some still living in the town and district can be traced back through documents over many years, but few have origins here earlier than the 18th century. It is rare indeed to find the family names of the 16th century still present in the area. The mobility of population has been greater than is sometimes supposed.

Fordingbridge's medieval growth was based on trade, and although the markets and fairs have faded away, the modern town is still dependant upon the well-being of its commercial heart for its prosperity. Recent developments have done much to modernise the town centre and to improve its appearance, helping to create the pleasant and welcoming environment that shops and businesses need to be successful.

The large workforces of the 19th and early 20th centuries no longer exist. Thompsons' factories at East and West Mills, and Neaves' near the station ceased trading many years ago. Present day businesses are relatively small, and there are now no employers of comparable size.

Today power is in the hands of the various councils at County, District and Parish level. Hampshire County Council was established in 1888 and the parish council in 1894. The New Forest District Council is a product of Local Government reorganisation in 1974, when it absorbed the former Ringwood and Fordingbridge Rural District Council.

What then of the future? Of immediate concern, in the summer of 2001, is the establishment of the New Forest National Park. The bulk of the town seems likely to be excluded, although Horseport, and the old open-field of Lulsey with its adjacent meadows to the south of Bowerwood Road, may be within it. The long term effects on the town are difficult to quantify, although increased income from tourism could be one consequence.

How will Fordingbridge deal with even greater traffic pressure? Will its population continue to rise? Will it be able to attract sufficient industries and businesses to provide adequate employment opportunities without the need for large scale commuting? Indeed, what will the town look like in a hundred years time? Even if change continues at the present rate, we can surely assume that there would still be much that we could recognise.

Most of the buildings in this photograph of the High Street in about 1902 are immediately identifiable today, although uses have changed.

Compare it with the modern photograph on page 151.

Will the same be true, though, *in a thousand years*? There is little from the early years of the second millennium that exists today, and it would be optimistic in the extreme to expect that much from our time will be here at the beginning of the fourth millennium. Assuming that the human race avoids planetary ecological disaster, will there even be a town called Fordingbridge in a thousand years? No amount of speculation will produce the answers, but we would be seriously lacking in imagination, if, after looking back over the past millennia, we did not also wonder about the next.

APPENDIX - Previous publications

Two previous attempts have been made to write general histories of Fordingbridge. The first, *The History of Fordingbridge and Neighbourhood* by **Reginald Hannen**, ran to three editions between 1883 and 1909 and has been the subject of a modern facsimile reprint. Like his father before him, the author was Steward of the Manor of Fordingbridge, and had an intimate knowledge of the town and its people. His chapters on the town provide a unique insight into the later 19th century, long experience having enabled him to record facts that are both fascinating and dependable. Sadly the same cannot be said of his section on the early history of the area, which includes much that is fanciful. (Reginald Hannen is pictured above, by courtesy of his grandson.)

The Story of Fordingbridge in Fact and Fancy by A. T. Morley Hewitt was produced in 1966 as a collection of historical and archaeological information, which had been assembled by the writer during his 42 years residency in the town as an estate agent. While there is some attempt to cover the various periods of the town's development, it is largely an assemblage of interesting facts and anecdotes, not all of which are historically correct. There is, nevertheless, much of value which can be selected from the text. Unfortunately, there is little real effort to analyse the information in depth and the book lacks maps or plans. Morley Hewitt (pictured right) made considerable use of Hannen's work and supplemented it by drawing together material from many sources, some of which were then relatively obscure.

A little book, *Tales of the Hundred of Ford*, tells eight stories, best considered as fictional accounts relating to historical events or legends of the locality. The third edition was published in 1928 and it has recently been reprinted as a series of slim booklets. The only authorship recorded on the title page is *'Transcribed in memory of his sister, Margaret, by her brother'*, but it has been attributed to Reginald Hannen's father, John. The Author's Preface claims that the whole work was transcribed from an old leather-bound-book predating 1790 – but even the preface reads like fiction. (See our notes about some of its inaccuracies on pages 92 and 95.)

Small specialist books have appeared during the 1990s, detailing the histories of the Turks Football Club and of the Fire Service in the town. To these must be added booklets on the parish church and on the Catholic Church. All of these are listed below and may be consulted in the town's library.

The present authors have previously published other works on Fordingbridge (see page 172). Two volumes, both now out of print, dealt with specific periods in the history of the town. Some material from *Tudor Fordingbridge* is incorporated into this book, modified due to the resurfacing of 'lost' documents since the book was published in 1993. *Victorian Journal – Fordingbridge 1837-1901* reproduced many fascinating items from the local newspaper over this period, and some of these stories have also made their way into this book.

Our two other books are primarily collections of old photographs. *Fordingbridge and District – a Pictorial History* mainly covers the period 1860-1960, while *James Coventry – Gentleman Photographer* showcases the work of a local amateur photographer who lived in Fordingbridge in the 1890s (see page 123).

Other Published Books on Fordingbridge

The History of Firefighting in Fordingbridge, 1864-1994, Peter White, 1994

The Turks, 1868-1993, Norman Gannaway, 1993

St Mary's, Fordingbridge – a Short Description of the Church, Thomas Wright Little (vicar, 1915-1935), 1952

St Mary's, Fordingbridge by John Lovering, undated

St Mary and St Philip, Fordingbridge, An Outline History, M.A.R., 1993

Tales of the Hundred of Ford, 4th edition, June 1977, publ. by J G and D L Fredericks

Philpott of Fordingbridge, Lawrence Reed, 1993

A Jefferis Family of Fordingbridge, David Jefferis, 1998 (photocopied volume)

New Forest Explosives, Anthony Passmore (ed), 1993, publ Hants Field Club

Glossary

If a word appearing in an inventory does not appear in the glossary, it is probably an odd spelling of a familiar word. Often, just pronouncing it aloud will reveal its meaning - e.g. coultes for colts, beakon for bacon

advowson	the right to appoint the incumbent of a church
alimbicke	*alembic* - distilling apparatus
almaine rivets	light, rivetted armour, invented in Germany
amphora	large pottery vessel for transporting wine or garum (fish paste)
andiers	*andiron* - a fire dog
antiphoner	books of anthems
awlblade	the metal part of a pointed instrument for boring small holes
baffine	a coarse cloth
balet	probably half a bale
baudrick	*baldric* - a warrior's belt or shoulder sash
bedcoard	cords stretched across the frame of a bed to support the mattress
bond tenant	an un-free tenant - one bound to do service to the Lord of the Manor
borryer	*boring iron* - tool for boring holes
boulster	chisel
broche	a spit
brokage	*brokerage* - as in the Brokage Books of Southampton, being the accounts of the Bargate broker which detail tolls on goods entering and leaving the town
butteres	tool for paring horses' hoofs before shoeing
bychornes	anvils
chaffing-dishe	vessel holding charcoal for warming plates at table
chantry chapel	a chapel, usually within a church, for the chanting of masses for the soul of the benefactor
chapmen	itinerant dealers or pedlars
civitas	the lands of a self-governing tribal community during the Roman occupation
clerestory	an upper storey in a church, with its own row of windows
close	an enclosed field (i.e. fenced or hedged)
clyftes	clefts - splitting tools
coffer	a chest
coole	*coal* (as in *Smythes Coole* – the coal used by a blacksmith)
coppie houlde	*copyhold* - a tenancy of a property held by virtue of a copy of an agreement entered on a Court Roll (q.v.)
corselet	piece of armour covering the body
cotrell, cotterell	iron bar for hanging pots over a fire
coupell	pair of cruck beams used in medieval house construction
court roll	the written record of the proceedings of a manorial court
covell	*a cowl* - large vessel with 'ears' for handles
daguerreotype	an early photograph produced by mercury vapour development of silver iodide exposed on a copper plate
deanery	group of parishes presided over by a Dean
demesne	land owned and farmed by or for the Lord of the Manor
dogg	an andiron
donge pyke	dung fork
doule stake	*dowel stake* - wooden block for making dowels
durans	stout, durable cloth
eithen	harrows
ell	a cloth measure of 45 inches
estray	a stray beast
extent	a detailed valuation of a manor

fatchys	*vetches* or peas
firkins	cask holding 9 gallons of ale etc.
fleashooke	*flesh hook* - a meat hook
fulling mill	a water mill in which woollen cloth is fulled (scoured and beaten by hammers) to cleanse it
fustian	coarse, twilled cotton fabric
gredyron	*grid-iron* - platform of iron bars for cooking meat over a fire
groundsills	lowest horizontal timbers of a structure
guilt salt	a gilded salt-cellar
hayward	manorial official responsible for the upkeep of hedges and ditches and for the pasturage belonging to tenants
hide	an area of land originally deemed sufficient to maintain a household. In theory as much as 120 acres, but in practice often as low as 40 acres in parts of central southern England
hoggesheade	*hogshead* - a large barrel holding 52½ gallons of ale etc.
hollande	linen fabric originally made in Holland
holmnes	a fustian (q.v.) made at Ulm in Germany
hundred	administrative unit based on the old Saxon one of an area occupied by a hundred households
husbandman	a working farmer
inter-ties	a short timber, binding together upright posts
joyne stools	stool joined together with wooden dowels
keeve	tub used in brewing
kyne	cattle
kytts	circular wooden tubs for butter, milk, or washing clothes
lay rector	a lay person holding the tithes of a parish and probably the advowson (q.v.) (see also *rector*)
leese	*leas* - meadows or pastures
lentfeigs	*Lenten figs* - the first crop of the year
linturne	? *lantern*
locoram	coarse, loosely woven linen, for poor quality shirts etc.
Logion	collection of early sayings of Jesus
manor	administrative unit consisting of the landed estate of the Lord of that manor
mayles	eyelet holes
mercer	a dealer in textiles and small wares
messuage	a dwelling and its adjoining lands
morrion	an open helmet without visor or lower face covering
nayle tacles	equipment for making nails
nayling stake	small anvil used by nail makers
packthredd	thread for tying parcels
pallett bedstead	small bed with straw-filled mattress
parcel	a piece or part
pax	a tablet kissed by the priest and congregation during Mass
peson	peas
pie powder court	market court - from *'pieds poudreux'* (dusty feet) - referring to itinerant traders
pillities	*pillowties* - pillow cases
piscina	niche and drain near altar for emptying water used to wash sacred vessels
pontage	tax levied to finance the upkeep of a bridge
pooles	probably the clay and wood-lined 'tanks' used by tanners for soaking animal skins
porringer	bowls for soup or porridge

portesse	portable daily service book
pothengles	*pot-hanger*
powdring tubbes	tubs for curing meat with salt and spices
prytchell	sharp pointed instrument for punching holes in horse-shoes
puncheon	*pancheon* - a coarse earthenware pan
pye	rule book for determining church office of the day
pyx, pyxis	vessel for holding the consecrated wafer
reconsiliacion	re-consecration of a church after its closure for building work
rector	a clergyman of a parish where the tithes are not held by a layman (see also *lay rector*)
rood loft	a preaching gallery containing an image of Christ on the cross, usually set across the nave-chancel arch
rother beasts	cattle
sacring-bell	a small bell used in Catholic churches to call attention to the more solemn parts of the Mass
saferon	*saffron* - small crocus used as flavouring
scaffoll	(probably) scaffolding
seak	*sack* - a Spanish wine
searche	a small fine seive
secutare	*secretaire* - a writing desk
shambles	butchers' market stalls
shutes, shutts	piglets
skillet	small long-handled pan with three feet
smytbylls	smith's cutting tools
sornyer	searing iron (?branding iron for cattle etc.)
spyncer	pincers
tableboard	table
teaster	*tester* - canopy over a four-poster bed, made of wood or fabric
tenement	a dwelling, or part of it, used by one family - or more generally a holding of land including a dwelling
tithes	a tenth of the produce of land and stock, payable annually to the church
trendle, trendale	a round or oval table
trendle wheel	a wheel suspended horizontally from the church roof and holding lighted candles
trivett, tryvet	a three-footed support for a vessel to be stood on a fire
trucklebed	low bed on small wheels or truckles, which could be pushed under a high bed when not in use
tunnill	a cask
turbary, right of	right to dig turf for fuel
tynning dish	tin dish
tything	a district of a parish, originally containing ten householders, each responsible for the behaviour of the rest
tythingman	the chief man of a tithing
univallate	single ditched
vicar	a parson who receives only the smaller tithes or a salary
victualler	a supplier of provisions, usually with licence to sell alcoholic drink
villein	a villager, free but bound to the Lord of the Manor for service
vyoll glass	a glass phial
wattle and daub	clay or mud plastered onto interwoven twigs for walling
wymshete	*winnowing sheet* - a large sheet on which corn was winnowed to separate the chaff
yeoman	a small farmer, above the class of labourer and below that of gentleman
yoating fawte	vat for soaking grain for brewing

Monetary Values through the Centuries

The currency system in use from medieval times until decimalisation in 1971 was based on pounds, shilling and pence – abbreviated £, s and d.

12 pence = 1 shilling

20 shillings = 1 pound

Thus there were 240 pence in the pound, so that pence in use today are equivalent to 2.4 old pence. The table, below left, shows some equivalent values.

While there were different ways of writing amounts, including the simple *2/6* for two shillings and sixpence, we have standardised (even within transcribed documents) on the more understandable style of *2s. 6d.* However, if an amount was quoted as *44s. 4d.* we have not changed it to *£2. 4s. 4d.*

Attempting conversion from 'old money' into present-day values is not especially meaningful, even within the twentieth century. However, some kind of yardstick is useful when looking at costs and values in previous centuries. On page 41 we learn that a pound of figs was valued at 3d in 1597 – could the average working man have afforded to buy them? A builder's labourer might have expected to earn around 8d a day, so they would probably have been a considerable luxury at that level of society.

The second table, below right, is adapted from the researches of H. P. Brown and S. V. Hopkins (*A Perspective on Wages and Prices*, London, 1981) and is included as the approximate yardstick proposed. But there must be all kinds of provisos. Craftsman and labourers might not have been able to find work every day; the sizes of their families are not known; their rents would vary with all kinds of factors; expectations, even in food and clothing, would vary greatly, both with time and with levels of society.

Pre-1971	Post-1971
6d.	2½p.
1s. 0d.	5p.
2s.6d.	12½p.
5s.0d.	25p.
6s.8d.	33½p.
10s.0d.	50p.
£1.0s.0d.	£1.00

Period	Daily wage, building craftsman	Daily wage, building labourer
13th century	3d.	1d.
14th century	3d. - 5d.	1½d. - 3d.
15th century	5d. - 6d.	3d. - 4d.
16th century	6d. - 1s. 0d.	4d. - 8d.
17th century	1s. 0d. - 1s. 8d.	8d. - 1s. 2d.
18th century	1s. 8d. - 3s. 0d.	1s. 2d. - 1s. 10d.
19th century	3s. 0d. - 6s. 8d.	1s. 11d. - 4s. 2d.
1950	£1. 8s. 4d	£1. 3s. 9d.

Acknowledgements and Picture Credits

Extensive research over many years lies behind the production of this volume. Many people have contributed in a variety of ways; sadly, it is not possible to mention all of them individually. The authors wish to express their gratitude to all who have lent family papers and photographs, shared their memories of the town, or discussed aspects of the town's history.

Special thanks must go to the County Archivist and her staff at the Hampshire Record Office in Winchester. Their help and advice on many occasions has been extremely valuable. In particular, they have permitted us to include reproductions of the following documents : engraving of the church, ref.138M84W/161, p.49; Churchwardens Accounts, ref.44M81M/PW1, p.53; engraving of the Bulkeley brass, ref.Top.Fordingbridge2/9, p.59; Militia Substitute Paper, ref.24M82/PO17/3, p.90; Tithe Map, p.96; Poor Rate Bill, ref.24M82/PW54/10229, p.109; Carrier Card, ref.44M69/G1/187e(i), p.115; also the photographs by James Coventry, ref.33M84, on pp.4, 76, 95 (lower), 118 (upper), 123 (lower) and 124.

Archivists at collections in other parts of the country, notably at King's College, Cambridge and at the Cornwall County Record Office, as well as those listed p.166, have also given valuable advice and/or provided useful material. The archivist at Hatfield House provided the extracts from John Norden's map of Cranborne Chase which appear on the front cover and on p.61 – our gratitude goes to the Marquess of Salisbury for permission to use these extracts. Fordingbridge Junior School holds the Log Books of the National School and allowed us to quote material from them.

Organisations which provided illustrations and/or gave permission for their use include: the British Publishing Company for the map on p.2; the Ordnance Survey for the aerial photograph of Castle Ditches on p.7; Cranborne Ancient Technology Centre for Jake Keen's photograph of Iron Age round-houses, p.8; Hampshire Museums Service for the drawing of Rockbourne Roman Villa, p.11; Winchester Museums Service for the photograph of the Byzantine 'bucket', p.13; Fordingbridge Infants School for the photograph on p.145(lower).

The cartoons on pages 63 and 119 were drawn by Phil Anderton of Hexham and we wish to thank him for his careful and humorous completion of our commission – and his research concerning football goalposts! Ernest Major of the Willis Museum provided information about the probable Basingstoke strip.

The facsimile of the Domesday Book entry, p.14, was taken from the 1982 edition, volume 4, *Hampshire* (General Editor, John Morris; County Editors, Frank and Caroline Thorn). It is reproduced by kind permission of the publishers, Phillimore and Co. Ltd., Shopwyke Barn, Chichester, PO20 6BG.

Individuals who loaned photographs or provided other illustrations include: the late Dennis Sloper, drawing of a Paleolithic axe, p.6; Stephen Moody, drawings of Mesolithic flints, p.6; Harold Hanna, photograph of Neolithic flints, p.6; Chris Gifford, photograph of the Saxon brooch, p.13; John Dawes, 1779 title page, p.92; Sir Edward Hulse, photograph of cyclist, p.112; Jean Cormack, photographs of the Thompson and Westlake families, p.122 and p.127(upper two); Martin Hannen, family photographs and poster, pp.125, 126, 160 (also other family papers including John Hannen Junior's yeomanry notebook, quoted on p.98); Mr Windless, aerial photograph, p.131; Penny Copland Griffiths, photograph of Morley Hewitt, p.160.

The following photographs and postcards are from Anthony Light's personal collection: back cover(both), 16(both), 30(lower), 36, 51, 94, 95(upper), 100, 105, 109, 115(upper), 123, 127, 128(top and lower two), 132, 134, 142(left), 157, 159. Other postcards and photographs were loaned by: Mr P. Gulliver, p.112; Jill Bostock, pp.129(lower right), 142(right); Lesley Allison, pp.33, 99, 115(lower), 117, 118, 133; Jack Weaving, p.141. Pictures from the Shering Collection were used with the permission of Fordingbridge Museum: 30(lower), 107, 123(middle), 129(upper).

The modern photographs on the following pages were taken by Gerald Ponting : 9, 18, 19(right), 27, 28, 30(top), 38(both), 46(both), 50, 51(lower), 58, 68(both), 69(both), 70, 79, 81, 82, 84, 94(lower), 104, 105(lower three), 109(right), 116, 120, 127(lower right), 128(Star and Crown), 129(lower two), 130(all), 133(lower), 139(both), 144(both), 145(top 4), 146, 147, all 15 photos on pages150-154, 155(bottom).

The maps on pages 10, 16, 17, 24, 25, 32, 68 and 109 were drawn by Anthony Light; he also took the Greyhound excavation photograph on p.19(left). With the help of his wife, Elizabeth, he was responsible for the drawings on pages 23, 26(all), 27, 42(all), 44(all), 57(both), 71.

The sketch on p.45 and the globe on p.155 came from copyright-free clip-art collections.

The authors also wish to thank: Julia Norman and Martin Poole of NFDC and Alison Fowler and Francis Cooper of HWT for advice on the text of pages 155-157; Mrs E. Baggaley of Branksome China for information about the former cinema; Reverend Timothy Daykin and the Churchwardens of St Mary's Fordingbridge and St Mary's, Breamore for permission to include photographs taken in those churches; Barbara Burbridge and Barbara Hillier for proof-reading the text at different stages; the staff of Hobbs the Printers for their unfailing co-operation in the production of the book; and the proprietors of the Fordingbridge Bookshop for their support of our publications over many years.

Our wives, Elizabeth Light and Elizabeth Ponting, have taken an interest in this project over a considerable period and it could not have been completed without their support in many ways, both directly and indirectly.

Sources and References

Documents concerning the town are to be found in many archives, primarily the Hampshire Record Office at Winchester and the Public Record Office at Kew. King's College, Cambridge, and the Cornwall Record Office also have important Fordingbridge documents, as do collections in Nottingham, Derbyshire, London and Wiltshire. Locally, the archives of Breamore House, the Shering Collection at Fordingbridge Museum and a number of private collections have further information. The Salisbury Local Studies Library holds every edition of the *Salisbury and Winchester Journal* on microfilm, a valuable and extensive source for the later centuries.

Major Sources and References for the Medieval period

Public Record Office at Kew -
The Domesday Survey of 1086 (published)
Inquisitions Post Mortem for the Brune family and others together with the associated 'Extents' of the Manors. Classes C132, C133, C135, C140 and E152.
Various Crown Papers including Pipe Rolls, Placito de Bianco and the Patent Rolls which include grants of Pontage for the Great Bridge. Some of these are published.
Taxation Rolls, mainly in class E179, including the Lay Subsidies of 1327 and 1333 which name individual taxpayers.
Breamore Priory Deed of 1347 (PRO E326/3596).

Hampshire County Record Office at Winchester -
The Manorial Account Roll for 1276-7, 79M95/1
Churchwardens' Account Book 1490-1518, 44M81/PW1
Hundred Rolls and Court Books for Burgate Manor including those for 1405/6, 1M53/1 and 1429, 79M95/2

King's College, Cambridge
Good series of Account Rolls and Court Rolls for Woodfidley, together with a few miscellaneous documents.

Nottingham University Library
A series of 14th- and 15th-century deeds in the Willoughby family papers relating to a few properties in Fordingbridge and Horseport. MID 2568-2599

Breamore House Muniments
Deeds of the 14th and 15th centuries relating to East Mill Manor.

Miscellaneous deeds are held in a number of repositories, notably the Public Record Office, the British Library and the Derbyshire County Record Office.

Major Sources and References for the 16th century

Public Record Office -
Taxation Rolls, notably the Benevolence of 1543, E179/173/242.
Militia Musters for 1522, Class E36/19, and for 1569, SP12/59.
Wills proved in the Prerogative Court of Canterbury.
Various property deeds, some of which are published in 'Ancient Deeds'.
Chancery Rolls which include records of some court cases.
John Bulkeleys' disputes with William Dodington are recorded in Star Chamber Proceedings D15 and D33-39.
'... new work on the bell tower' mentioned in a will of 1483 (PRO 7 Logge)
'... tower of the church of Fordingbridge', in a will of 1504 (PRO 15 Holgrave).
Will of John Molens, Lord of the Manor of Sandhill, dated 1483 (PRO 7 Logge)
Inventory of Church Goods (PRO E117/2)

King's College, Cambridge -
Numerous Court Rolls, Accounts and miscellaneous documents relating to Woodfidley Manor; a good Survey of the Manor for 1575; Embellishment of the Church exterior (KC FOR/3),

Hampshire County Record Office -
> Court Books of the Manor of Ford, Court Rolls and Books of the Hundred, and Estreat Rolls of both, all in the Coventry papers, 1M53.
> Wills and Inventories of numerous inhabitants, with much good detail.
> Churchwardens Accounts, mainly for the early years of the century in HRO44M81/PW1-2.
> Rentals of the Manor of Forde in the Coventry papers, 1M53/221, 224.
> Survey of the Manor 1593 -fiche copy of the Cornwall Record Office document PB4/158/1.
> Bequests to the church from Richard Asley and from '*the village of Gorley*', 1515
>> (HRO 44M81/PW1).
> 1581 lease to Nicholas Bounde (HRO 152M85/2)
> Nicholas Norris's inventory (HRO 1587 Ad 45)

Major Sources and References for the 17th century

Public Record Office
> Various Taxation Rolls, mainly in class E175.
> Hearth Taxes 1664-5, E176/565 (Published in Hampshire Record Series, Vol 11) and 1674, E176/569.
> Wills proved in the Prerogative Court of Canterbury.

Hampshire Record Office -
> Parish Registers from 1640 onwards with numerous Poor Law papers, including Rate lists, accounts, apprenticeship indentures etc. in 24M82
> Churchwardens Accounts 1603-1648, with gaps. 44M81/PW3-8.
> The Account of 1639 (HRO 24M82/PW1)
> Numerous wills and inventories.
> Quarter Sessions papers.
> Bulkeley inventory (HRO 1M53/1371)
> Battalion of the Hampshire Militia, poor relief (HRO 24M82/PO17/1)

Cornwall Record Office (Also held as micro-fiche copy at Hampshire Record Office)
> Court Books of the Manor of Fordingbridge from 1654-1700 (PB4/144/4-5)

King's College, Cambridge
> Accounts, Court papers of Woodfidley, with numerous subsidiary documents.

Hatfield House archives : John Norden's map of Cranborne Chase (CPM Supp. 18)

Abstract of Claims in the New Forest 1680 - published volume with sections relating to Fordingbridge and most other local manors and villages.

Major Sources and References for the 18th Century

Hampshire Record Office –
> The Hampshire Directory 1784 and the Universal British Directory of 1792.
> Fordingbridge Parish Records 24M82, including the Registers of Births,
Marriages and Deaths, the Poor Law Records and various miscellaneous documents.
> Wills of many local people.
> Quarter Sessions papers and Calendars of Prisoners.
> Land Tax Records for various years in the last three decades of the century.
> Parish Council Records including Overseers Books from 1731, in 63M92
> Miscellaneous deeds including the St Cross records (HRO 111M94W), Barton Field
>> (HRO 34M73M/E/T1) and Middle Croft and Bridge Street (HRO40M78M/E/T10-T20)
> Building the Smallpox House (HRO 24M82/PO
> William Sutton service card (HRO 44M69/G1/187e (i))
> Account from Edmund Dale, blacksmith, dated 1757 (HRO 24M82/PW10/66)
> Account of Bricks for the Smallpox house 1741/2 (HRO 24M82/PO5)
> Workhouse purchase from Mary Windover, 1755. (HRO 62M92/PO2)
> Extending the workhouse (HRO 24M82/PV1)
> Charges Disbursed by the Constable 1742 (HRO 24M82/PO5)
> Militia substitute paper (HRO 24M82/PO17/3)

King's College, Cambridge
> Court Books and related papers for Woodfidley Manor, with Accounts, Leases etc.

Cornwall Record Office
> Manor of Fordingbridge Court Books, Rentals and a few miscellaneous documents in the Prideaux Brune papers (PB4)
>> (Also held as micro-fiche copy at Hampshire Record Office).

Public Record Office
> Assize Records covering the whole century.
> Wills of the Prerogative Court of Canterbury

Guildhall Library Record Office
> Sun Fire Office Policies, Ms 17817/15, and records of other insurance companies, with many Fordingbridge policies from 1717 onwards.

Miscellaneous deeds can be found in other repositories, including the Wiltshire Record Office, and in private collections.

Major Sources and References for the 19th Century

Public Record Office
> Assize Records
> Wills of the Prerogative Court of Canterbury
> Salisbury and Dorset Junction Railway Board Minutes etc (RAIL 594 etc)
> Militia records of local men, 1870s onwards (WO68/379)

Hampshire Record Office
> Parish Records including Registers of Births, Marriages and Deaths, Churchwardens' papers, Poor Law etc. (HRO 24M82).
> The Tithe Map of 1840 and accompanying Schedule.
> Board of Guardians Minute Books 1835-1919 (HRO PL3/9/1-26)
> Parish Council Minute Books from 1895 (HRO 63M92)
> District Council Clerk's Books (HRO 88M76/DDC 1-11 & 88M76/DDC2)
> Burgate Estate Papers and Coventry family records (HRO 8M59 & 212M87)
> Trade Directories from 1832 onwards.
> Census Returns with names 1801-1831 (HRO 24M82/PO 20-21)
> Census Returns 1841-1891 held on fiche and microfilm
>> (Some are also available in Salisbury, Fordingbridge and Ringwood Libraries)
> Wills of many Fordingbridge people
> Ordnance Survey Maps of the Fordingbridge district - incomplete series of various editions and sizes. (Some Libraries hold copies of large and small scale maps.)
> Deeds and associated papers relating to the Quaker Meeting House (HRO 24M54/321) and also burial records and plan of graveyard.
> Minute Book of the Highways Board 1863-77 (HRO 88M76/DH1)
> Quarter Sessions Records and Calendars of Prisoners
> Plans of the new Workhouse 1883 (HRO 111M86/116)
> Church attendances 24M82/PZ/11
> Extracts from the minutes of a meeting of subscribers to the National Schools held in the schoolroom July 2nd 1879 (HRO 24M82/PJ3)
> Arms returned to the Ordnance Store Portsmouth (HRO 21M57)
> Poor Rate bill, 1871 (HRO 24M82 PW54/10)
> Many other miscellaneous deeds, photographs, bills, posters etc.
> Engraving of Fordingbridge church by G N Shepherd published by Jas Robbins, College Street, Winchester (HRO 138M84W/16 (i))

King's College, Cambridge
> Woodfidley Manor Court Books, accounts and miscellaneous papers including a good Survey and map of 1859, FOR/30

Breamore House Muniments
> Rules of the local Troop (Misc.33)

Salisbury Local Studies Library
> Complete series of the *Salisbury and Winchester Journal* on microfilm.

Cornwall Record Office
    Rental of Fordingbridge manor 1878 in PB4/149
      (Also held as micro-fiche copy at Hampshire Record Office).

The Shering collection at the Fordingbridge Museum includes 19th-century material.
Main Libraries usually have examples of 19th-century Hampshire Directories.
Some Record Offices and Libraries outside Hampshire hold local documents.
Many other miscellaneous documents are still held privately, and others doubtless still await discovery.

Index

Names of individuals are indexed only where they take 'centre stage' at one point or another in our story. Those who appear only briefly, in quotations or in lists do not, in general, appear in this index.

About the Authors

Anthony Light and Gerald Ponting have been working together on the history of the Fordingbridge area since 1986. Most of their books and booklets have been published by their own imprint of Charlewood Press.

Anthony lives at Alderholt and runs a family market garden at Burgate. He was educated at Breamore Primary School and at Bishop Wordsworth's School, Salisbury. He has been deeply involved in local history and amateur archaeology for many years, and has worked extensively on the Hulse family muniments at Breamore House. He has directed a number of excavations both in this area and further afield. Of particular importance to our knowledge of Fordingbridge is the season of excavation which he directed in 1989 on the site of the former Greyhound Hotel in the heart of the town, when many medieval features were revealed (see page 19). His extensive documentary research is the foundation for this and the other books which he and Gerald have written and published.

Gerald lives in Chandler's Ford. He is a free-lance writer, photographer and lecturer and also a Blue Badge Tourist Guide. He was brought up in Breamore and, like Anthony, attended the village school there before going on to Bishop Wordsworth's. Following study at the Universities of Southampton and Leicester, Gerald's career as a biology teacher took him first to Suffolk. Here he became interested in local history, ultimately resulting in a published history of Kesgrave, near Ipswich. During the ten years that he lived on the Isle of Lewis, he published a number of books about the Standing Stones of Callanish, and received a British Archaeological Award for researches there. On returning to Hampshire, he taught at The Burgate School, Fordingbridge, for eight years before taking early retirement. In addition to undertaking most of the technical work on Charlewood Press's books, Gerald also operates the imprint of Millers Dale Publications.

List of Publications

A WALK THROUGH HISTORICAL BREAMORE by Anthony Light and Gerald Ponting, 1987, Charlewood Press

* *THE TRAGEDIES OF THE DODINGTONS* by Anthony Light and Gerald Ponting, 1991, Charlewood Press

* *TUDOR FORDINGBRIDGE* by Anthony Light and Gerald Ponting, 1993, Charlewood Press

BREAMORE - A SHORT HISTORY AND GUIDE by Anthony Light and Gerald Ponting, 1994, Charlewood Press

FORDINGBRIDGE AND DISTRICT - A PICTORIAL HISTORY by Anthony Light and Gerald Ponting, 1994, Phillimore

THE HISTORY OF THE BURGATE SCHOOL, 1957-1995 by Gerald Ponting, 1996, Burgate School

A WALK THROUGH OLD FORDINGBRIDGE by Anthony Light and Gerald Ponting, 2nd ed., 1997, Charlewood Press

* *VICTORIAN JOURNAL – FORDINGBRIDGE 1837–1901* by Anthony Light and Gerald Ponting, 1997, Charlewood Press

* *CHANDLER'S FORD – YESTERDAY AND TODAY* by Barbara Hillier and Gerald Ponting, 1998, Millers Dale Publications

ROMSEY YESTERDAY AND TODAY by Barbara Burbridge and Gerald Ponting, 1999, Millers Dale Publications

JAMES COVENTRY, GENTLEMAN PHOTOGRAPHER by Anthony Light and Gerald Ponting, 1999, Charlewood Press

A WALK TO BREAMORE MIZ-MAZE by Anthony Light and Gerald Ponting, 2nd ed., 2000, Charlewood Press

LANDMARK VISITORS GUIDE – NEW FOREST by Gerald Ponting, 2000, Landmark Publishing

A COIN HOARD FROM ROMAN BREAMORE by Anthony Light and Gerald Ponting, 2001, Charlewood Press

FORDINGBRIDGE IN OLD PICTURE POSTCARDS by Anthony Light and Gerald Ponting, forthcoming, European Library

CALLANISH – and other Ancient Sites in the Outer Hebrides by Gerald Ponting, forthcoming, Wooden Books

* – out of print